Patterns of Democracy

Patterns of
Democracy

*Government Forms and Performance in
Thirty-Six Countries*

Arend Lijphart

Yale University Press   New Haven and London

Published with assistance from the Louis
Stern Memorial Fund

Designed by James J. Johnson
and set in Melior type by Keystone
Typesetting, Inc.
Printed in the United States of America.

Library of Congress Cataloging-in-
Publication Data

Lijphart, Arend.
    Patterns of democracy : government
forms and performance in thirty-six
countries / Arend Lijphart.
        p.   cm.
    Includes bibliographical references and
index.
    ISBN 978-0-300-07893-0 (pbk.)
ISBN 0-300-07894-3 (cloth)
    1. Democracy.   2. Comparative
government.   I. Title.
JC421.L542   1999
320.3—DC21   99-12365

A catalogue record for this book is available
from the British Library.

The paper in this book meets the guidelines
for permanence and durability of the
Committee on Production Guidelines for
Book Longevity of the Council on Library
Resources.

for

Gisela

and for our grandchildren

Connor,

Aidan,

Arel,

Caio, *and*

Senta,

in the hope that the next century—their century—
will be more democratic, more peaceful, kinder, and gentler than
ours has been

Contents

Preface   ix

1   Introduction   1
2   The Westminster Model of Democracy   9
3   The Consensus Model of Democracy   31
4   Thirty-Six Democracies   48
5   Party Systems: Two-Party and Multiparty Patterns   62
6   Cabinets: Concentration Versus Sharing of
    Executive Power   90
7   Executive-Legislative Relations: Patterns of
    Dominance and Balance of Power   116
8   Electoral Systems: Majority and Plurality Methods
    Versus Proportional Representation   143
9   Interest Groups: Pluralism Versus Corporatism   171
10 Division of Power: The Federal-Unitary and
    Centralized-Decentralized Contrasts   185
11 Parliaments and Congresses: Concentration Versus
    Division of Legislative Power   200
12 Constitutions: Amendment Procedures and
    Judicial Review   216

13 Central Banks: Independence Versus Dependence   232

14 The Two-Dimensional Conceptual Map of Democracy 243

15 Macro-Economic Management and the Control of
        Violence: Does Consensus Democracy Make a
        Difference?   258

16 The Quality of Democracy and a "Kinder, Gentler"
        Democracy: Consensus Democracy Makes a Difference 275

17 Conclusions and Recommendations   301

Appendix A. Two Dimensions and Ten Basic Variables,
1945–96 and 1971–96   311

Appendix B. Alternative Measure of Multipartism,
Cabinet Composition, and Disproportionality,
1945–96 and 1971–96   315

References   317

Index   341

Preface

My book *Democracies,* published in 1984, was a comparative study of twenty-one democracies in the period 1945–80. Its most important findings were (1) that the main institutional rules and practices of modern democracies—such as the organization and operation of executives, legislatures, party systems, electoral systems, and the relationships between central and lower-level governments—can all be measured on scales from majoritarianism at one end to consensus on the other, (2) that these institutional characteristics form two distinct clusters, and (3) that, based on this dichotomous clustering, a two-dimensional "conceptual map" of democracy can be drawn on which each of the democracies can be located. My original plan for a second edition was to reinforce this theoretical framework and the empirical findings mainly by means of an update to the mid-1990s—an almost 50 percent increase in the total time span—with only a few additional corrections and adjustments.

When I began work on the revision, however, I realized that it offered me a great opportunity for much more drastic improvements. I decided to add not just the updated materials but also fifteen new countries, new operationalizations of the institutional variables, two completely new institutional variables, an attempt to gauge the stability of the countries' positions on the conceptual map, and an analysis of the performance of the different types of democracy with regard to a large number of public policies. As a result, while *Patterns of Democracy* grew out of *Democracies,* it has become an entirely new book rather than a second edition.

For those readers who are familiar with *Democracies,* let me describe the principal changes in *Patterns of Democracy* in somewhat greater detail:

1. *Patterns of Democracy* covers thirty-six countries—fifteen more than the twenty-one countries of *Democracies.* This new set of thirty-six countries is not just numerically larger but considerably more diverse. The original twenty-one democracies were all industrialized nations and, with one exception (Japan), Western countries. The fifteen new countries include four European nations (Spain, Portugal, Greece, and Malta), but the other eleven—almost one-third of the total of thirty-six—are developing countries in Latin America, the Caribbean, Africa, Asia, and the Pacific. This greater diversity provides a critical test of the two-dimensional pattern found in *Democracies.* A minor change from *Democracies* is that I dropped the French Fourth Republic (1946–58) because it lasted only twelve years—in contrast with the minimum of almost twenty years of democracy for all other cases; in this book, "France" means the Fifth Republic from 1958 on.

2. In *Democracies,* I analyzed the twenty-one democracies from their first national elections in or soon after 1945 until the end of 1980. *Patterns of Democracy* extends this period until the middle of 1996. For the original countries (except France), the starting-point is still the second half of the 1940s; for the others, the analysis begins with their first elections upon the achievement of independence or the resumption of democracy—ranging from 1953 (Costa Rica) to 1977 (India, Papua New Guinea, and Spain).

3. The two new institutions analyzed in *Patterns of Democracy* are interest groups and central banks (Chapters 9 and 13). Two other variables that were discussed prominently in *Democ-*

racies and given chapters of their own—the issue dimensions of partisan conflict and referendums—are "demoted" in *Patterns of Democracy*. I now discuss them more briefly in Chapters 5 and 12, and I have dropped the issue dimensions as one of the five elements of the first cluster of characteristics because, unlike all the other variables, it is not an institutional characteristic. The first cluster still consists of five variables, however, because the interest group system is now added to it. The second cluster is expanded from three to five elements: I split the variable of constitutional rigidity versus flexibility into two separate variables—the difficulty of constitutional amendment and the strength of judicial review—and I added the variable of central bank independence.

4. I critically reviewed the operationalization of all of the institutional characteristics, and I found that almost all could be, and should be, improved. My overriding objective was to maximize the validity of my quantitative indicators—that is, to capture the "reality" of the political phenomena, which are often difficult to quantify, as closely as possible. One frequent problem was that I was faced with two alternative operationalizations that appeared to be equally justified. In such cases, I consistently chose to "split the difference" by combining or averaging the alternatives instead of more or less arbitrarily picking one instead of the other. In the end, only the operationalization of the party system variable—in terms of the effective number of parliamentary parties—survived almost (but not completely) intact from *Democracies*. All of the others were modified to a significant extent.

5. In *Democracies*, I placed my democracies on the conceptual map of democracy on the basis of their average institutional practices in the thirty to thirty-five years under consideration; I did not raise the question of how much change may have occurred over time. Chapter 14 of *Patterns of Democracy* does look into this matter by dividing the approximately fifty years from 1945 to 1996 into separate periods of 1945–70 and 1971–96 and

by showing how much—or how little—twenty-six of the democracies (those with a sufficient number of years in the first period) shifted their positions on the conceptual map from the first to the second period.

6. Perhaps the most important new subject covered in *Patterns of Democracy* is the "so what?" question: does the type of democracy make a difference for public policy and for the effectiveness of government? Chapter 15 investigates the relationship between the degree of consensus democracy and how successful governments are in their macroeconomic management (such as economic growth and the control of inflation and unemployment) and the control of violence. Chapter 16 looks at several indicators of the quality of democracy (such as women's representation, equality, and voter participation) and the records of the governments with regard to welfare policies, environmental protection, criminal justice, and economic aid to developing countries.

7. I began *Democracies* with sketches of British and New Zealand politics as illustrative examples of the Westminster model of democracy and similar brief accounts of Swiss and Belgian democracy as examples of the consensus model. *Patterns of Democracy* updates these four sketches and adds Barbados and the European Union as two further examples of the respective models.

8. *Democracies* presented the relationships between the different variables by means of tables with cross-tabulations. In *Patterns of Democracy,* I generally use scattergrams that show these relationships and the positions of each of the thirty-six democracies in a much clearer, more accurate, and visually more attractive fashion.

9. *Patterns of Democracy* adds an appendix with the values on all ten institutional variables and the two overall majoritarian-consensus dimensions for the entire period 1945–96 and for the shorter period 1971–96. The ready availability of these basic data as part of the book should facilitate replications

that other scholars may want to perform as well as the use of these data for further research.

It would have been impossible for me to analyze the thirty-six countries covered in *Patterns of Democracy* without the help of a host of scholarly advisers—and almost impossible without the invention of email! I am extremely grateful for all of the facts and interpretations contributed by my advisers and for their unfailingly prompt responses to my numerous queries.

On the Latin American democracies, I received invaluable assistance from Octavio Amorim Neto, John M. Carey, Brian F. Crisp, Michael J. Coppedge, Jonathan Hartlyn, Gary Hoskin, Mark P. Jones, J. Ray Kennedy, Scott Mainwaring, and Matthew S. Shugart. Ralph R. Premdas was a key consultant on the Caribbean democracies, together with Edward M. Dew, Neville R. Francis, Percy C. Hintzen, and Fragano S. Ledgister. Pradeep K. Chhibber and Ashutosh Varshney helped me solve a number of puzzles in the politics of India. With regard to some of the small and underanalyzed countries, I was particularly dependent on the willingness of area and country experts to provide facts and explanations: John D. Holm, Bryce Kunimoto, Shaheen Mozaffar, and Andrew S. Reynolds on Botswana; John C. Lane on Malta; Hansraj Mathur and Larry W. Bowman on Mauritius; and Ralph Premdas (again) as well as Ben Reilly and Ron May on Papua New Guinea.

Nathaniel L. Beck, Susanne Lohmann, Sylvia Maxfield, Pierre L. Siklos, and Steven B. Webb advised me on central banks; Miriam A. Golden, Stephan Haggard, Neil J. Mitchell, Daniel R. Nielson, Adam Przeworski, and Alan Siaroff on interest groups; and Martin Shapiro and Alec Stone on judicial review. On other countries and subjects I benefited from the help and suggestions of John S. Ambler, Matthew A. Baum, Peter J. Bowman, Thomas C. Bruneau, Gary W. Cox, Markus M. L. Crepaz, Robert G. Cushing, Robert A. Dahl, Larry Diamond, Panayote E. Dimitras, Giuseppe Di Palma, James N. Druckman,

xiv   PREFACE

Svante O. Ersson, Bernard Grofman, Arnold J. Heidenheimer, Charles O. Jones, Ellis S. Krauss, Samuel H. Kernell, Michael Laver, Thomas C. Lundberg, Malcolm Mackerras, Peter Mair, Jane Mansbridge, Marc F. Plattner, G. Bingham Powell, Jr., Steven R. Reed, Manfred G. Schmidt, Kaare Strom, Wilfried Swenden, Rein Taagepera, Paul V. Warwick, and Demet Yalcin.

In October 1997, I gave an intensive two-week seminar, largely based on draft materials for *Patterns of Democracy*, at the Institute for Advanced Studies in Vienna; I am grateful for the many helpful comments I received from Josef Melchior, Bernhard Kittel, and the graduate students who participated in the seminar sessions. In April and May 1998, I gave similar lectures and seminars at several universities in New Zealand: the University of Canterbury in Christchurch, the University of Auckland, Victoria University of Wellington, and the University of Waikato in Hamilton. Here, too, I benefited from many useful reactions, and I want to thank Peter Aimer, Jonathan Boston, John Henderson, Martin Holland, Keith Jackson, Raymond Miller, Nigel S. Roberts, and Jack Vowles in particular.

James N. Druckman expertly executed the factor analysis reported in Chapter 14. Ian Budge, Hans Keman, and Jaap Woldendorp provided me with their new data on cabinet formation before these were published. Several other scholars also generously shared their not yet published or only partly published data with me: data on the composition of federal chambers from Alfred Stepan and Wilfried Swenden's Federal Databank; data on the distance between governments and voters collected by John D. Huber and G. Bingham Powell, Jr.; and Christopher J. Anderson and Christine A. Guillory's data on satisfaction with democracy. Last, but certainly not least, I am very grateful for the work of my research assistants Nastaran Afari, Risa A. Brooks, Linda L. Christian, and Stephen M. Swindle.

CHAPTER 1

Introduction

There are many ways in which, in principle, a democracy can be organized and run; in practice, too, modern democracies exhibit a variety of formal governmental institutions, like legislatures and courts, as well as political party and interest group systems. However, clear patterns and regularities appear when these institutions are examined from the perspective of how majoritarian or how consensual their rules and practices are. The majoritarianism-consensus contrast arises from the most basic and literal definition of democracy—government by the people or, in representative democracy, government by the representatives of the people—and from President Abraham Lincoln's famous further stipulation that democracy means government not only *by* but also *for* the people—that is, government in accordance with the people's preferences.[1]

Defining democracy as "government by and for the people" raises a fundamental question: who will do the governing and to whose interests should the government be responsive when the people are in disagreement and have divergent preferences?

1. As Clifford D. May (1987) points out, credit for this definition should probably go to Daniel Webster instead of Lincoln. Webster gave an address in 1830—thirty-three years before Lincoln's Gettysburg address—in which he spoke of a "people's government, made for the people, made by the people, and answerable to the people."

One answer to this dilemma is: the majority of the people. This is the essence of the majoritarian model of democracy. The majoritarian answer is simple and straightforward and has great appeal because government by the majority and in accordance with the majority's wishes obviously comes closer to the democratic ideal of "government by and for the people" than government by and responsive to a minority.

The alternative answer to the dilemma is: as many people as possible. This is the crux of the consensus model. It does not differ from the majoritarian model in accepting that majority rule is better than minority rule, but it accepts majority rule only as a *minimum* requirement: instead of being satisfied with narrow decision-making majorities, it seeks to maximize the size of these majorities. Its rules and institutions aim at broad participation in government and broad agreement on the policies that the government should pursue. The majoritarian model concentrates political power in the hands of a bare majority—and often even merely a plurality instead of a majority, as Chapter 2 will show—whereas the consensus model tries to share, disperse, and limit power in a variety of ways. A closely related difference is that the majoritarian model of democracy is exclusive, competitive, and adversarial, whereas the consensus model is characterized by inclusiveness, bargaining, and compromise; for this reason, consensus democracy could also be termed "negotiation democracy" (Kaiser 1997, 434).

Ten differences with regard to the most important democratic institutions and rules can be deduced from the majoritarian and consensus principles. Because the majoritarian characteristics are derived from the same principle and hence are logically connected, one could also expect them to occur together in the real world; the same applies to the consensus characteristics. All ten variables could therefore be expected to be closely related. Previous research has largely confirmed these expectations—with one major exception: the variables cluster in two clearly separate dimensions (Lijphart 1984, 211–22; 1997a,

196–201). The first dimension groups five characteristics of the arrangement of executive power, the party and electoral systems, and interest groups. For brevity's sake, I shall refer to this first dimension as the *executives-parties dimension*. Since most of the five differences on the second dimension are commonly associated with the contrast between federalism and unitary government—a matter to which I shall return shortly—I shall call this second dimension the *federal-unitary dimension*.

The ten differences are formulated below in terms of dichotomous contrasts between the majoritarian and consensus models, but they are all variables on which particular countries may be at either end of the continuum or anywhere in between. The majoritarian characteristic is listed first in each case. The five differences on the executives-parties dimension are as follows:

1. Concentration of executive power in single-party majority cabinets versus executive power-sι aring in broad multiparty coalitions.
2. Executive-legislative relationships in which the executive is dominant versus executive-legislative balance of power.
3. Two-party versus multiparty systems.
4. Majoritarian and disproportional electoral systems versus proportional representation.
5. Pluralist interest group systems with free-for-all competition among groups versus coordinated and "corporatist" interest group systems aimed at compromise and concertation.

The five differences on the federal-unitary dimension are the following:

1. Unitary and centralized government versus federal and decentralized government.
2. Concentration of legislative power in a unicameral legislature versus division of legislative power between two equally strong but differently constituted houses.

3. Flexible constitutions that can be amended by simple majorities versus rigid constitutions that can be changed only by extraordinary majorities.

4. Systems in which legislatures have the final word on the constitutionality of their own legislation versus systems in which laws are subject to a judicial review of their constitutionality by supreme or constitutional courts.

5. Central banks that are dependent on the executive versus independent central banks.

One plausible explanation of this two-dimensional pattern is suggested by theorists of federalism like Ivo D. Duchacek (1970), Daniel J. Elazar (1968), Carl J. Friedrich (1950, 189–221), and K. C. Wheare (1946). These scholars maintain that federalism has primary and secondary meanings. Its primary definition is: a guaranteed division of power between the central government and regional governments. The secondary characteristics are strong bicameralism, a rigid constitution, and strong judicial review. Their argument is that the guarantee of a federal division of power can work well only if (1) both the guarantee and the exact lines of the division of power are clearly stated in the constitution and this guarantee cannot be changed unilaterally at either the central or regional level—hence the need for a rigid constitution, (2) there is a neutral arbiter who can resolve conflicts concerning the division of power between the two levels of government—hence the need for judicial review, and (3) there is a federal chamber in the national legislature in which the regions have strong representation—hence the need for strong bicameralism; moreover, (4) the main purpose of federalism is to promote and protect a decentralized system of government. These federalist characteristics can be found in the first four variables of the second dimension. As stated earlier, this dimension is therefore called the federal-unitary dimension.

The federalist explanation is not entirely satisfactory, however, for two reasons. One problem is that, although it can explain the clustering of the four variables in one dimension, it does not explain why this dimension should be so clearly distinct from the other dimension. Second, it cannot explain why the variable of central bank independence is part of the federal-unitary dimension. A more persuasive explanation of the two-dimensional pattern is the distinction between "collective agency" and "shared responsibility" on one hand and divided agencies and responsibilities on the other suggested by Robert E. Goodin (1996, 331).[2] These are both forms of diffusion of power, but the first dimension of consensus democracy with its multiparty face-to-face interactions *within* cabinets, legislatures, legislative committees, and concertation meetings between governments and interest groups has a close fit with the collective-responsibility form. In contrast, both the four federalist characteristics and the role of central banks fit the format of diffusion by means of institutional separation: division of power between separate federal and state institutions, two separate chambers in the legislature, and separate and independent high courts and central banks. Viewed from this perspective, the first dimension could also be labeled the joint-responsibility or joint-power dimension and the second the divided-responsibility or divided-power dimension. However, although these labels would be more accurate and theoretically more meaningful, my original labels—"executives-parties" and "federal-unitary"—have the great advantage that they are easier to remember, and I shall therefore keep using them throughout this book.

The distinction between two basic types of democracy, majoritarian and consensus, is by no means a novel invention in political science. In fact, I borrowed these two terms from Robert G. Dixon, Jr. (1968, 10). Hans Hattenhauer and Werner Kaltefleiter (1986) also contrast the "majority principle" with

2. A similar distinction, made by George Tsebelis (1995, 302), is that between "institutional veto players," located in different institutions, and "partisan veto players" like the parties within a government coalition.

consensus, and Jürg Steiner (1971) juxtaposes "the principles of majority and proportionality." G. Bingham Powell (1982) distinguishes between majoritarian and broadly "representational" forms of democracy and, in later work, between two "visions of liberal democracy": the Majority Control and the Proportionate Influence visions (Huber and Powell 1994). Similar contrasts have been drawn by Robert A. Dahl (1956)—"populistic" versus "Madisonian" democracy; William H. Riker (1982)—"populism" versus "liberalism"; Jane Mansbridge (1980)—"adversary" versus "unitary" democracy; and S. E. Finer (1975)—"adversary politics" versus centrist and coalitional politics.

Nevertheless, there is a surprisingly strong and persistent tendency in political science to equate democracy solely with majoritarian democracy and to fail to recognize consensus democracy as an alternative and equally legitimate type. A particularly clear example can be found in Stephanie Lawson's (1993, 192–93) argument that a strong political opposition is "the *sine qua non* of contemporary democracy" and that its prime purpose is "to become the government." This view is based on the majoritarian assumption that democracy entails a two-party system (or possibly two opposing blocs of parties) that alternate in government; it fails to take into account that governments in more consensual multiparty systems tend to be coalitions and that a change in government in these systems usually means only a partial change in the party composition of the government—instead of the opposition "becoming" the government.

The frequent use of the "turnover" test in order to determine whether a democracy has become stable and consolidated betrays the same majoritarian assumption. Samuel P. Huntington (1991, 266–67) even proposes a "two-turnover test," according to which "a democracy may be viewed as consolidated if the party or group that takes power in the initial election at the time of transition [to democracy] loses a subsequent election and turns over power to those election winners, and if those election winners then peacefully turn over power to the winners of a later election." Of the twenty long-term democracies analyzed in this book, all of which are undoubtedly stable and consolidated democratic systems, no fewer than four—Germany, Luxembourg, the Netherlands, and Switzerland—fail even the one-turnover test during the half-century from the late 1940s to 1996, that is, they experienced many cabinet changes but never a complete turnover, and eight—the same four countries plus Belgium, Finland, Israel, and Italy—fail the two-turnover test.

This book will show that pure or almost pure majoritarian democracies are actually quite rare—limited to the United Kingdom, New Zealand (until 1996), and the former British colonies in the Caribbean (but only with regard to the executives-parties dimension). Most democracies have significant or even predominantly consensual traits. Moreover, as this book shows, consensus democracy may be considered more democratic than majoritarian democracy in most respects.

The ten contrasting characteristics of the two models of democracy, briefly listed above, are described in a preliminary fashion and exemplified by means of sketches of relatively pure cases of majoritarian democracy—the United Kingdom, New Zealand, and Barbados—and of relatively pure cases of consensus democracy—Switzerland, Belgium, and the European Union—in Chapters 2 and 3. The thirty-six empirical cases of democracy, including the five just mentioned (but not the European Union), that were selected for the comparative analysis are systematically introduced in Chapter 4. The ten institutional variables are then analyzed in greater depth in the nine chapters that comprise the bulk of this book (Chapters 5 to 13). Chapter 14 summarizes the results and places the thirty-six democracies on a two-dimensional "conceptual map" of democracy; it also analyzes shifts on this map over time and shows that most countries occupy stable positions on the map. Chapters 15 and 16 ask the "so what?" question: does the type of democracy make a difference, especially with regard to effective economic policymaking and the quality of democracy? These chapters show that there are only small differences with regard to governing effectiveness but that consensus systems tend to score significantly higher on a wide array of indicators of democratic quality. Chapter 17 concludes with a look at the policy implications of the book's findings for democratizing and newly democratic countries.

CHAPTER 2

The Westminster Model of Democracy

In this book I use the term *Westminster model* interchangeably with *majoritarian model* to refer to a general model of democracy. It may also be used more narrowly to denote the main characteristics of *British* parliamentary and governmental institutions (Wilson 1994; Mahler 1997)—the Parliament of the United Kingdom meets in the Palace of Westminster in London. The British version of the Westminster model is both the original and the best-known example of this model. It is also widely admired. Richard Rose (1974, 131) points out that, "with confidence born of continental isolation, Americans have come to assume that their institutions—the Presidency, Congress and the Supreme Court—are the prototype of what should be adopted elsewhere." But American political scientists, especially those in the field of comparative politics, have tended to hold the British system of government in at least equally high esteem (Kavanagh 1974).

One famous political scientist who fervently admired the Westminster model was President Woodrow Wilson. In his early writings he went so far as to urge the abolition of presidential government and the adoption of British-style parliamentary government in the United States. Such views have also been held by many other non-British observers of British politics, and many features of the Westminster model have been exported to other countries: Canada, Australia, New Zealand, and most of Britain's former colonies in Asia, Africa, and the Caribbean when they became independent. Wilson (1884, 33) referred to parliamentary government in accordance with the Westminster model as "the world's fashion."

The ten interrelated elements of the Westminster or majoritarian model are illustrated by features of three democracies that closely approximate this model and can be regarded as the majoritarian prototypes: the United Kingdom, New Zealand, and Barbados. Britain, where the Westminster model originated, is clearly the first and most obvious example to use. In many respects, however, New Zealand is an even better example—at least until its sharp turn away from majoritarianism in October 1996. The third example—Barbados—is also an almost perfect prototype of the Westminster model, although only as far as the first (executives-parties) dimension of the majoritarian-consensus contrast is concerned. In the following discussion of the ten majoritarian characteristics in the three countries, I emphasize not only their conformity with the general model but also occasional deviations from the model, as well as various other qualifications that need to be made.

The Westminster Model in the United Kingdom

1. Concentration of executive power in one-party and bare-majority cabinets. The most powerful organ of British government is the cabinet. It is normally composed of members of the party that has the majority of seats in the House of Commons, and the minority is not included. Coalition cabinets are rare. Because in the British two-party system the two principal parties are of approximately equal strength, the party that wins the elections usually represents no more than a narrow majority, and the minority is relatively large. Hence the British one-party and bare-majority cabinet is the perfect embodiment of the principle of majority rule: it wields vast amounts of political power to rule as the representative of and in the interest of a majority that is not of overwhelming proportions. A large minority is excluded from power and condemned to the role of opposition. Especially since 1945, there have been few exceptions to the British norm of one-party majority cabinets. David Butler (1978, 112) writes that "clear-cut single-party government has been much less prevalent than many would suppose," but most of the deviations from the norm—coalitions of two or more parties or minority cabinets—occurred from 1918 to 1945. The most recent instance of a coalition cabinet was the 1940–45 wartime coalition formed by the Conservatives, who had a parliamentary majority, with the Labour and Liberal parties, under Conservative Prime Minister Winston Churchill. The only instances of minority cabinets in the postwar period were two minority Labour cabinets in the 1970s. In the parliamentary election of February 1974, the Labour party won a plurality but not a majority of the seats and formed a minority government dependent on all other parties not uniting to defeat it. New elections were held that October and Labour won an outright, albeit narrow, majority of the seats; but this majority was eroded by defections and by-election defeats, and the Labour cabinet again became a minority cabinet in 1976. It regained a temporary legislative majority in 1977 as a result of the pact it negotiated with the thirteen Liberals in the House of Commons: the Liberals agreed to support the cabinet in exchange for consultation on legislative proposals before their submission to Parliament. No Liberals entered the cabinet, however, and the cabinet therefore continued as a minority instead of a true coalition cabinet. The so-called Lab-Lib pact lasted until 1978, and in 1979 Labour Prime Minister James Callaghan's minority cabinet was brought down by a vote of no confidence in the House of Commons.

2. *Cabinet dominance.* The United Kingdom has a parliamentary system of government, which means that the cabinet is dependent on the confidence of Parliament. In theory, because the House of Commons can vote a cabinet out of office, it

"controls" the cabinet. In reality, the relationship is reversed. Because the cabinet is composed of the leaders of a cohesive majority party in the House of Commons, it is normally backed by the majority in the House of Commons, and it can confidently count on staying in office and getting its legislative proposals approved. The cabinet is clearly dominant vis-à-vis Parliament.

Because strong cabinet leadership depends on majority support in the House of Commons and on the cohesiveness of the majority party, cabinets lose some of their predominant position when either or both of these conditions are absent. Especially during the periods of minority government in the 1970s, there was a significant increase in the frequency of parliamentary defeats of important cabinet proposals. This even caused a change in the traditional view that cabinets must resign or dissolve the House of Commons and call for new elections if they suffer a defeat on either a parliamentary vote of no confidence or a major bill of central importance to the cabinet. The new unwritten rule is that only an explicit vote of no confidence necessitates resignation or new elections. The normalcy of cabinet dominance was largely restored in the 1980s under the strong leadership of Conservative Prime Minister Margaret Thatcher.

Both the normal and the deviant situations show that it is the disciplined two-party system rather than the parliamentary system that gives rise to executive dominance. In multiparty parliamentary systems, cabinets—which are often coalition cabinets—tend to be much less dominant (Peters 1997). Because of the concentration of power in a dominant cabinet, former cabinet minister Lord Hailsham (1978, 127) has called the British system of government an "elective dictatorship."[1]

1. In presidential systems of government, in which the presidential executive cannot normally be removed by the legislature (except by impeachment), the same variation in the degree of executive dominance can occur, depending on exactly how governmental powers are separated. In the United States, president and Congress can be said to be in a rough balance of power, but presidents in France and in some of the Latin American countries are considerably more powerful. Guillermo O'Donnell (1994, 59–60) has proposed the term "delega-

3. Two-party system. British politics is dominated by two large parties: the Conservative party and the Labour party. Other parties also contest elections and win seats in the House of Commons—in particular the Liberals and, after their merger with the Social Democratic party in the late 1980s, the Liberal Democrats—but they are not large enough to be overall victors. The bulk of the seats are captured by the two major parties, and they form the cabinets: the Labour party from 1945 to 1951, 1964 to 1970, 1974 to 1979, and from 1997 on, and the Conservatives from 1951 to 1964, 1970 to 1974, and in the long stretch from 1979 to 1997. The hegemony of these two parties was especially pronounced between 1950 and 1970: jointly they never won less than 87.5 percent of the votes and 98 percent of the seats in the House of Commons in the seven elections held in this period.

The interwar years were a transitional period during which the Labour party replaced the Liberals as one of the two big parties, and in the 1945 election, the Labour and Conservative parties together won about 85 percent of the votes and 92.5 percent of the seats. Their support declined considerably after 1970: their joint share of the popular vote ranged from only 70 percent (in 1983) to less than 81 percent (in 1979), but they continued to win a minimum of 93 percent of the seats, except in 1997, when their joint seat share fell to about 88.5 percent. The Liberals were the main beneficiaries. In alliance with the Social Democratic party, they even won more than 25 percent of the vote on one occasion (in the 1983 election) but, until 1997, never more than fourteen seats by themselves and twenty-three seats in alliance with the Social Democrats. In the 1997 election, however, the Liberal Democrats captured a surprising forty-six seats with about 17 percent of the vote.

---

tive democracy"—akin to Hailsham's "elective dictatorship"—for systems with directly elected and dominant presidents; in such "strongly majoritarian" systems, "whoever wins election to the presidency is thereby entitled to govern as he or she sees fit, constrained only by the hard facts of existing power relations and by a constitutionally limited term of office."

A corollary trait of two-party systems is that they tend to be one-dimensional party systems; that is, the programs and policies of the main parties usually differ from each other mainly with regard to just one dimension, that of socioeconomic issues. This is clearly the case for the British two-party system. The principal politically significant difference that divides the Conservative and Labour parties is disagreement about socioeconomic policies: on the left-right spectrum, Labour represents the left-of-center and the Conservative party the right-of-center preferences. This difference is also reflected in the pattern of voters' support for the parties in parliamentary elections: working-class voters tend to cast their ballots for Labour candidates and middle-class voters tend to support Conservative candidates. The Liberals and Liberal Democrats can also be placed easily on the socioeconomic dimension: they occupy a center position.

There are other differences, of course, but they are much less salient and do not have a major effect on the composition of the House of Commons and the cabinet. For instance, the Protestant-Catholic difference in Northern Ireland is the overwhelmingly dominant difference separating the parties and their supporters, but Northern Ireland contains less than 3 percent of the population of the United Kingdom, and such religious differences are no longer politically relevant in the British part of the United Kingdom (England, Scotland, and Wales). Ethnic differences explain the persistence of the Scottish National party and the Welsh nationalists, but these parties never manage to win more than a handful of seats. The only slight exception to the one-dimensionality of the British party system is that a foreign-policy issue—British membership in the European Community—has frequently been a source of division both within and between the Conservative and Labour parties.

4. Majoritarian and disproportional system of elections. The House of Commons is a large legislative body with a membership that has ranged from 625 in 1950 to 659 in 1997. The mem-

bers are elected in single-member districts according to the plurality method, which in Britain is usually referred to as the "first
past the post" system: the candidate with the majority vote or, if
there is no majority, with the largest minority vote wins.

This system tends to produce highly disproportional results.
For instance, the Labour party won an absolute parliamentary
majority of 319 out of 635 seats with only 39.3 percent of the
vote in the October 1974 elections, whereas the Liberals won
only 13 seats with 18.6 percent of the vote—almost half the Labour vote. In the five elections since then, from 1979 to 1997, the
winning party has won clear majorities of seats with never more
than 44 percent of the vote. All of these majorities have been
what Douglas W. Rae (1967, 74) aptly calls "manufactured majorities"—majorities that are artificially created by the electoral
system out of mere pluralities of the vote. In fact, all the winning
parties since 1945 have won with the benefit of such manufactured majorities. It may therefore be more accurate to call the
United Kingdom a *pluralitarian democracy* instead of a majoritarian democracy. The disproportionality of the plurality
method can even produce an overall winner who has failed to
win a plurality of the votes: the Conservatives won a clear seat
majority in the 1951 election not just with less than a majority of
the votes but also with fewer votes than the Labour party had
received.

The disproportional electoral system has been particularly
disadvantageous to the Liberals and Liberal Democrats, who
have therefore long been in favor of introducing some form of
proportional representation (PR). But because plurality has
greatly benefited the Conservatives and Labour, these two major
parties have remained committed to the old disproportional
method. Nevertheless, there are some signs of movement in the
direction of PR. For one thing, PR was adopted for all elections in Northern Ireland (with the exception of elections to the
House of Commons) after the outbreak of Protestant-Catholic
strife in the early 1970s. For another, soon after Labour's elec-

tion victory in 1997, Prime Minister Tony Blair's new cabinet decided that the 1999 election of British representatives to the European Parliament would be by PR—bringing the United Kingdom in line with all of the other members of the European Union. PR will also be used for the election of the new regional assemblies for Scotland and Wales. Moreover, an advisory Commission on Voting Systems, chaired by former cabinet member Lord Jenkins, was instituted to propose changes in the electoral system, including the possibility of PR, for the House of Commons. Clearly, the principle of proportionality is no longer anathema. Still, it is wise to heed the cautionary words of Graham Wilson (1997, 72), who points out that the two major parties have a long history of favoring basic reforms, but only until they gain power; then "they back away from changes such as electoral reform which would work to their disadvantage."

5. *Interest group pluralism.* By concentrating power in the hands of the majority, the Westminster model of democracy sets up a government-versus-opposition pattern that is competitive and adversarial. Competition and conflict also characterize the majoritarian model's typical interest group system: a system of free-for-all pluralism. It contrasts with interest group corporatism in which regular meetings take place between the representatives of the government, labor unions, and employers' organizations to seek agreement on socioeconomic policies; this process of coordination is often referred to as *concertation,* and the agreements reached are often called *tripartite* pacts. Concertation is facilitated if there are relatively few, large, and strong interest groups in each of the main functional sectors—labor, employers, farmers—and/or if there is a strong peak organization in each of the sectors that coordinates the preferences and desired strategies for each sector. Pluralism, in contrast, means a multiplicity of interest groups that exert pressure on the government in an uncoordinated and competitive manner.

Britain's interest group system is clearly pluralist. The one exception is the 1975 Social Contract on wages and prices concluded between the Labour government, the main labor union federation (the Trades Union Congress), and the main employers' federation (the Confederation of British Industry). This contract fell apart two years later when the government failed to get union agreement to accept further wage restraints and imposed wage ceilings unilaterally. The 1980s were characterized even more by grim confrontations between Margaret Thatcher's Conservative government and the labor unions—the very opposite of concertation and corporatism. As Michael Gallagher, Michael Laver, and Peter Mair (1995, 370) point out, Britain is "decidedly not a corporatist system" for two important reasons: "The first is the general lack of integration of both unions and management into the policymaking process. The second is the apparent preference of both sides for confrontational methods of settling their differences."

6. *Unitary and centralized government.* The United Kingdom is a unitary and centralized state. Local governments perform a series of important functions, but they are the creatures of the central government and their powers are not constitutionally guaranteed (as in a federal system). Moreover, they are financially dependent on the central government. There are no clearly designated geographical and functional areas from which the parliamentary majority and the cabinet are barred. The Royal Commission on the Constitution under Lord Kilbrandon concluded in 1973: "The United Kingdom is the largest unitary state in Europe and among the most centralised of the major industrial countries in the world" (cited in Busch 1994, 60). More recently, Prime Minister Tony Blair called the British system "*the* most centralised government of any large state in the western world" (cited in Beer 1998, 25).

Two exceptions should be noted. One is that Northern Ireland was ruled by its own parliament and cabinet with a high degree of autonomy—more than what most states in federal systems have—from 1921, when the Republic of Ireland became independent, until the imposition of direct rule from London in

1972. It is also significant, however, that Northern Ireland's autonomy could be, and was, eliminated in 1972 by Parliament by means of a simple majoritarian decision. The second exception is the gradual movement toward greater autonomy for Scotland and Wales—"devolution," in British parlance. But it was not until September 1997 that referendums in Scotland and Wales finally approved the creation of autonomous and directly elected Scottish and Welsh assemblies and that Prime Minister Blair could proclaim the end of the "era of big centralized government" (cited in Buxton, Kampfner, and Groom 1997, 1).

7. *Concentration of legislative power in a unicameral legislature.* For the organization of the legislature, the majoritarian principle of concentrating power means that legislative power should be concentrated in a single house or chamber. In this respect, the United Kingdom deviates from the pure majoritarian model. Parliament consists of two chambers: the House of Commons, which is popularly elected, and the House of Lords, which consists mainly of members of the hereditary nobility but also contains a large number of so-called life peers, appointed by the government. Their relationship is asymmetrical: almost all legislative power belongs to the House of Commons. The only power that the House of Lords retains is the power to delay legislation: money bills can be delayed for one month and all other bills for one year. The one-year limit was established in 1949; between the first major reform of 1911 and 1949, the Lords' delaying power was about two years, but in the entire period since 1911 they have usually refrained from imposing long delays.

Therefore, although the British bicameral legislature deviates from the majoritarian model, it does not deviate much: in everyday discussion in Britain, "Parliament" refers almost exclusively to the House of Commons, and the highly asymmetric bicameral system may also be called near-unicameralism. Moreover, the Lords' power may well be reduced further. Especially in the Labour party, there is strong sentiment in favor of reforms that range from eliminating the voting rights of the hereditary members to the abolition of the House of Lords. The change from near-unicameralism to pure unicameralism would not be a difficult step: it could be decided by a simple majority in the House of Commons and, if the Lords objected, merely a one-year delay.

8. *Constitutional flexibility.* Britain has a constitution that is "unwritten" in the sense that there is not one written document that specifies the composition and powers of the governmental institutions and the rights of citizens. These are defined instead in a number of basic laws—like the Magna Carta of 1215, the Bill of Rights of 1689, and the Parliament Acts of 1911 and 1949—common law principles, customs, and conventions. The fact that the constitution is unwritten has two important implications. One is that it makes the constitution completely flexible because it can be changed by Parliament in the same way as any other laws—by regular majorities instead of the supermajorities, like two-thirds majorities, required in many other democracies for amending their written constitutions. One slight exception to this flexibility is that opposition by the House of Lords may force a one-year delay in constitutional changes.

9. *Absence of judicial review.* The other important implication of an unwritten constitution is the absence of judicial review: there is no written constitutional document with the status of "higher law" against which the courts can test the constitutionality of regular legislation. Although Parliament normally accepts and feels bound by the rules of the unwritten constitution, it is not formally bound by them. With regard to both changing and interpreting the constitution, therefore, Parliament—that is, the parliamentary majority—can be said to be the ultimate or sovereign authority. In A. V. Dicey's (1915, 37–38) famous formulation, parliamentary sovereignty "means neither more nor less than this, namely, that Parliament . . . has, under the English constitution, the right to make or unmake any law whatever; and, further, that no person or body is recognised by

the law of England as having a right to override or set aside the legislation of Parliament."

One exception to parliamentary sovereignty is that when Britain entered the European Community—a supranational instead of merely an international organization—in 1973, it accepted the Community's laws and institutions as higher authorities than Parliament with regard to several areas of policy. Because sovereignty means supreme and ultimate authority, Parliament can therefore no longer be regarded as fully sovereign. Britain's membership in the European Community—now called the European Union—has also introduced a measure of judicial review both for the European Court of Justice and for British courts: "Parliament's supremacy is challenged by the right of the Community institutions to legislate for the United Kingdom (without the prior consent of Parliament) and by the right of the courts to rule on the admissibility (in terms of Community law) of future acts of Parliament" (Coombs 1977, 88). Similarly, Britain has been a member of the European Convention on Human Rights since 1951, and its acceptance of an optional clause of this convention in 1966 has given the European Court of Human Rights in Strasbourg the right to review and invalidate any state action, including legislation, that it judges to violate the human rights entrenched in the convention (Cappelletti 1989, 202; Johnson 1998, 155–58).

   10. A central bank controlled by the executive. Central banks are responsible for monetary policy, and independent banks are widely considered to be better at controlling inflation and maintaining price stability than banks that are dependent on the executive. However, central bank independence is clearly in conflict with the Westminster model's principle of concentrating power in the hands of the one-party majority cabinet. As expected, the Bank of England has indeed not been able to act independently and has instead been under the control of the cabinet. During the 1980s, pressure to make the Bank of England more autonomous increased. Two Conservative chancellors of the exchequer tried to convince their colleagues to take this big step away from the Westminster model, but their advice was rejected (Busch 1994, 59). It was not until 1997—one of the first decisions of the newly elected Labour government—that the Bank of England was given the independent power to set interest rates.

The Westminster Model in New Zealand

Many of the Westminster model's features have been exported to other members of the British Commonwealth, but only one country has adopted virtually the entire model: New Zealand. A major change away from majoritarianism took place in 1996 when New Zealand held its first election by PR, but the New Zealand political system before 1996 can serve as a second instructive example of how the Westminster model works.

1. Concentration of executive power in one-party and bare-majority cabinets. For six decades, from 1935 to the mid-1990s, New Zealand had single-party majority cabinets without exceptions or interruptions. Two large parties—the Labour party and the National party—dominated New Zealand politics, and they alternated in office. The one-party majority cabinet formed after the last plurality election in 1993 suffered a series of defections and briefly became a quasi-coalition cabinet (a coalition with the recent defectors), then a one-party minority cabinet, and finally a minority coalition—but all of these unusual cabinets occurred in the final phase of the transition to the new non-Westminster system (Boston, Levine, McLeay, and Roberts 1996, 93–96). The only other deviations from single-party majority government happened much earlier: New Zealand had a wartime coalition cabinet from 1915 to 1919, and another coalition was in power from 1931 to 1935.

2. Cabinet dominance. In this respect, too, New Zealand was a perfect example of the Westminster model. Just as during most of the postwar period in the United Kingdom, the combination of the parliamentary system of government and a two-party system with cohesive parties made the cabinet predominate over the legislature. In the words of New Zealand political scientist Stephen Levine (1979, 25–26), the "rigidly disciplined two-party system has contributed to the concentration of power within the Cabinet, formed from among the Members of Parliament . . . belonging to the majority party."

3. Two-party system. Two large parties were in virtually complete control of the party system, and only these two formed cabinets during the six decades from 1935 to the mid-1990s: the Labour party (1935–49, 1957–60, 1972–75, and 1984–90) and the National party (1949–57, 1960–72, 1975–84, and after 1990). Party politics revolved almost exclusively around socioeconomic issues—Labour represented left-of-center and the National party right-of-center political preferences. Moreover, unlike in Britain, third parties were almost absent from the New Zealand House of Representatives. In eleven of the seventeen elections from 1946 to 1993, the two large parties divided all of the seats; in five elections, only one other party gained one or two seats; and in 1993, two small parties gained two seats each (out of ninety-nine). New Zealand's two-party system was therefore an almost pure two-party system.

4. Majoritarian and disproportional system of elections. The House of Representatives was elected according to the plurality method in single-member districts. The only unusual feature was that there were four special large districts, geographically overlapping the regular smaller districts, that were reserved for the Maori minority (comprising about 12 percent of the population). These four districts entailed a deviation from the majoritarianism of the Westminster model because their aim was to guarantee minority representation. From 1975 on, all Maori voters have had the right to register and vote either in the regular district or in the special Maori district in which they reside.

As in the United Kingdom, the plurality system produced severely disproportional results, especially in 1978 and 1981. In the 1978 election, the National party won a clear majority of fifty-one out of ninety-two seats even though it won neither a majority of the popular vote—its support was only 39.8 percent—nor a plurality, because Labour's popular vote was 40.4 percent; the Social Credit party's 17.1 percent of the vote yielded only one seat. In 1981, the National party won another parliamentary majority of forty-seven out of ninety-two seats and again with fewer votes than Labour, although the respective percentages were closer: 38.8 and 39.0 percent; Social Credit now won 20.7 percent of the popular vote—more than half of the votes gained by either of the two big parties—but merely two seats. Moreover, all of the parliamentary majorities from 1954 on were manufactured majorities, won with less than majorities of the popular vote. In this respect, New Zealand was, like the United Kingdom, more a pluralitarian than a majoritarian democracy.

5. *Interest group pluralism.* New Zealand's interest group system, like Britain's, is clearly pluralist. Also, again like Britain, New Zealand has had high strike levels—indicative of confrontation instead of concertation between labor and management. In comparative studies of corporatism and pluralism, many scholars have tried to gauge the precise degree to which the interest group systems of the industrialized democracies are corporatist or pluralist. Their judgments differ considerably with regard to a few of these countries, but on Great Britain and New Zealand there is little disagreement: both belong on the extreme pluralist end of the pluralist-corporatist spectrum. New Zealand, moreover, is generally judged to be slightly more pluralist than Britain (Lijphart and Crepaz 1991). Hence in this respect, too, New Zealand is the somewhat better example of the Westminster model.

6. *Unitary and centralized government.* The "Act to grant a Representative Constitution to the Colony of New Zealand," passed by the British parliament in 1852, created six provinces with considerable autonomous powers and functions vis-à-vis

the central government, but these provinces were abolished in 1875. Today's governmental system is unitary and centralized—not as surprising, of course, for a country with a population of less than four million than for the United Kingdom with its much larger population of about sixty million people.

7. *Concentration of legislative power in a unicameral legislature.* For about a century, New Zealand had a bicameral legislature, consisting of an elected lower house and an appointed upper house, but the upper house gradually lost power. Its abolition in 1950 changed the asymmetrical bicameral system into pure unicameralism.

8. *Constitutional flexibility.* Like the United Kingdom, New Zealand lacks a single written constitutional document. Its "unwritten" constitution has consisted of a number of basic laws—like the Constitution Acts of 1852 and 1986, the Electoral Acts of 1956 and 1993, and the Bill of Rights Act of 1990—conventions, and customs.[2] Some key provisions in the basic laws are "entrenched" and can be changed only by three-fourths majorities of the membership of the House of Representatives or by a majority vote in a referendum; however, this entrenchment can always be removed by regular majorities, so that, in the end, majority rule prevails. Hence, like the British parliament, the parliament of New Zealand is sovereign. Any law, including laws that "amend" the unwritten constitution, can be adopted by regular majority rule. As one of New Zealand's constitutional law experts puts it, "The central principle of the Constitution is that there are no effective legal limitations on what Parliament may enact by the ordinary legislative process" (Scott 1962, 39).

9. *Absence of judicial review.* Parliamentary sovereignty also means, as in Britain, that the courts do not have the right of judicial review. The House of Representatives is the sole judge of the constitutionality of its own legislation.

10. *A central bank controlled by the executive.* Andreas

2. The Constitution Act of 1852 and Electoral Act of 1956 were superseded by the two later acts.

Busch (1994, 65) writes that historically New Zealand "has been a country with . . . a very low degree of central bank independence," and for the period until 1989, he gives the Reserve Bank of New Zealand his lowest rating—indicating even less autonomy than that of the Bank of England. This situation was changed radically by the Reserve Bank Act of 1989. Price stability was now defined as the primary aim of monetary policy, and the central bank was given the sole responsibility not to exceed the target rate of inflation, the precise level of which has to be negotiated between the central bank and the minister of finance. Inflation levels have decreased dramatically in New Zealand: measured in terms of the consumer price index, inflation was at double-digit levels during six years in the 1980s, but it was only 2 percent on average from 1991 to 1997 (OECD 1998, 240). Greater central bank independence must be given at least some of the credit for this success.

With only two exceptions—the parliamentary seats reserved for the Maori minority and the earlier shift to central bank autonomy—democracy in New Zealand was, until 1996, more clearly majoritarian and hence a better example of the Westminster model than British democracy. In fact, especially in view of the minority cabinets and frequent defeats of cabinet proposals in Britain in the 1970s, Richard Rose could legitimately claim that New Zealand was "the only example of the true British system left" (personal communication, April 8, 1982). However, the adoption of PR and the first PR election of parliament in October 1996 entailed a radical shift away from the Westminster model.

The two major parties were opposed to PR, but they both unintentionally contributed to its adoption. The first impetus was the Labour party's unhappiness with the results of the 1978 and 1981 elections, mentioned above, in which the National party won parliamentary majorities not only with less than 40 percent of the popular vote but with fewer votes than the Labour party had received. When Labour was returned to power in 1984, it appointed a Royal Commission on the Electoral System to recommend improvements. The commission's terms of reference were very broad, however, and it recommended not just small adjustments but a radical change to PR as well as a referendum on whether to adopt it. The government tried to deflect this proposal by turning it over to a parliamentary committee, which, as expected, rejected PR and instead merely recommended minor changes. The election campaign of 1987 put PR back on the political agenda: the Labour prime minister promised to let the voters decide the issue by referendum, but his party retreated from this pledge after being reelected. Seeking to embarrass Labour, the National party opportunistically made the same promise in the 1990 campaign, and when they won the election, they could not avoid honoring it. The voters then twice endorsed PR in referendums held in 1992 and 1993 (Jackson and McRobie 1998).

The form of PR that was adopted and used in the 1996 election was a system, modeled after the German system, in which sixty-five members are elected by plurality in single-member districts—including five special Maori districts—and fifty-five members by PR from party lists; a crucial provision is that this second set of fifty-five seats is allocated to the parties in a way that makes the overall result as proportional as possible. Therefore, although the New Zealand term for this system is the "mixed member proportional" (MMP) system, implying that it is a mixture of PR and something else, it is in fact clearly and fully a PR system.[3]

The first PR election instantly transformed New Zealand politics in several respects (Vowles, Aimer, Banducci, and Karp 1998). First, the election result was much more proportional than those of the previous plurality elections. The largest party, the National party, was still overrepresented, but by less than three percentage points; it won 33.8 percent of the vote and 36.7

3. Each voter has two votes, one for a district candidate and one for a party list. To avoid excessive fragmentation, parties must win either a minimum of 5 percent of the list votes or at least one district seat to qualify for list seats.

percent of the seats. Second, the election produced a multiparty system with an unprecedented six parties gaining representation in parliament. Third, unlike in any other postwar election, no party won a majority of the seats. Fourth, an ethnic dimension was added to the party system: the New Zealand First party, led by a Maori and winning seventeen seats, including all five of the special Maori seats, became the main representative of the Maori minority (although it was not a specifically Maori party nor supported exclusively by Maori voters). The Christian Coalition almost succeeded in making the party system even more multidimensional by adding a religious issue dimension, but its vote fell just short of the required 5 percent threshold. Fifth, in contrast with the long line of previous single-party majority cabinets, a two-party coalition cabinet was formed by the National and New Zealand First parties.

Because of these significant deviations from the majoritarian model, post-1996 New Zealand is no longer a good, let alone the best, example of the "true British system." Hence, in Kurt von Mettenheim's (1997, 11) words, "the United Kingdom [now] appears to be the only country to have retained the central features of the Westminster model." It should be noted, however, that all of the post-1996 changes in New Zealand have to do with the executives-parties dimension of the majoritarian model, comprising the first five of the ten characteristics of the model, and that, especially with regard to this first dimension, several other former British colonies continue to have predominantly Westminster-style institutions. A particularly clear and instructive example is Barbados.

The Westminster Model in Barbados

Barbados is a small island state in the Caribbean with a population of about a quarter of a million. It has a "strongly homogeneous society" that is mainly of African descent (Duncan 1994, 77). It gained its independence from Britain in 1966, but there continues to be "a strong and pervasive sense of British tradition and culture" (Banks, Day, and Muller 1997, 69)—including British *political* traditions. Barbados is often called the "Little England" of the Caribbean.

1. *Concentration of executive power in one-party and bare-majority cabinets.* Since independence in 1966, Barbados has had single-party majority cabinets. Its two large parties—the Barbados Labour party (BLP) and the Democratic Labour party (DLP)—have been the overwhelmingly dominant forces in Barbados politics, and they have alternated in office. Unlike in the British and New Zealand cases, there are no exceptions or qualifications to this pattern that need to be noted. In fact, the pattern extends back to colonial times. Ever since the establishment of universal suffrage and cabinet government in the early 1950s, the sequence of single-party majority cabinets has been unbroken.

2. *Cabinet dominance.* Barbadian cabinets have been at least as dominant as those of the two earlier examples of the Westminster model. The term *elective dictatorship,* coined by Lord Hailsham for Britain also fits the Barbados system well (Payne 1993, 69). One special reason for the predominance of the cabinet in Barbados is the small size of the legislature. The Barbadian House of Assembly had only twenty-four members from 1966 to 1981; this number was increased only slightly to twenty-seven in 1981 and twenty-eight in 1991. Many of the legislators are therefore also cabinet ministers, which in turn means that, as Trevor Munroe (1996, 108) points out, almost one-third of the members of the legislature "are in effect constitutionally debarred from an independent and critical stance in relation to the executive."

3. *Two-party system.* The same two large parties have controlled the party politics of Barbados since independence, and they have formed all of the cabinets: the DLP from 1966 to 1976 and from 1986 to 1994, and the BLP between 1976 to 1986 and from 1994 on. These two parties differ from each other mainly

on socioeconomic issues, with the BLP occupying the right-of-center and the DLP the left-of-center position on the left-right spectrum. In five of the seven elections since 1966, no third parties won any seats; only one small party won two seats in 1966, and another small party won one seat in 1994. The strength of the two-party system is also illustrated by the fate of the four members of parliament who defected from the ruling DLP in 1989 and formed a separate party. As Tony Thorndike (1993, 158) writes, this new party "did not long survive the logic of the 'first past the post' Westminster system and the two-party culture of Barbados. In elections in January 1991 it lost all its four seats."

4. *Majoritarian and disproportional system of elections.* In the elections before independence, including the 1966 election, which was held several months before formal independence took place, Barbados used the plurality method but not in the usual single-member districts. Instead, two-member districts were used (Emmanuel 1992, 6; Duncan 1994, 78); these tend to increase the disproportionality of the election results because, in plurality systems, disproportionality increases as the number of representatives elected per district increases. Since 1971, all elections have been by plurality in single-member districts, but electoral disproportionality has remained high. For instance, in 1971 the DLP won three-fourths of the seats with 57.4 percent of the votes, and in 1986 it won twenty-four of the twenty-seven seats (88.9 percent) with 59.4 percent of the votes. In three of the elections since 1966, the parliamentary majorities were "manufactured" from pluralities of the vote, but in the other four elections the seat majorities were genuinely "earned" with popular vote majorities. On balance, therefore, Barbados has been less of a pluralitarian democracy than Britain and New Zealand. Moreover, unlike the other two countries, Barbados has not experienced any instances of a parliamentary majority won on the basis of a second-place finish in the popular vote.

5. *Interest group pluralism.* Again like the United Kingdom

and New Zealand, Barbados has had an interest group system that is pluralist rather than corporatist. In recent years, however, there has been a trend toward corporatist practices. In 1993, the government, business leaders, and labor unions negotiated a pact on wages and prices, which included a wage freeze. This agreement was replaced two years later by a new and more flexible tripartite pact.

6–10. The characteristics of the second (federal-unitary) dimension of the majoritarian model. Barbados has a unitary and centralized form of government—hardly surprising for a small country with only a quarter of a million people—but as far as the other four characteristics of the federal-unitary dimension are concerned, it does not fit the pure majoritarian model. It has a bicameral legislature consisting of a popularly elected House of Assembly and an appointed Senate that can delay but not veto—a case of asymmetrical bicameralism. It has a written constitution that can be amended only by two-thirds majorities in both houses of the legislature. The constitution explicitly gives the courts the right of judicial review. Finally, the central bank of Barbados has a charter that gives it a medium degree of autonomy in monetary policy (Cukierman, Webb, and Neyapti 1994, 45).

Anthony Payne (1993) argues that the former British colonies in the Caribbean are characterized not by Westminster systems but by "Westminster adapted." As illustrated by Barbados—but by and large also true for the other Commonwealth democracies in the region—this adaptation has affected mainly the second dimension of the Westminster model. On the first (executives-parties) dimension, the Westminster model has remained almost completely intact. The fact that Barbados deviates from majoritarianism with regard to most of the characteristics of the federal-unitary dimension does not mean, of course, that it deviates to such an extent that it is a good example of the contrasting model of consensus democracy. In order to illustrate the consensus model, I turn in the next chapter to the examples of Switzerland, Belgium, and the European Union.

CHAPTER 3

The Consensus Model of Democracy

The majoritarian interpretation of the basic definition of democracy is that it means "government by the *majority of the people*." It argues that majorities should govern and that minorities should oppose. This view is challenged by the consensus model of democracy. As the Nobel Prize–winning economist Sir Arthur Lewis (1965, 64–65) has forcefully pointed out, majority rule and the government-versus-opposition pattern of politics that it implies may be interpreted as undemocratic because they are principles of exclusion. Lewis states that the primary meaning of democracy is that "all who are affected by a decision should have the chance to participate in making that decision either directly or through chosen representatives." Its secondary meaning is that "the will of the majority shall prevail." If this means that winning parties may make all the governmental decisions and that the losers may criticize but not govern, Lewis argues, the two meanings are incompatible: "to exclude the losing groups from participation in decision-making clearly violates the primary meaning of democracy."

Majoritarians can legitimately respond that, under two conditions, the incompatibility noted by Lewis can be resolved. First, the exclusion of the minority is mitigated if majorities and minorities alternate in government—that is, if today's minority can become the majority in the next election instead of being condemned to permanent opposition. This is how the British, New Zealand, and Barbadian two-party systems have worked. In Barbados, alternation has operated perfectly since independence in 1966: neither of the two main parties has won more than two elections in a row. In Britain and New Zealand, however, there have been long periods in which one of the two main parties was kept out of power: the British Labour party during the thirteen years from 1951 to 1964 and the eighteen years from 1979 to 1997, the New Zealand National party for fourteen years from 1935 to 1949, and New Zealand Labour for twelve years from 1960 to 1972.

Even during these extended periods of exclusion from power, one can plausibly argue that democracy and majority rule were not in conflict because of the presence of a second condition: the fact that all three countries are relatively homogeneous societies and that their major parties have usually not been very far apart in their policy outlooks because they have tended to stay close to the political center. One party's exclusion from power may be undemocratic in terms of the "government *by* the people" criterion, but if its voters' interests and preferences are reasonably well served by the other party's policies in government, the system approximates the "government *for* the people" definition of democracy.

In less homogeneous societies neither condition applies. The policies advocated by the principal parties tend to diverge to a greater extent, and the voters' loyalties are frequently more rigid, reducing the chances that the main parties will alternate in exercising governmental power. Especially in *plural societies*—societies that are sharply divided along religious, ideological, linguistic, cultural, ethnic, or racial lines into virtually separate subsocieties with their own political parties, interest groups, and media of communication—the flexibility necessary for majoritarian democracy is likely to be absent. Under these conditions, majority rule is not only undemocratic but also dangerous, because minorities that are continually denied access to power will feel excluded and discriminated against and may lose their allegiance to the regime. For instance, in the plural society of Northern Ireland, divided into a Protestant majority and a Catholic minority, majority rule meant that the Unionist party representing the Protestant majority won all the elections and formed all of the governments between 1921 and 1972. Massive Catholic protests in the late 1960s developed into a Protestant-Catholic civil war that could be kept under control only by British military intervention and the imposition of direct rule from London.

In the most deeply divided societies, like Northern Ireland, majority rule spells majority dictatorship and civil strife rather than democracy. What such societies need is a democratic regime that emphasizes consensus instead of opposition, that includes rather than excludes, and that tries to maximize the size of the ruling majority instead of being satisfied with a bare majority: consensus democracy. Despite their own majoritarian inclinations, successful British cabinets have recognized this need: they have insisted on PR in all elections in Northern Ireland (except those to the House of Commons) and, as a precondition for returning political autonomy to Northern Ireland, on broad Protestant-Catholic power-sharing coalitions. PR and power-sharing are also key elements in the agreement on Northern Ireland reached in 1998. Similarly, Lewis (1965, 51–55, 65–84) strongly recommends PR, inclusive coalitions, and federalism for the plural societies of West Africa. The consensus model is obviously also appropriate for less divided but still heterogeneous countries, and it is a reasonable and workable alternative to the Westminster model even in fairly homogeneous countries.

The examples I use to illustrate the consensus model are Switzerland, Belgium, and the European Union—all multiethnic entities. Switzerland is the best example: with one exception it approximates the pure model perfectly. Belgium also provides a good example, especially after it formally became a federal state in 1993; I therefore pay particular attention to the pattern of Belgian politics in the most recent period. The European Union (EU) is a supranational organization—more than just an international organization—but it is not, or not yet, a sovereign state. Because of the EU's intermediate status, analysts of the European Union disagree on whether to study it as an international organization or an incipient federal state, but the latter approach is increasingly common (Hix 1994). This is also my approach: if the EU is regarded as a federal state, its institutions are remarkably close to the consensus model of democracy. I discuss the Swiss and Belgian prototypes first and in tandem with each other and then turn to the EU example.

The Consensus Model in Switzerland and Belgium

The consensus model of democracy may be described in terms of ten elements that stand in sharp contrast to each of the ten majoritarian characteristics of the Westminster model. Instead of concentrating power in the hands of the majority, the consensus model tries to share, disperse, and restrain power in a variety of ways.

1. Executive power-sharing in broad coalition cabinets. In contrast to the Westminster model's tendency to concentrate executive power in one-party and bare-majority cabinets, the consensus principle is to let all or most of the important parties share executive power in a broad coalition. The Swiss seven-member national executive, the Federal Council, offers an excellent example of such a broad coalition: the three large parties— Christian Democrats, Social Democrats, and Radical Democrats —each of which has held about one-fourth of the seats in the lower house of the legislature during the post–World War II era, and the Swiss People's party, with about one-eighth of the seats, share the seven executive positions proportionately according to the so-called magic formula of 2:2:2:1, established in 1959. An additional criterion is that the linguistic groups be represented in rough proportion to their sizes: four or five German-speakers, one or two French-speakers, and frequently an Italian-speaker. Both criteria are informal rules but are strictly obeyed.

The Belgian constitution offers an example of a formal requirement that the executive include representatives of the large linguistic groups. For many years, it had already been the custom to form cabinets with approximately equal numbers of ministers representing the Dutch-speaking majority and the French-speaking minority. This became a formal rule in 1970, and the new federal constitution again stipulates that "with the possible exception of the Prime Minister, the Council of Ministers [cabinet] includes as many French-speaking members as Dutch-speaking members" (Alen and Ergec 1994). Such a rule does not apply to the partisan composition of the cabinet, but there have only been about four years of one-party rule in the postwar era, and since 1980 all cabinets have been coalitions of between four and six parties.

2. Executive-legislative balance of power. The Swiss political system is neither parliamentary nor presidential. The relationship between the executive Federal Council and the legislature is explained by Swiss political scientist Jürg Steiner (1974, 43) as follows: "The members of the council are elected individually for a fixed term of four years, and, according to the Constitution, the legislature cannot stage a vote of no confidence during that period. If a government proposal is defeated by Parliament, it is not necessary for either the member sponsoring this proposal or the Federal Council as a body to resign." This formal separation of powers has made both the executive and the legislature more independent, and their relationship is much more balanced than cabinet-parliament relationships in the British, New Zealand, and Barbadian cases in which the cabinet is clearly dominant. The Swiss Federal Council is powerful but not supreme.

Belgium has a parliamentary form of government with a cabinet dependent on the confidence of the legislature, as in the three prototypes of the Westminster model. However, Belgian cabinets, largely because they are often broad and uncohesive coalitions, are not at all as dominant as their Westminster counterparts, and they tend to have a genuine give-and-take relationship with parliament. The fact that Belgian cabinets are often short-lived attests to their relatively weak position: from 1980 to 1995, for instance, there were six cabinets consisting of different multiparty coalitions—with an average cabinet life of only about two and a half years.

3. Multiparty system. Both Switzerland and Belgium have multiparty systems without any party that comes close to majority status. In the 1995 elections to the Swiss National Council, fifteen parties won seats, but the bulk of these seats—162 out of 200—were captured by the four major parties represented on the Federal Council. Switzerland may therefore be said to have a four-party system.

Until the late 1960s, Belgium was characterized by a three-party system consisting of two large parties—Christian Democrats and Socialists—and the medium-sized Liberals. Since then, however, these major parties have split along linguistic lines and several new linguistic parties have attained prominence, creating an extreme multiparty system: about a dozen parties have usually been able to win seats in the Chamber of Representatives, and nine of these have been important enough to be included in one or more cabinets.

The emergence of multiparty systems in Switzerland and Belgium can be explained in terms of two factors. The first is that the two countries are plural societies, divided along several lines of cleavage. This multiplicity of cleavages is reflected in the multidimensional character of their party systems. In Switzerland, the religious cleavage divides the Christian Democrats, mainly supported by practicing Catholics, from the Social Democrats and Radicals, who draw most of their support from Catholics who rarely or never attend church and from Protestants. The socioeconomic cleavage further divides the Social Democrats, backed mainly by the working class, from the Radical Democrats, who have more middle-class support. The Swiss People's party is especially strong among Protestant farmers. The third source of cleavage, language, does not cause much further division in the Swiss party system, although the Swiss People's party's support is mainly in German-speaking Switzerland, and the three large parties are relatively loose alliances of cantonal parties *within* which the linguistic cleavage is a significant differentiator (McRae 1983, 111–14).

Similarly, the religious cleavage in Catholic Belgium divides the Christian Social parties, representing the more faithful Catholics, from the Socialists and Liberals, representing rarely practicing or non-practicing Catholics. The Socialists and Liberals are divided from each other by class differences. In contrast with Switzerland, the linguistic cleavage in Belgium has caused further splits both by dividing the above three groupings, which used to be Belgium's three dominant parties, into separate and smaller Dutch-speaking and French-speaking parties and by creating several additional small linguistic parties (McRae 1986, 130–48).

4. Proportional representation. The second explanation for the emergence of multiparty systems in Switzerland and Belgium is that their proportional electoral systems have not inhibited the translation of societal cleavages into party-system cleavages. In contrast with the plurality method, which tends to overrepresent large parties and to underrepresent small parties, the basic aim of proportional representation (PR) is to divide the parliamentary seats among the parties in proportion to the votes they receive. The lower houses of both legislatures are elected by PR.

5. Interest group corporatism. There is some disagreement among experts on corporatism about the degree of corporatism in Switzerland and Belgium, mainly because the labor unions in these two countries tend to be less well organized and less influential than business. This disagreement can be resolved, however, by distinguishing between two variants of corporatism: social corporatism in which the labor unions predominate and liberal corporatism in which business associations are the stronger force. Peter J. Katzenstein (1985, 105, 130) uses Switzerland and Belgium as two exemplars of the latter, and he concludes that Switzerland "most clearly typifies the traits characteristic of liberal corporatism." Both countries clearly show the three general elements of corporatism: tripartite concertation, relatively few and relatively large interest groups, and the prominence of peak associations. Gerhard Lehmbruch (1993, 52) writes that "the strength of Swiss peak associations is remarkable, and it is generally acknowledged that the cohesion of Swiss interest associations is superior to that of Swiss political parties." Moreover, Klaus Armingeon (1997) argues that, although the extent and effectiveness of corporatism in many European countries has been declining in the 1990s, it continues to be strong in Switzerland.

6. *Federal and decentralized government.* Switzerland is a federal state in which power is divided between the central government and the governments of twenty cantons and six so-called half-cantons, produced by splits in three formerly united cantons. The half-cantons have only one instead of two representatives in the Swiss federal chamber, the Council of States, and they carry only half the weight of the regular cantons in the voting on constitutional amendments; in most other respects, however, their status is equal to that of the full cantons. Switzerland is also one of the world's most decentralized states.

Belgium was a unitary and centralized state for a long time, but from 1970 on it gradually moved in the direction of both decentralization and federalism; in 1993, it formally became a federal state. The form of federalism adopted by Belgium is a "unique federalism" (Fitzmaurice 1996) and one of "Byzantine complexity" (McRae 1997, 289), because it consists of three geo-graphically defined regions—Flanders, Wallonia, and the bilin-gual capital of Brussels—and three nongeographically defined cultural communities—the large Flemish and French commu-nities and the much smaller German-speaking community. The main reason for the construction of this two-layer system was that the bilingual area of Brussels has a large majority of French-speakers, but that it is surrounded by Dutch-speaking Flanders. There is a considerable overlap between regions and commu-nities, but they do not match exactly. Each has its own legisla-ture and executive, except that in Flanders the government of the Flemish community also serves as the government of the Flemish region.

7. *Strong bicameralism.* The principal justification for in-stituting a bicameral instead of a unicameral legislature is to give special representation to minorities, including the smaller states in federal systems, in a second chamber or upper house. Two conditions have to be fulfilled if this minority represen-tation is to be meaningful: the upper house has to be elected on a different basis than the lower house, and it must have real power—ideally as much power as the lower house. Both of these conditions are met in the Swiss system: the National Council is the lower house and represents the Swiss people, and the Coun-cil of States is the upper or federal chamber representing the cantons, with each canton having two representatives and each half-canton one representative. Hence the small cantons are much more strongly represented in the Council of States than in the National Council. Moreover, as Wolf Linder (1994, 47) writes, the "absolute equality" of the two chambers is a "sacro-sanct rule" in Switzerland.

The two Belgian chambers of parliament—the Chamber of Representatives and the Senate—had virtually equal powers in prefederal Belgium, but they were both proportionally consti-tuted and hence very similar in composition. The new Senate, elected for the first time in 1995, especially represents the two cultural-linguistic groups, but it is still largely proportionally constituted and not designed to provide overrepresentation for the French-speaking and German-speaking minorities.[1] Moreover, its powers were reduced in comparison with the old Senate; for instance, it no longer has budgetary authority (Senelle 1996, 283). Hence the new federal legislature of Belgium exemplifies a relatively weak rather than strong bicameralism.

8. Constitutional rigidity. Both Belgium and Switzerland have a written constitution—a single document containing the basic rules of governance—that can be changed only by special majorities. Amendments to the Swiss constitution require the approval in a referendum of not only a nationwide majority of the voters but also majorities in a majority of the cantons. The half-cantons are given half weight in the canton-by-canton calculation; this means that, for instance, a constitutional amendment can be adopted by 13.5 cantons in favor and 12.5 against. The requirement of majority cantonal approval means that the populations of the smaller cantons and half-cantons, with less than 20 percent of the total Swiss population, can veto constitutional changes.

In Belgium, there are two types of supermajorities. All constitutional amendments require the approval of two-thirds majorities in both houses of the legislature. Moreover, laws pertaining to the organization and powers of the communities and regions have a semiconstitutional status and are even harder to adopt and to amend: in addition to the two-thirds majorities in

1. Most senators—forty out of seventy-one—are directly elected from two multimember districts that are partly defined in nongeographical terms—one comprising Flanders and Dutch-speakers in Brussels and the other Wallonia and French-speaking Bruxellois. The remaining thirty-one senators are indirectly elected or coopted in different ways. The overall linguistic composition is: forty-one Dutch-speakers, twenty-nine French-speakers, and one German-speaker. A further curious provision is that any adult children of the king are "senators by right."

both houses, they require the approval of majorities within the Dutch-speaking group as well as within the French-speaking group in each of the houses. This rule gives the French-speakers an effective minority veto.

9. *Judicial review.* Switzerland deviates in one respect from the pure consensus model: its supreme court, the Federal Tribunal, does not have the right of judicial review. A popular initiative that tried to introduce it was decisively rejected in a 1939 referendum (Codding 1961, 112).[2]

There was no judicial review in Belgium either until 1984, when the new Court of Arbitration was inaugurated. The court's original main responsibility was the interpretation of the constitutional provisions concerning the separation of powers between the central, community, and regional governments. Its authority was greatly expanded by the constitutional revision of 1988, and the Court of Arbitration can now be regarded as a genuine constitutional court (Alen and Ergec 1994, 20–22; Verougstraete 1992, 95).

10. *Central bank independence.* Switzerland's central bank has long been regarded as one of the strongest and most independent central banks, together with the German Bundesbank and the Federal Reserve System in the United States. In contrast, the National Bank of Belgium was long one of the weakest central banks. However, its autonomy was substantially reinforced in the early 1990s, roughly at the same time as the transition to a federal system, but mainly as a result of the Maastricht Treaty, signed in 1992 and ratified in 1993, which obligated the EU member states to enhance the independence of their central banks. Robert Senelle (1996, 279) concludes that the Belgian central bank now enjoys a "high degree of autonomy . . . in the conduct of its monetary policy."

2. National laws can, however, be challenged in a different manner: if, within ninety days of the passage of a law, a minimum of fifty thousand citizens demand a referendum on it, a majority of Swiss voters can reject it.

The Consensus Model in the European Union

The principal institutions of the European Union do not fit the classification into executive, legislative, judicial, and monetary organs as easily as those of the five sovereign states discussed so far. This is especially true for the European Council, which consists of the heads of government of the fifteen member states, meeting at least twice a year; it can exert great political influence, and most of the major steps in the development of the European Community and, since 1993, of the European Union have been initiated by the European Council. Of the other institutions, the European Commission serves as the executive of the EU and can be compared to a cabinet; the European Parliament is the lower house of the legislature; and the Council of the European Union can be regarded as the upper house. The responsibilities of the European Court of Justice and the European Central Bank are clear from their names.

1. Executive power-sharing in broad coalition cabinets. The European Commission consists of twenty members, each with a specific ministerial responsibility, appointed by the governments of the member states. The five largest states—Germany, the United Kingdom, France, Italy, and Spain—appoint two commissioners apiece, and each of the other ten members appoints one commissioner. Because all fifteen nations that belong to the EU are represented on it, the Commission is a broad and permanent internation coalition. In practice, the Commission is also a coalition that unites the left, center, and right of the political spectrum in Europe. A telling example is that, in the mid-1990s, the two British commissioners were Conservative Leon Brittan and former Labour party leader Neil Kinnock—politicians who are extremely unlikely ever to serve together in a British cabinet.

2. Executive-legislative balance of power. After each five-yearly parliamentary election, the new European Commission must be approved by a vote in the European Parliament. Parliament also has the power to dismiss the Commission, but only by a two-thirds majority. Parliament has strong budgetary powers, but although its other legislative powers were enhanced by the Amsterdam Treaty of 1997, they remain relatively weak. In comparison with the Commission, the Parliament's role appears to be subordinate. This judgment of executive-legislative relationships changes, however, when we add the Council of the European Union—composed of ministers from the governments of the fifteen member states—to the picture. George Tsebelis and Jeannette Money (1997, 180) call the Council "the European equivalent of [an] upper house." The Council is also clearly the strongest of the three institutions. Overall, therefore, the Commission is much more like the equal partner in the consensus model than the dominant cabinet in the Westminster model.

   3. Multiparty system. The 626-member European Parliament had eight officially recognized parties (comprising the minimum of 18 members required for recognition) in 1996. The largest of these was the Party of European Socialists with about 34 percent of the seats in Parliament—far short of a parliamentary majority. The next largest was the European People's party (mainly Christian Democrats) with about 29 percent of the seats. None of the other parties held more than 10 percent of the seats. The political fragmentation is even greater than appears from this multiparty pattern because the parties in the European Parliament are considerably less cohesive and disciplined than the parties in the national parliaments. The partisan composition of the "upper house," the Council of the European Union, changes as the cabinets of the member countries change, and it also depends on the subject matter being discussed, which determines which particular minister will attend a particular session; for instance, if farm policies are on the Council's agenda, the national ministers of agriculture are likely to attend. In practice, however, the Council is also a multiparty body.

   4. Proportional representation. The European Parliament has been directly elected since 1979. It is supposed to be elected

in each country according to a uniform electoral system, but the member countries have not been able to agree on such a system. Nevertheless, the prevalent method is some variant of PR, and PR is used in all of the member countries and in Northern Ireland. The only exception has been the election by plurality of the British representatives from the United Kingdom, but in 1997 the new Labour cabinet decided that the 1999 European Parliament elections in the United Kingdom would be entirely by PR. Even then, however, there will still be a significant degree of disproportionality as a result of the overrepresentation of the small states and the underrepresentation of the large states in the European Parliament. At the extremes, Germany has ninety-nine and Luxembourg six representatives in the European Parliament, even though Germany's population is about two hundred times larger than Luxembourg's. In this respect, the European Parliament combines in one legislative chamber the principles of proportional representation and of equal national representation that, for instance, in Switzerland are embodied in two separate houses of the legislature.

5. *Interest group corporatism.* The EU has not yet developed a full-fledged corporatism, largely because the most important socioeconomic decisions are still made at the national level or subject to national vetoes. As the EU becomes more integrated, the degree of corporatism is bound to increase. In the title of Michael J. Gorges's (1996) book *Euro-Corporatism?* the question mark is deliberate, and Gorges answers the question mainly in the negative for the present situation, but he also sees significant corporatist elements in certain sectors as well as a clear trend toward greater corporatism. One important factor is that the European Commission has long favored a corporatist mode of negotiating with interest groups. For instance, it sponsored a series of tripartite conferences during the 1970s, and although these did not lead to the institutionalization of tripartite bargaining, "the Commission never abandoned its goal of promoting a dialogue between the social partners and of improving their partici-

pation in the Community's decision-making process" (Gorges 1996, 139). Another indication of the EU's inclination toward corporatism is that one of its formal institutions is the advisory Economic and Social Committee, which consists of interest group representatives appointed by the member governments.

6. *Federal and decentralized government.* Compared with other international organizations, the supranational EU is highly unified and centralized, but compared with national states—even as decentralized a state as Switzerland—the EU is obviously still more "confederal" than federal as well as extremely decentralized.

7. *Strong bicameralism.* The two criteria of strong bicameralism are that the two houses of a legislature be equal in strength and different in composition. The EU's legislature fits the second criterion without difficulty: the Council has equal representation of the member countries and consists of representatives of the national governments, whereas the Parliament is directly elected by the voters and the national delegations are weighted by population size. In national legislatures, deviations from equal power tend to be to the advantage of the lower house. In the EU it is the other way around: the upper house (Council) is considerably more powerful than the lower house (Parliament)—not fully in accordance with the consensus model, but even less with the majoritarian model.[3]

8. *Constitutional rigidity.* The EU's "constitution" consists of the founding Treaty of the European Economic Community, signed in Rome in 1957, and a series of both earlier and subsequent treaties. Because these are international treaties, they can be changed only with the consent of all of the signatories. Hence they are extremely rigid. In addition, most important decisions in the Council require unanimity; on less important matters, it has become more common since the 1980s to make decisions by

3. Another notable example of at least a slight asymmetry favoring the upper house is the U.S. Congress in which the Senate has special powers over treaties and appointments.

"qualified majority voting," that is, by roughly two-thirds majorities and by means of a weighted voting system (similar to the weighted allocation of seats in the European Parliament).

9. Judicial review. A key EU institution is the European Court of Justice. The Court has the right of judicial review and can declare both EU laws and national laws unconstitutional if they violate the various EU treaties. Moreover, the Court's approach to its judicial tasks has been creative and activist. Martin Shapiro and Alec Stone (1994, 408) write that "clearly the two most politically influential constitutional courts in Europe are those of Germany and the Community [EU]. . . . There are few instances as observable and as important as the ECJ [European Court of Justice] case of a court building itself as a political institution, and building the whole set of institutions of which it is a part."

10. Central bank independence. The European Central Bank, which started operating in 1998, was designed to be a highly independent central bank; indeed, the *Economist* (November 8, 1997) wrote that "its constitution makes it the most independent central bank in the world." However, its independence was compromised to some extent when the first bank president was appointed in 1998. In order to maximize the president's authority, the appointment is formally for an eight-year term, but the first president had to pledge to resign well before the end of his term, probably after about four years, as part of a political deal between France, which had insisted on its own candidate, and the other EU members.

In the beginning of this chapter, I emphasized that the majoritarian model was incompatible with the needs of deeply divided, plural societies. The EU is clearly such a plural society: "Deep-seated and long-standing national differences, of which language is only one, have not and will not disappear in Europe" (Kirchner 1994, 263). Hence it is not surprising that the EU's institutions conform largely to the consensus instead of the majoritarian model. Many observers predict that the EU will eventually become a federal state, especially as a result of the adoption of a common currency. For instance, Martin Feldstein (1997, 60) asserts that the "fundamental long-term effect of adopting a single currency [will] be the creation of a political union, a European federal state with responsibility for a Europe-wide foreign and security policy as well as for what are now domestic economic and social policies." If and when the EU develops into a sovereign European state, its institutions are likely to change— the European Parliament, for instance, will probably become a more powerful legislative chamber—but it is not likely to stray far from the consensus model, and it is almost certain to take the form of a *federal* United States of Europe.

CHAPTER 4

Thirty-Six Democracies

The remainder of this book is a systematic comparison of the thirty-six countries (with populations of at least a quarter of a million) that were democratic in the middle of 1996 and that had been continuously democratic since 1977 or earlier. Each democracy is analyzed from its first democratic election in or after 1945 until June 30, 1996; the time span for the thirty-six democracies therefore varies from fifty-one years (1945–96) to nineteen years (1977–96). In this chapter, I explain the criteria for selecting the thirty-six democracies and for choosing the minimum of nineteen years of democratic experience. I also discuss the principal social and economic characteristics that can be expected to influence the types of democracy and democratic performance of the thirty-six countries.

Definitions of Democracy

Although political scientists have disagreed on some of the details of defining and measuring democracy (Beetham 1994, Inkeles 1991), the eight criteria proposed by Robert A. Dahl (1971, 3) in his seminal book *Polyarchy* still command widespread support: (1) the right to vote, (2) the right to be elected, (3) the right of political leaders to compete for support and votes, (4) elections that are free and fair, (5) freedom of association, (6) freedom of expression, (7) alternative sources of information, and (8) institutions for making public policies depend on votes and other expressions of preference. These requirements are already implied by Lincoln's simple definition of democracy as government by the people (or by representatives of the people) and for the people. For instance, "by the people" implies universal suffrage, eligibility for public office, and free and fair elections; and elections cannot be free and fair unless there is freedom of expression and association both before and between elections. Similarly, "for the people" implies Dahl's eighth criterion of responsiveness by the government to the voters' preferences. Nevertheless, it is instructive to spell out the specific criteria especially for the purpose of deciding which countries qualify as democracies and which countries do not.

Democracy, as defined by Dahl, is a twentieth-century phenomenon, and Göran Therborn (1977, 11–17) credits Australia and New Zealand with having established the first genuinely democratic systems of government in the first decade of the twentieth century. New Zealand has the strongest claim because, as early as 1893, it was the first country to institute truly universal suffrage, that is, the right to vote for both men and women *and* for the Maori minority; women, however, did not have to right to be candidates for public office until 1919. Australia adopted suffrage for both men and women in 1902, but Aboriginal Australians—admittedly a small minority comprising about 2 percent of the total population—could not vote in federal elections until 1962 (Inter-Parliamentary Union 1995, 61, 193).

Table 4.1 lists the countries that can be regarded as democratic in 1996 and as having been democratic for at least nineteen years; these are the thirty-six countries analyzed in this book, classified by the decade and first year from which the analysis of each country starts. In order to decide which countries qualify as democracies, I relied to a large extent—following the example of many other researchers—on the ratings for all

Table 4.1   The thirty-six democracies included in this study, classified by decade and first year of the period (until the middle of 1996) analyzed

Decade	First year analyzed	Democracies
1940s	1945	Austria, Canada, Denmark, Finland, Luxembourg, Norway, United Kingdom
	1946	Australia, Belgium, Iceland, Italy, Japan, Netherlands, New Zealand, United States
	1947	Switzerland
	1948	Ireland, Sweden
	1949	Germany, Israel
1950s	1953	Costa Rica
	1958	Colombia, France, Venezuela
1960s	1961	Trinidad and Tobago
	1962	Jamaica
	1965	Botswana
	1966	Barbados, Malta
1970s	1972	Bahamas
	1974	Greece
	1976	Mauritius, Portugal
	1977	India, Papua New Guinea, Spain

countries in the world that Freedom House has produced since 1972 (Gastil 1989, 50–61). In the Freedom House surveys, countries are rated as free, partly free, or not free, and these ratings are based on two sets of criteria similar to those suggested by Dahl: political rights, such as the right to participate in free and competitive elections, and civil liberties, such as freedom of speech and association. Hence the "free" countries can also be regarded as democratic countries.

There are four borderline cases: India, Papua New Guinea, Colombia, and Venezuela. In the Freedom House Survey Team's

(1996) judgment, based especially on the high levels of political violence and corruption in these countries, they slipped from "free" to only "partly free" in the early 1990s. For India this judgment is probably too severe, given India's huge size and the fact that most violence has been confined to the periphery of the country, but there is little doubt that democracy has been operating far from perfectly in any of the four countries in recent years. A different survey of the world's political systems in 1994, which uses a ten-point scale with 10 as the highest rating, rates the four countries below the perfect 10—a score that *is* given to the bulk of the countries in Table 4.1. On the other hand, the four borderline cases still have reasonably high scores, and several other countries are also rated lower than 10. Colombia receives a score of 9—the same as Israel and Spain; India, Papua New Guinea, and Venezuela receive an 8—the same as France and Trinidad and Tobago (Jaggers and Gurr 1995). In Mark J. Gasiorowski's (1996, 480–81) dataset tracking political regime changes through 1992, all four countries are judged to have retained a democratic regime until the end of 1992.

Writing at the end of the 1980s, Larry Diamond (1989, 1) judged India to be "the most surprising and important case of democratic endurance in the developing world" and stated that Papua New Guinea had "manifested a remarkably vibrant and resilient democratic system." Their democratic performance deteriorated in the 1990s but, in my opinion, not sufficiently to warrant the conclusion that they cannot be regarded as democratic any longer. It is also preferable to err on the side of inclusion because India is the world's most populous democracy and because all four countries make the set of democracies analyzed in this book much more interesting and diverse: India and Papua New Guinea are the least developed of the thirty-six countries and they are among the most ethnically divided societies. Colombia and Venezuela are two of only five presidential democracies and the only South American democracies, among the thirty-six countries.[1] (By the end of 1998, India, Venezuela, and Papua New Guinea had been readmitted to Freedom House's "free" countries.)

I am also somewhat lenient with regard to several other countries that are on the list of long-term democracies in Table 4.1 in spite of the absence of fully universal suffrage—the most fundamental of democratic requisites. In pre-1971 Switzerland, women did not yet have the right to vote. In Australia, as noted earlier, Aborigines could not vote until 1962. And, in spite of President Bill Clinton's claim in his 1993 inaugural address that the United States is "the world's oldest democracy" (*New York Times,* January 21, 1993, A11), universal suffrage was not firmly established in the United States until the passage of the Voting Rights Act in 1965. The principle of universal suffrage was also violated by the United Kingdom, France, the Netherlands, and Belgium while these countries were colonial powers, by the three Allied Powers while they were occupying Germany and Japan, and by post-1967 Israel on account of its control over the occupied territories.[2] Focusing on the post-1945 period minimizes these problems because the colonial empires were rapidly dissolved and because women finally received the right to vote in Belgium, France, and Italy.

In comparative analyses of democracy, the smallest and least populous ministates are usually excluded; the cutoff point tends to vary between populations of one million and of a quarter of a million. Here, too, I opted to be inclusive by selecting the lower cutoff point.

1. This book is not designed to contribute to the scholarly debate about the viability of parliamentary versus presidential regimes (see Linz and Valenzuela 1994, Power and Gasiorowski 1997). Nevertheless, it seems significant that there are merely five presidential systems among the thirty-six long-term democracies as of 1996 and that two of these are borderline cases of democracy.

2. Postwar control of conquered countries or areas is the least serious violation of the universal-suffrage standard because such control is meant to be temporary; the longer such control lasts, however, the more it creates a dilemma for democracy.

There are two reasons for the requirement that countries be not just democratic but democratic for an extended period. The substantive reason is that it provides assurance that the democracies studied are not ephemeral entities but reasonably stable and consolidated democratic systems. The second reason is procedural: in order to study, for instance, the results that elections tend to have, the kinds of cabinets that tend to be formed, and the durability of these cabinets in a particular country, we need to be able to measure more than just one or a few of these elections and cabinets. Obviously somewhat arbitrarily, I first selected twenty years as the minimum time span but then relaxed this criterion slightly so as to be able to include India, Papua New Guinea, and Spain.

Table 4.1 shows the first year of the period analyzed for each of the thirty-six democracies. Generally, this is the year of the first democratic election since 1945 or since independence. In countries where democracy was interrupted in the postwar period—in France in 1958, Greece from 1967 to 1974, India from 1975 to 1977, and Venezuela from 1948 to 1958—it is the election year that marks the resumption of democracy. In the countries that became independent in the 1960s and 1970s, it is the year of the election held closest to the achievement of independence—which in three cases means the election in the year before independence (Trinidad and Tobago, Botswana, and the Bahamas).[3] The only exception is Mauritius, which held a democratic election in 1967, one year before formal independence in 1968, but where democracy lapsed for several years in the early 1970s: a state of emergency was in force from 1971 to 1976; opposition leaders were imprisoned; labor unions were banned; and the 1972 election was postponed to 1976 (Bowman 1991,

3. Trinidad and Tobago—for brevity's sake hereinafter simply referred to as "Trinidad"—and Jamaica became independent in 1962, Malta in 1964, Barbados and Botswana in 1966, Mauritius in 1968, the Bahamas in 1973, and Papua New Guinea in 1975.

Table 4.2 The twenty-five other democracies (with populations over 250,000), as of January 1996, classified by decade and year of democratization

Decade	Year of democratization	Democracies
1970s	1978	Solomon Islands
1980s	1980	Ecuador
	1981	Cyprus
	1984	Argentina
	1985	Uruguay
	1988	Korea
1990s	1990	Chile, Czech Republic, Hungary, Namibia, Poland
	1991	Benin, Bulgaria, Cape Verde, Lithuania, Mongolia, Slovenia
	1993	Estonia, Guyana
	1994	Latvia, Malawi, Panama, Slovakia, South Africa
	1995	Mali

Source: Based on information in Freedom House Survey Team 1996 and earlier volumes of the *Freedom in the World* annual survey

73–74, Bräutigam 1997, 50). The 1976 election marks the restoration of democracy, and Mauritius is therefore included in the analysis from 1976 on.

The requirement of a minimum time span of nineteen years of democratic experience necessarily means that quite a few democracies had to be omitted from the analysis. Fortunately, as Table 4.2 shows, this number is not very great. The table lists the twenty-five countries that the Freedom House Survey Team (1996) judged to be democratic as of January 1996, and it provides the year from which democracy lasted continuously in each of the countries until 1996. Shortening the required time span from nineteen years to ten would have resulted in the inclusion of only five more countries: the Solomon Islands, Ecuador, Cyprus (the Greek part of the island), Argentina, and Uruguay. Moreover, the twenty-five more recent democracies are generally smaller countries; no country has a population larger than fifty million, and only Korea's and South Africa's populations exceed forty million. Of the combined total population of the sixty-one democracies—more than two billion people—the thirty-six older democracies contain more than 87 percent.[4]

Thirty-Six Diverse Democracies

Our set of thirty-six democracies includes representatives of each of the three waves of democratization identified by Samuel P. Huntington (1991, 13–26). Using a rather lenient definition of "universal" suffrage—the right to vote for at least 50 percent of adult males[5]—Huntington sees a long first wave starting as early as 1828 and lasting until 1926, a short second wave from 1943 to 1962, and a third wave starting in 1974; two reverse waves, in which democracy collapsed in many countries, occurred between the three waves of democratization. Several countries that experienced reverse waves participated in more than one forward wave; among our thirty-six democracies, Greece is the one case of involvement in all three forward waves and in both reverse waves. All of the countries listed in Table 4.1 as having been continuously democratic since the 1940s, except Israel, were already part of the first of Huntington's waves. About half were also in the second wave: those in which democracy failed in the first reverse wave, like Germany and Italy, and countries where democracy was interrupted by German occupation during the Second World War.

The countries listed in Table 4.1 as having been democratic since the 1950s and 1960s belong to the second wave; for the

4. If we exclude India with its huge population of almost one billion people, the percentage of the combined population in the remaining thirty-five older democracies is still more than 77 percent.

5. Huntington (1991, 14) concedes that he includes both democratic and "semidemocratic" systems.

Table 4.3 Population sizes (in thousands) and levels of development of thirty-six democracies, classified by extent of pluralism, c. 1995

	Population (000s) 1995	Human development index 1994		Population (000s) 1995	Human development index 1994
Plural societies			**Nonplural societies**		
India	929,358	0.446	Japan	125,213	0.940
Spain	39,199	0.934	United Kingdom	58,533	0.931
Canada	29,606	0.960	Venezuela	21,671	0.861
Belgium	10,146	0.932	Australia	18,054	0.931
Switzerland	7,039	0.930	Greece	10,467	0.923
Israel	5,521	0.913	Portugal	9,927	0.890
Papua New Guinea	4,302	0.525	Sweden	8,830	0.936
Trinidad	1,287	0.880	Denmark	5,220	0.927
Mauritius	1,128	0.831	Norway	4,354	0.943
			New Zealand	3,601	0.937
Semiplural societies			Ireland	3,586	0.929
United States	263,119	0.942	Costa Rica	3,399	0.889
Germany	81,869	0.924	Jamaica	2,522	0.736
France	58,060	0.946	Botswana	1,450	0.673
Italy	57,204	0.921	Malta	372	0.887
Colombia	36,813	0.848	Bahamas	276	0.894
Netherlands	15,460	0.940	Iceland	268	0.942
Austria	8,054	0.932	Barbados	266	0.907
Finland	5,110	0.940			
Luxembourg	410	0.899			

Source: Based on data in World Bank 1997, 16–17, and United Nations Development Programme 1997, 146–48

1960s group, democratization came about as a result of decolonization. Huntington uses 1962 as the year in which the second wave ended, but Botswana, Barbados, Malta, and even the Bahamas (not independent until 1973) should be included in the second wave. The end of the Portuguese dictatorship in 1974 initiated the third wave, which also encompasses the other democracies in the 1970s group (except the Bahamas) and which continued in the 1980s and 1990s, especially in Latin America and Eastern Europe (Table 4.2).

The twenty democracies that have been continuously democratic since the 1940s (or earlier) are a rather homogeneous group in several key respects, except their degree of pluralism: they are all economically developed, industrialized, and urbanized; with the exception of Japan, they belong to the Western Judeo-Christian world; and most are geographically concentrated in the North Atlantic area. However, the addition of the second-wave and third-wave democracies adds a great deal of diversity. Three major differences are highlighted in Table 4.3: the degree to which the thirty-six democracies are plural societies, their levels of socioeconomic development, and their population sizes.

The first difference is the degree of societal division. This variable is commonly operationalized as the number and relative sizes of the ethnic groups in different countries (Ordeshook and Shvetsova 1994, Amorim Neto and Cox 1997). This ethnic-groups measure captures an important element of societal division; for instance, *ceteris paribus,* a country consisting of three ethnic groups of equal size is less divided than one with four such equal groups, and a country with two ethnic groups comprising 90 and 10 percent of the population is less divided than one with two groups of 50 percent each. Another advantage is that it can be precisely quantified.[6]

6. The measure used by Ordeshook and Shvetsova (1994) and Amorim Neto and Cox (1997) is the "effective number of ethnic groups," which is conceptually similar to the effective number of political parties that I introduce and explain in Chapter 5.

Its disadvantage is that it leaves out a number of important aspects of division. First, ethnic divisions are not the only relevant differences; in particular, religious cleavages, such as those between Hindus, Muslims, and Sikhs in India, may be as important or even more important. Second, the measure could, in principle, be adjusted so as to include religious as well as ethnic differences, but it would then still miss important cleavages *within* religious groups, such as the difference between faithfully practicing Catholics on one hand and infrequently and non-practicing Catholics on the other and the related split between prochurch and anticlerical forces that has historically shaped much of the politics of France, Italy, and Colombia.

Third, it fails to take the depth of division into account. It is misleading, for instance, to treat the Protestant-Catholic division of Northern Ireland on a par with that in Switzerland, Germany, and the Netherlands; or to equate ethnic divisions in which linguistic differentiation is relatively unimportant, such as between Welsh and English or Frisians and Dutch, with ethnic divisions that coincide with sharp linguistic divisions, as in Belgium, Switzerland, India, Spain, and Finland. Fourth, it fails to indicate the extent to which the ethnic, religious, and possibly other groups differentiate themselves organizationally. A high degree of this can historically be seen in Austria, Belgium, the Netherlands, and Israel, where religious and ideological groups have organized themselves into more or less separate subsocieties with their own political, socioeconomic, cultural, educational, and recreational associations.

The threefold classification into plural, semiplural, and non-plural societies in Table 4.3 takes all these considerations into account. It is obviously a more subjective and much rougher measure than one based exclusively on the number and sizes of ethnic groups, but it is also a more valid and meaningful measure. Three further comments on the trichotomous classification are in order. First, all but one of the plural societies are linguistically divided countries; India, with its more than a dozen officially recognized languages is an extreme case, and Papua New Guinea is even more fragmented along linguistic lines. The population of Mauritius is about two-thirds of Indian and one-third of African descent; the Indian community is a microcosm of the linguistic and religious divisions of India. Israel is a plural society not just because of the division between Jewish and Arab citizens but even more as a result of the sharp split between religious and secular Jews. The only exceptional case is Trinidad, where there is a common language but where "an all-pervasive and fundamental cleavage . . . dominates Trinidadian society: the Creole-cum-colored portion versus the Indian portion" (Premdas 1993, 100).

Second, the threefold classification reflects the situation in the mid-1990s, but it would not have looked very different if it had been based on a much longer time span. The only exceptions would be Austria, the Netherlands, and Luxembourg, which are classified as semiplural here but which should have been rated as plural in the first two postwar decades, when their religious and ideological segments were organizationally much more distinct. Third, it is important not to equate "nonplural" with "homogeneous": most of the nonplural societies are religiously divided to at least some extent and most contain at least one or more small minorities. Examples that have already been mentioned earlier are the ethnic minorities in the United Kingdom, Australia, and New Zealand. Another example is Botswana, which is often regarded as the most homogeneous state in Africa but where there is a significant ethnic minority, the Kalanga, and where the dominant Tswana ethnic group is divided internally into eight tribes.

Table 4.3 also indicates the level of socioeconomic development in the thirty-six democracies. This variable has traditionally been operationalized as gross national product (GNP) per capita, although it has long been recognized that GNP per capita is a flawed measure because of its excessive sensitivity to exchange rate fluctuations and its exaggeration of the poverty of less developed nations. A considerable improvement is to adjust per capita GNP for the different price levels in different countries, yielding so-called purchasing power parities (Dogan 1994, 44–46). A further big improvement is the human development index, designed by the United Nations Development Programme (1997, 44) in the early 1990s: "It is a composite index of achievements in basic human capabilities in three fundamental dimensions—a long and healthy life, knowledge, and a decent standard of living." The three variables on which the index are based are income, life expectancy, and educational attainment. It is a more accurate indicator of development because it is more broadly based than the two older measures, and it has already found wide acceptance among social scientists (Diamond 1992, 100–102, Lane and Ersson 1994a, 214–28, Vanhanen 1997, 75–79).

The human development index can, in principle, range from a high of 1 to a low of 0. As Table 4.3 shows, based on 1994 data, most of the countries that are commonly regarded as highly developed and industrialized have indices higher than 0.9; those of most of the developing countries are between 0.8 and 0.9, but four nations have much lower indices: the lowest is India (0.446), followed in ascending order by Papua New Guinea, Botswana, and Jamaica.

By far the greatest difference among the thirty-six countries is in their population sizes. Table 4.3 highlights these differences by listing the countries in each of the three degree-of-pluralism categories in descending order of size. India is by far the largest country with a population approaching one billion; according to the 1995 World Bank figures, India's population was larger than the combined populations of the thirty-five other countries. Another way to emphasize these enormous differences is to calculate India's weekly population growth from its annual growth of about eighteen million people; its population increase *per week* is about 350,000—more than the entire populations of three of the thirty-six democracies: the Bahamas, Barbados, and Iceland.

The above variables are important in this comparative analysis because they can be expected to influence the form of democracy adopted in different countries as well as their democratic performance. For instance, I have hinted in previous chapters that consensus democracy is especially appropriate for plural societies and that federalism makes more sense for large than for small countries. Moreover, the level of development is likely to have an effect on the macroeconomic performance of governments. These relationships are explored in Chapters 14 and 15.

The three variables are only weakly correlated among each other. It is logical to expect larger countries to be more heterogeneous than smaller countries (Dahl and Tufte 1973, 13–14); indeed, population size (logged) and degree of pluralism in our thirty-six democracies are positively correlated, but the correlation coefficient is a mere 0.26, which is statistically significant only at the 10 percent level. Plural societies tend to be less developed (r=−0.24, significant at the 10 percent level), but this relationship is driven largely by the two cases of India and Papua New Guinea. Larger countries are somewhat less developed than smaller countries (r=−0.10), but the relationship is very weak and not statistically significant. Finally, the length of continuous democratic experience between 1945 and 1996 (measured by decade, as indicated in Table 4.1) is very strongly correlated with development—the older democracies are the wealthier countries (r=0.57, significant at the 1 percent level)—but there is no significant relationship with either population size or degree of pluralism.

CHAPTER 5

Party Systems
Two-Party and Multiparty Patterns

The first of the ten variables that characterize the majoritarian-consensus contrast, presented in Chapter 1, was the difference between single-party majority governments and broad multiparty coalitions. This first difference can also be seen as the most important and typical difference between the two models of democracy because it epitomizes the contrast between concentration of power on one hand and power-sharing on the other. Moreover, the factor analysis reported in Chapter 14 shows that it correlates more strongly with the "factor" representing the first (executives-parties) dimension than any of the other four variables that belong to this dimension. It would therefore make sense to devote this chapter—the first of nine chapters that will discuss the ten basic variables[1]—to this first and most typical variable.

For practical reasons, however, it is necessary to discuss the subject of party systems first. The classification of cabinets—single-party cabinets versus multiparty coalition cabinets, and bare-majority cabinets versus minority cabinets and cabinets that have "unnecessary" parties in them—depends a great deal on how political parties and the numbers of parties in party systems are defined. Hence these definitional problems have to

1. Two of the variables—constitutional rigidity and judicial review—will be discussed in one chapter (Chapter 12).

be solved before the question of cabinet types can be properly addressed. It is worth noting, however, that the type of party system is also a strong component of the executives-parties dimension. To preview the factor analysis in Chapter 14 once more, the party-system variable correlates with the first "factor" almost as strongly as the type of cabinet and more strongly than the remaining three variables.[2]

Two-party systems typify the majoritarian model of democracy and multiparty systems the consensus model. The traditional literature on party systems is staunchly majoritarian and emphatically favors the two-party system. Two-party systems are claimed to have both direct and indirect advantages over multiparty systems. The first direct benefit is that they offer the voters a clear choice between two alternative sets of public policies. Second, they have a moderating influence because the two main parties have to compete for the swing voters in the center of the political spectrum and hence have to advocate moderate, centrist policies. This mechanism is especially strong when large numbers of voters are located in the political center, but its logic continues to operate even when opinions are more polarized: at the two ends of the spectrum, the parties will lose some of their supporters, who will decide to abstain instead of voting for what is, to them, a too moderate program, but a vote gained in the center, taken away from the other party, is still twice as valuable as a vote lost by abstention. Both claims are quite plausible—but also contradictory: if the programs of the two parties are both close to the political center, they will be very similar to each other and, instead of offering a meaningful "choice" to the voters, are more likely to "echo" each other.[3]

2. In *Democracies,* party systems actually emerged as the strongest element of the first "factor," and the type of cabinet was in second place (Lijphart 1984, 214).

3. Most two-party theorists do not make both of the competing claims simultaneously. The advantage of party moderation is typically asserted by the American school of thought, whereas the claim of a clear-cut choice reflects the British two-party school.

In addition, two-party systems are claimed to have an important indirect advantage: they are necessary for the formation of single-party cabinets that will be stable and effective policymakers. For instance, A. Lawrence Lowell (1896, 70, 73–74), one of the first modern political scientists, wrote that the legislature must contain "two parties, and two parties only, . . . in order that the parliamentary form of government should permanently produce good results." He called it an "axiom in politics" that coalition cabinets are short-lived and weak compared with one-party cabinets: "the larger the number of discordant groups that form the majority the harder the task of pleasing them all, and the more feeble and unstable the position of the cabinet."

In the next two chapters I confirm Lowell's hypothesis linking party systems to types of cabinets and his "axiom" that single-party majority cabinets are more durable and dominant than coalition cabinets. The majoritarians' preference for two-party systems is therefore clearly and logically linked to their preference for powerful and dominant one-party cabinets. Furthermore, in Chapter 8 I show a strong link between party systems and electoral systems, which further explains the majoritarians' strong preference for plurality, instead of PR, because of its bias in favor of larger parties and its contribution to the establishment and maintenance of two-party systems. However, whether this syndrome of majoritarian features actually translates into more capable and effective policy-making than its consensual counterpart is another matter entirely. Lowell simply assumes that concentrated strength means effective decision-making; in Chapter 15 I show that this assumption is largely incorrect.

In this chapter I first address the question of how the number of parties in party systems should be counted and argue that the "effective number of parliamentary parties" is the optimal measure. I also try to solve the problem of how to treat factionalized parties as well as closely allied parties: should such parties be treated as one party or as more than one party? Next, the average effective numbers of parliamentary parties in our thirty-six democracies are presented and discussed; these numbers exhibit a wide range—from well below two to almost six parties. Finally, the numbers of parties are related to the numbers and types of issue dimensions that divide the parties.

The Effective Number of Parties

Pure two-party systems with, in Lowell's words quoted above, "two parties, and two parties only," are extremely rare. In Chapter 2, the party systems of Britain, New Zealand, and Barbados were also described as two-party systems in spite of the usual presence of one or more additional small parties in the legislature. Is this a correct description, or should it be modified in some way? This question points to the most important problem in determining the number of parties in a party system: whether to count small parties and, if not, how large a party has to be in order to be included in the count.

One well-known solution was proposed by Giovanni Sartori (1976, 122–23). He suggests, first of all, that parties that fail to win seats in parliament be disregarded, that the relative strengths of the other parties be measured in terms of parliamentary seats, and that not all parties regardless of size can be counted, but that one cannot establish an arbitrary cut-off point of, say, 5 or 10 percent above which parties are counted and below which they should be ignored. These preliminary assumptions are unexceptionable. More controversial are his "rules for counting." He argues that only those parties should be counted as components of the party system that are "relevant" in terms of having either "coalition potential" or "blackmail potential." A party has coalition potential if it has participated in governing coalitions (or, of course, in one-party governments) or if the major parties regard it as a possible coalition partner. Parties that are ideologically unacceptable to all or most of the other coalition partners, and that therefore lack coalition potential, must still be counted if they are large enough. Examples are the strong French and Italian Communist parties until the 1970s. This is Sartori's "subsidiary counting rule based on the power of intimidation, or more exactly, the *blackmail potential* of the opposition-oriented parties."[4]

Sartori's criteria are very useful for distinguishing between the parties that are significant in the political system and those that play only a minor role; the section on the issue dimensions of partisan conflict, later on in this chapter, uses them for this purpose. But they do not work well for counting the number of parties in a party system. First, although Sartori's criteria are based on two variables, size and ideological compatibility, size is the crucial factor. Only sufficiently large parties can have blackmail potential, but sufficiently large size is also the chief determinant of coalition potential: very small parties with only a few seats in the legislature may be quite moderate and hence ideologically acceptable to most other parties, but they rarely possess coalition potential because they simply do not have sufficient "weight" to contribute to a cabinet. Hence the parties to be counted, whether or not they are ideologically compatible, are mainly the larger ones. Second, although size figures so prominently in Sartori's thinking, he does not use this factor to make further distinctions among the relevant parties: for instance, both the Christian Democratic party that dominated Italian politics until the 1990s and its frequent but very small coalition partner, the Republican party, which has never won more than 5 percent of the lower house seats, are counted equally.

To remedy this defect, Jean Blondel (1968, 184–87) proposed a classification of party systems that takes into account both

4. Sartori (1976, 123) is too critical of his own criterion of coalition potential when he states that it is merely "postdictive," since "the parties having a coalition potential, coincide, in practice, with the parties that have in fact entered, at some point in time, coalition governments." For instance, immediately after the first electoral success of the Dutch party Democrats '66 in 1967, it was widely regarded as an acceptable coalition partner, although it did not actually enter a cabinet until 1973.

Table 5.1 Classification of party systems based on the numbers and relative sizes of political parties

Party systems	Hypothetical examples of seat shares	Effective number of parties
Two-party system	55 – 45	2.0
Two-and-a-half party system	45 – 40 – 15	2.6
Multiparty system with a dominant party	45 – 20 – 15 – 10 – 10	3.5
Multiparty system without a dominant party	25 – 25 – 25 – 15 – 10	4.5

Source: Adapted from Blondel 1968, 184–87

their number and their relative sizes. His four categories are shown in Table 5.1. Two-party systems are dominated by two large parties, although there may be some other small parties in parliament. Blondel's examples include our British and New Zealand prototypes. If, in addition to the two large parties, there is a considerably smaller party but one that may have coalition potential and that plays a significant political role—such as the German and Luxembourg Liberals, the Irish Labour party, and the Canadian New Democrats—Blondel calls this a "two-and-a-half" party system. Systems with more than two-and-a-half significant parties are multiparty systems, and these can be subdivided further into multiparty systems with and without a dominant party. Examples of the former are pre-1990 Italy with its dominant Christian Democratic party and the three Scandinavian countries with their strong Socialist parties. Representative instances of party systems without a dominant party are Switzerland, the Netherlands, and Finland.

The concepts of a "dominant" party and a "half" party are extremely useful in highlighting, respectively, the relatively strong and relatively weak position of one of the parties compared with the other important parties in the system, but they are obviously rather imprecise. What we need is an index that tells us exactly how many parties there are in a party system, taking their relative sizes into account. Such an index was developed by Markku Laakso and Rein Taagepera (1979) and is now widely used by comparativists in political science: the effective number of parties. This number (N) is calculated as follows:

$$N = \frac{1}{\sum s_i^2}$$

in which s_i is the proportion of seats of the i-th party.[5]

It can easily be seen that in a two-party system with two equally strong parties, the effective number of parties is exactly 2.0. If one party is considerably stronger than the other, with, for instance, respective seat shares of 70 and 30 percent, the effective number of parties is 1.7—in accordance with our intuitive judgment that we are moving away from a pure two-party system in the direction of a one-party system. Similarly, with three exactly equal parties, the effective-number formula yields a value of 3.0. If one of these parties is weaker than the other two, the effective number of parties will be somewhere between 2.0 and 3.0, depending on the relative strength of the third party. In the hypothetical example of the two-and-a-half party system in Table 5.1—with three parties holding 45, 40, and 15 percent of the parliamentary seats—the effective number of parties is in fact very close to two and a half, namely 2.6.

In all cases where all the parties are exactly equal, the effective number will be the same as the raw numerical count.

5. It is also possible to calculate the effective number of parties based on their vote shares instead of their seat shares, but I consistently use seat shares because this study's focus is on the strengths and patterns of parties in parliaments and on their effects on the formation of cabinets. The effective number of parties (N) carries the same information as Douglas W. Rae and Michael Taylor's (1970, 22–44) index of fragmentation (F) and can easily be calculated from F as follows:

$$N = \frac{1}{1-F}$$

The advantage of N is that it can be visualized more easily as the number of parties than the abstract Rae-Taylor index of fragmentation.

When the parties are not equal in strength, the effective number will be lower than the actual number. This can also be seen in Table 5.1. The two hypothetical examples of multiparty systems contain five parties each. When there is a dominant party, the effective number of parties is only 3.5. Without a dominant party, the seat shares are more equal and the effective number increases to 4.5, close to the raw number of parties in which all parties are counted regardless of size.

Closely Allied Parties

The problem of how to count parties of different sizes is solved by using the effective-number measure. This measure, however, does not solve the question of what a political party is. The usual assumption in political science is that organizations that call themselves "political parties" are, in fact, political parties. This assumption works well for most parties and most countries but is problematic in two situations: parties that are so tightly twinned that they look more like one party than two parties and, conversely, parties that are so factionalized that they look more like two or more parties than one party. The former problem is less difficult to solve than the latter. Let me turn to the relatively easier issue first.

The cases in point are the following five closely allied parties: the Christian Democratic Union (CDU) and Christian Social Union (CSU) in Germany, the Liberal and National parties in Australia, and, in Belgium, the two Christian Democratic parties that resulted from a split along linguistic lines in 1968, the two similarly divided Liberal parties since 1971, and the two Socialist parties since 1978. In particular, the two German and two Australian parties are often treated as single parties. For instance, Blondel (1968, 185) regards the Liberals and Nationals as one party when he calls the Australian party system a two-party instead of a two-and-a-half party system, and he treats the CDU and CSU as one party when he calls the German system a two-and-a-half instead of a two-and-two-halves party system. Another example is Manfred G. Schmidt's (1996, 95) statement that the three "major established parties" in Germany are "the CDU-CSU, the SPD [Socialists] and the Liberals."

Four criteria can be applied to decide whether closely allied parties—which do have different names and separate party organizations—are actually two parties or more like one party. First, political parties normally compete for votes in elections; do the problematic five pairs of parties do so? The CDU and CSU do not compete for votes because they operate in different parts of the country: the CSU in Bavaria and the CDU in the rest of Germany. Neither do the three pairs of Belgian parties because they compete for votes in either Flanders or Wallonia and among either French-speakers or Dutch-speakers in Brussels. In the Australian single-member district elections, the pattern is mixed: Liberals and Nationals usually do not challenge an incumbent representative of the other party, but they may each nominate a candidate in Labor-held districts and in districts without an incumbent.

The second criterion revolves around the degree of cooperation between the parties in parliament and, in particular, whether the two parties form a single parliamentary party group and also caucus together. Only the CDU and CSU do so. Third, do the parties behave like separate parties in cabinet formations: are they either in the cabinet together or in opposition together, or can one be in the cabinet and the other in the opposition? In this respect, each of the five pairs operates strictly like a single party. The Australian example is particularly striking because, although the Liberals won clear seat majorities in the 1975, 1977, and 1996 elections, and could therefore have governed by themselves, they nevertheless included the Nationals in all three cabinets that they formed.

The fourth criterion is time: it only makes sense to consider counting tightly allied parties as one party if the close collaboration is of long standing. Both duration and degree of closeness distinguish the above five pairs of parties from other examples of electoral alliances that are mere "marriages of convenience." Electoral systems with single-member district elections give small and medium-sized parties a strong incentive to form such alliances, but these alliances tend to be ad hoc, temporary, and shifting; examples are France, India, and Mauritius.[6] Electoral alliances also occur in PR systems, such as, in Portugal, the three-party Democratic Alliance that presented a single list of candidates and was highly successful in the 1979 and 1980 elections but that reverted to mutually competitive parties from 1983 on. In Italy, too, after the switch to a less proportional system in 1994, groupings like the Freedom Alliance and Olive Tree Alliance have been, as their names indicate, mere party alliances and not parties.

Unfortunately, the four criteria do not provide an unequivocal answer to the question of how the five problematic pairs of parties in Australia, Belgium, and Germany should be treated. They are all genuinely somewhere in between two parties and one party. Therefore, instead of arbitrarily opting for either the one-party or two-party solution—or by simply flipping a coin!— I propose to split the difference: calculate two effective numbers of parties, based first on the two-party assumption and next on the one-party assumption, and average these two numbers. This means that each twinned pair of parties is counted like one-and-a-half parties. Like any compromise, it may not be the most elegant solution, but it reflects the reality of these partisan actors better than either of the more extreme options.

6. Like the Australian alternative vote system, the French two-ballot electoral system actually encourages parties not to merge but to make electoral alliances with like-minded parties (see Chapter 8). However, unlike the Australian Liberal-National alliance, the French Socialist-Communist and Gaullist-Republican alliances fail to meet the criteria for closely allied parties, especially because Socialist cabinets have usually not included the Communists and because Gaullists and Republicans have fiercely challenged each other in presidential elections, except in 1995, when there were two Gaullist candidates but no Republican candidate.

Factionalized Parties

I propose a similar solution for highly factionalized parties: the Liberal and Conservative parties in Colombia, the Indian Congress party, the Italian Christian Democrats, the Liberal Democratic party in Japan, and the Democratic party in the United States. These are not the only parties in modern democracies that lack perfect cohesion—in fact, it is generally wrong to view parties as "unitary actors" (Laver and Schofield 1990, 14–28)—but they are the most extreme cases in which analysts have tended to conclude that the party factions are very similar to separate parties. For instance, Japan experts generally view the factions of the Liberal Democratic party as "parties within the party" (Reed and Bolland 1999); Junichiro Wada (1996, 28) writes that the Liberal Democrats are "not a single party but a coalition of factions"; and Raymond D. Gastil (1991, 25) pointedly states that "the 'real' party system in Japan is the factional system within the Liberal Democratic party." The Christian Democrats in Italy, John B. Goodman (1991, 341) states, have been "more a collection of factions than a unified party."

John A. Peeler (1985, 102) describes the two large Colombian parties as "faction ridden" and states that "for most purposes the factions are the real political actors, not the parties." Jonathan Hartlyn (1989, 321) similarly concludes that "party factionalism" makes the party system of Colombia "resemble a multiparty system" more than a two-party system. Paul R. Brass (1990, 97) argues that it is more accurate to speak of the Indian "factional system" than of the Indian party system. And Klaus von Beyme (1985, 229) states that the United States Congress "has never had a two-party system and [that] all existing studies assume a four-party or at least three-party system. The Democrats especially generally act as two parties in Congress, the Southern Conservatives and the Northern Liberals."

These kinds of strong intraparty factions also tend to operate much like political parties during cabinet formations and in coalition cabinets. As mentioned earlier, coalition cabinets tend to be less durable than one-party cabinets. If factions behave like parties, we would also expect cabinets composed of factionalized parties to be less durable than cabinets with more cohesive parties. In an eight-nation comparative study, James N. Druckman (1996) found that this was indeed the case.

The big challenge in finding a compromise solution for counting factionalized parties is that the two numbers to be compromised are not immediately obvious: at one end, there is the one-party alternative, but what is the number of parties at the other end? In Italy and Japan, where the intraparty factions have been the most distinct and identifiable, the number of factions has been quite large: if these factions are counted as parties, measured in terms of the effective number of parties discussed earlier, both the Christian Democrats and the Liberal Democrats would have to be counted as five to six parties (based on data in Leonardi and Wertman 1989, 114–15, Baerwald 1986, 27). This is clearly excessive, since it would make the overall party systems of these two countries the most extreme multiparty systems in the world. My proposal for the alternative at the multiparty end is much more modest: treat each factionalized party as two parties of equal size. The compromise is then to average the effective number of parties based on the one-party assumption and the effective number based on the two-equal-parties assumption.

The upshot is that factionalized parties are counted as one-and-a-half parties—exactly the same solution that I proposed for closely allied parties. Of course, my solution for factionalized parties is both a rougher approximation and more unconventional—and therefore likely to be more controversial. However, especially because this book focuses on the degree of multipartism as one of the elements of concentration versus fragmentation of power, it is absolutely necessary that severe intraparty fragmentation be taken into account. My own only doubt is not whether an adjustment is necessary and justified, but whether the proposed adjustment is substantial enough.[7]

The Party Systems of Thirty-Six Democracies

Table 5.2 shows the effective numbers of parties in thirty-six democracies—based on the partisan composition of the lower, and generally most important, house of bicameral legislatures or the only chamber of unicameral legislatures[8]—averaged over all elections between 1945 and the middle of 1996. They are listed in decreasing order of effective party numbers. The range is very wide: from a high of 5.98 in Papua New Guinea to a low of 1.35 parties in Botswana. The mean for the thirty-six democracies is 3.16 and the median 3.12 parties.

7. Whether closely allied parties and factionalized parties are counted as one-and-a-half parties or, more conventionally, as two parties and one party, respectively, also affects how cabinets are classified (one-party versus coalition cabinets and minimal winning versus other types of cabinets) and it affects the calculation of electoral disproportionality. For readers who prefer the conventional definition of parties, which accepts the parties' own definition of "parties," Appendix B provides the values based on this alternative definition for the three variables in the period 1945–96 as well as the period 1971–96.

8. The effective number of parties is based on the parties in the legislature when it first meets after an election. In most cases, there is no difference between the seats won by parties in an election and the seats they occupy in the legislature. However, several minor changes have occurred in three countries. In Japan since the 1950s, several successful independent candidates have joined the Liberal Democrats after their election. Similar switches from independent status to membership in parliamentary parties and between parties have been rampant after elections in Papua New Guinea. In the Botswana lower house, four "specially" elected legislators are coopted by the popularly elected ones; this has increased the legislative majorities of the ruling Botswana Democratic party by four seats (Holm 1989, 197)—and it has necessarily also slightly decreased the effective number of parties, from 1.39 to 1.35. Two other minor measurement questions: (1) The two instances of elections boycotted by a major party—in Trinidad in 1971 and in Jamaica in 1983—resulted in the election of one-party legislatures; I disregarded these election results because they are quite atypical. (2) Any independent members of the legislatures were counted as tiny one-member parties—which means, of course, that they are virtually ignored in the calculation of the effective number of parties, which weights parties by their seat shares.

Toward the bottom of the list, as expected, we also find our prototypical cases of the United Kingdom, New Zealand, and Barbados. The average of 2.11 parties in the British House of Commons reflects the numerous small parties in this still basically two-party system. In New Zealand and Barbados, where there have been fewer third parties and where the winning party's seat share has tended to be relatively large, the average effective numbers are below 2.00. The same applies to the other three Commonwealth democracies in the Caribbean—Jamaica, Trinidad, and the Bahamas—to Malta, and especially to Botswana where the ruling party has been numerically dominant to an extreme degree. At the other end of the range, Switzerland is almost at the top. Belgium has only the eighth highest multipartism over the entire period; however, in the six elections since 1978, after all of the major parties had split along linguistic lines, the average effective number was 5.82 parties—slightly lower than the number in Papua New Guinea.[9]

Table 5.2 also indicates the range of variation within each of the thirty-six democracies by showing the lowest and the highest effective numbers of parties in all of their elections (the number of which is given in the last column). The Maltese pure two-party system with two, and only two, highly equal

9. This number reflects the one-and-a-half parties adjustment, discussed above. For the period since 1945, the adjusted number of parties is 4.32 (see Table 5.2), in between the two unadjusted numbers of 3.59 and 5.05. In the Belgian case, the adjustment has a considerable impact because it involves three to six party entities. Its impact is smaller in the Australian and German cases. Counting the CDU-CSU as one party yields an effective number of 2.64 parties; counting the CDU and CSU separately yields 3.23 parties. The average reported in the table is 2.93 parties. In Australia, counting the Liberals and Nationals as one party or as two parties yields 1.94 and 2.50, respectively—close to a pure two-party and a pure two-and-a-half party system—with the adjusted number of 2.22 parties representing something like a two-and-a-quarter party system. The adjustment for factionalized parties has the greatest impact on the Colombian party system because it affects both major parties. The conventional treatment yields 2.22 parties, compared with the adjusted number of 3.32 parties. The respective numbers for India are 3.34 and 4.11, for Italy 4.16 and 4.91, for Japan 3.08 and 3.71, and for the United States 1.93 and 2.40.

Table 5.2 Average, lowest, and highest effective numbers of
parliamentary parties resulting from elections in thirty-six
democracies and the number of elections on which these
averages are based, 1945–96

	Mean	Lowest	Highest	Number of elections
Papua New Guinea	5.98	2.69	10.83	4
Switzerland	5.24	4.71	6.70	13
Finland	5.03	4.54	5.58	15
Italy	4.91	3.76	6.97	14
Netherlands	4.65	3.49	6.42	15
Israel	4.55	3.12	5.96	14
Denmark	4.51	3.50	6.86	21
Belgium	4.32	2.45	6.51	17
India	4.11	2.51	6.53	6
Iceland	3.72	3.20	5.34	16
Japan	3.71	2.58	5.76	19
France	3.43	2.49	4.52	10
Venezuela	3.38	2.42	4.88	8
Luxembourg	3.36	2.68	4.05	11
Norway	3.35	2.67	4.23	13
Portugal	3.33	2.23	4.26	8
Sweden	3.33	2.87	4.19	16
Colombia	3.32	2.98	4.84	14
Germany	2.93	2.48	4.33	13

parliamentary parties shows the least variation: between 1.97
and 2.00 in six elections. By far the greatest variation can be seen
in the four elections in Papua New Guinea: the original trend
appeared to be toward party system consolidation when the effective number of parties decreased from 4.46 in the first postin-
dependence election in 1977 to 2.69 in the second election in
1982, but this trend was reversed in 1987 and 1992 when the
numbers shot up to 5.95 and 10.83—especially the latter reflecting a large number of small parties and many independents in
the legislature.

Several countries have experienced long-term trends toward

Table 5.2 *Continued*

	Mean	Lowest	Highest	Number of elections
Ireland	2.84	2.38	3.63	15
Spain	2.76	2.34	3.02	7
Mauritius	2.71	2.07	3.48	6
Austria	2.48	2.09	3.73	16
Costa Rica	2.41	1.96	3.21	11
United States	2.40	2.20	2.44	25
Canada	2.37	1.54	2.86	16
Australia	2.22	2.08	2.30	21
Greece	2.20	1.72	2.40	8
United Kingdom	2.11	1.99	2.27	14
Malta	1.99	1.97	2.00	6
New Zealand	1.96	1.74	2.16	17
Trinidad	1.82	1.18	2.23	7
Barbados	1.76	1.25	2.18	7
Bahamas	1.68	1.45	1.97	5
Jamaica	1.62	1.30	1.95	7
Botswana	1.35	1.17	1.71	7

Source: Based on data in Mackie and Rose 1991, Mackie and Rose 1997, Nohlen 1993, Singh 1994, Lijphart 1994, and data provided by Pradeep K. Chhibber, Michael Coppedge, Brian F. Crisp, Gary Hoskin, Mark P. Jones, J. Ray Kennedy, Hansraj Mathur, Shaheen Mozaffar, Ben Reilly, and Andrew S. Reynolds

greater multipartism: especially Belgium, but also Austria, Colombia, Denmark, India, Italy, Norway, and Switzerland. In Germany, Israel, and Japan, the effective number of parties first declined gradually, but then increased again in the past two to three decades. Portugal is the only example of a clear trend toward fewer parties. In most of the other countries there is either little variation over time or fluctuation without any clear long-term trends. In fact, the lowest and highest effective numbers of parties were produced in back-to-back elections in no fewer than seven countries—Botswana, Canada, Costa Rica, France, New Zealand, Spain, and the United States.

The Issue Dimensions of Partisan Conflict

How can the contents and intensity of party programs and the issue dimensions of party systems be determined? Official party platforms or manifestos should be read with some skepticism, but they do offer some clues to where parties stand on public policies, especially if they are supplemented by other formal party pronouncements, debates in party conferences, and speeches by party leaders in parliament and elsewhere. Moreover, we can observe the actual policies pursued by a party when it is in power or the policies promoted by a party when it shares governmental power with one or more partners in a coalition (Budge, Robertson, and Hearl 1987, Laver and Hunt 1992, Klingemann, Hofferbert, and Budge 1994). Party programs must be distinguished from the characteristics of the voters that parties represent. For instance, the fact that a party receives exceptionally strong support from Catholic voters does not automatically make it a Catholic party or necessarily indicate that religion is an important issue dimension. And yet, there is usually a mutual relationship between a party program and the objective and subjective interests and needs of the party's supporters.

A second guideline for the identification of the issue dimensions of party systems is that the focus should be on the differences between rather than within parties. This means that some important sets of issues in a country may not constitute issue dimensions of its party system: they may divide parties internally instead of from each other. Third, the analysis will be restricted to the political issues dividing what Sartori (1976) calls the "relevant" parties—those with either coalition or blackmail potential. Finally, the focus will be on the durable issue dimensions of party systems; partisan differences that may emerge in one election but fade away soon afterward will be ignored.

The following seven issue dimensions can be observed in at least some of the thirty-six democratic party systems in the period 1945–96: (1) socioeconomic, (2) religious, (3) cultural-ethnic, (4) urban-rural, (5) regime support, (6) foreign policy, and (7) postmaterialist issues. Table 5.3 indicates which issue dimensions have been present in each of the thirty-six democracies. A distinction is made between dimensions of high salience (H) and those of only medium intensity or those that varied between high and low intensity over time (M). The judgments on which the table is based are necessarily subjective, but most are straightforward and uncontroversial. The few difficult cases are pointed out in the discussion of each of the issue dimensions.

1. The socioeconomic dimension. The socioeconomic issue dimension is listed first in Table 5.3 because it is the most important of the issue dimensions and because it was present in all of the democratic party systems in the period 1945–96. Many studies have shown that there are significant differences between the socioeconomic policies advocated and pursued by leftist-oriented and rightist-oriented parties and governments. Leftist governments have systematically produced a higher rate of growth of the public sector of the economy, larger central government budgets, more income equalization, greater efforts to reduce unemployment, and more emphasis on education, public health, and social welfare spending than rightist governments. The evidence can be summarized in the following statement by Edward R. Tufte (1978, 104): "The single most important determinant of variations in macroeconomic performance from one industrialized democracy to another is the location on the left-right spectrum of the governing political party. Party platforms and political ideology set priorities and help decide policy."

Left-right differences on socioeconomic issues have generally declined since the 1960s but not to the extent that, over the period under consideration for each country, this issue dimension can be said to have disappeared in any of the countries or even moderated from "high" to only "medium" salience in most

Table 5.3 Issue dimensions of thirty-six democratic party systems, 1945–96

	Socio-economic	Religious	Cultural ethnic	Urban-rural	Regime support	Foreign policy	Post-materialist	Number of dimensions
Finland	H	M	H	M	M	—	—	3.5
Belgium	H	H	H	—	—	—	—	3.0
Germany	H	H	M	—	—	—	M	3.0
India	H	H	M	—	M	—	—	3.0
Israel	H	H	—	—	—	H	—	3.0
Italy	H	H	—	—	M	M	—	3.0
Netherlands	H	H	—	—	—	—	H	3.0
Norway	H	M	H	M	—	—	M	3.0
Papua N.G.	H	M	H	—	—	M	—	3.0
Switzerland	H	H	M	M	—	—	—	3.0
France	H	M	—	—	M	M	—	2.5
Japan	H	M	—	—	M	M	—	2.5
Portugal	H	M	—	—	M	M	—	2.5
Colombia	H	M	—	M	M	—	—	2.5
Denmark	H	M	—	M	—	M	—	2.5
Spain	H	M	H	—	—	—	—	2.5
Sweden	H	M	—	M	—	—	M	2.5

Country								Total
Costa Rica	H	H	—	—	—	—	—	2.0
Luxembourg	H	H	—	—	—	—	—	2.0
Venezuela	H	H	—	—	—	—	—	2.0
Iceland	H	—	M	—	—	M	—	2.0
Malta	H	M	—	—	—	M	—	2.0
Mauritius	H	—	H	—	—	—	—	2.0
Ireland	H	—	—	—	—	M	—	1.5
Jamaica	H	—	—	—	—	M	—	1.5
United Kingdom	H	—	—	—	—	M	—	1.5
Canada	M	—	H	—	—	—	—	1.5
Trinidad	M	—	H	—	M	—	—	1.5
Australia	H	—	—	M	—	—	—	1.5
Austria	H	M	—	—	—	—	—	1.5
Botswana	H	—	—	—	M	—	—	1.5
Greece	H	—	M	—	—	—	—	1.5
Barbados	H	—	—	—	—	—	—	1.0
New Zealand	H	—	—	—	—	—	—	1.0
United States	M	—	M	—	—	—	—	1.0
Bahamas	M	—	—	—	—	—	—	0.5
Total	34.0	16.5	9.5	4.0	4.0	6.5	2.5	77.0

Note: H indicates an issue dimension of high salience and M a medium-salience dimension

countries. Table 5.3 assigns "medium" ratings only to the United States, Canada, the Bahamas, and Trinidad. When the thirty-six ratings are added up—with an H counted as 1.0 and an M as 0.5—the total is 34.0, as indicated in the bottom line of the table. This total score for the socioeconomic dimension is more than twice as high as the total score for any of the other dimensions; the socioeconomic dimension is also the only one that has been present to a significant extent in all thirty-six party systems—confirming Seymour Martin Lipset's (1960, 220) famous statement that elections can be seen as "the expression of the democratic class struggle."

2. *The religious dimension*. Differences between religious and secular parties constitute the second most important issue dimension. Such differences can be found in more than half of the thirty-six democracies. In twelve countries that are largely Catholic and/or Protestant, there are, or have long been, many parties that explicitly call themselves "Christian": Belgium, Costa Rica, Denmark, Finland, Germany, Italy, Luxembourg, the Netherlands, Norway, Sweden, Switzerland, and Venezuela. Where, in these twelve party systems, the religious-secular difference has been important throughout the period under consideration, a "high" rating is assigned in Table 5.3, and a "medium" score is assigned to the others. In six mainly Catholic countries, religious divisions have on average been less prominent and explicit but still merit at least a "medium" rating: Austria, Colombia, France, Malta, Portugal, and Spain. In three mainly non-Christian countries, a religious issue dimension has also been present. It has been, and continues to be, extremely important in Israel, where the National Religious party and other religious parties have long been highly effective advocates of orthodox religious policies, and in India, where the Bharatiya Janata party is usually described as a "Hindu nationalist" party. In Japan, the Komeito party became a significant political presence in the 1970s; it is the political representative of the Buddhist Soka Gakkai sect.

Like the socioeconomic issue dimension, the religious dimension has generally declined in importance in the post–World War II period. In the European countries with mixed Catholic and Protestant populations and histories of Catholic-Protestant antagonism, interreligious tensions have largely disappeared and the two groups have even tended to unite politically. The Christian Democratic Union of postwar Germany was founded as a joint Catholic-Protestant party. In the Netherlands, the Catholic party and the two main Protestant parties presented a joint list in the 1977 parliamentary elections and merged into a single party organization soon thereafter. Moreover, both the religious parties and their anticlerical opponents have moderated their claims and counterclaims to a large extent. However, religious and secular parties are still divided on a range of moral issues, such as questions of marriage and divorce, gay rights, birth control, abortion, sex education, pornography, and so on. These issues have become especially prominent since the late 1960s. Moreover, it was not until the second half of the period that the relatively small religious parties of Japan, Denmark, Finland, and Sweden became electorally important and not until the early 1990s that they clearly established their coalition potential by actually entering coalition cabinets.

3. *The cultural-ethnic dimension.* In their developmental theory of cleavage structures and party systems, Seymour Martin Lipset and Stein Rokkan (1967) identify four basic sources of party-system cleavages. These are, in addition to the socioeconomic and religious dimensions already discussed, cultural-ethnic cleavages and the division between rural-agrarian and urban-industrial interests. The cultural-ethnic dimension is of some importance in all nine of the countries described as plural societies in Chapter 4 except Israel. In most of these, cultural-ethnic issues have high salience. The two rather surprising exceptions are ethnically highly divided India and Switzerland; in these two countries the religious dimension is the much more salient differentiator at the national level.

In three of the semiplural societies, the cultural-ethnic dimension is of some importance, too. In Finland, the Swedish-speaking minority and the Swedish People's party are both very small, but the party has been an effective political actor and a frequent partner in coalition governments. Because the Christian Social Union of Bavaria is counted as a "half" party and also because of the emergence of the Party of Democratic Socialism as a specifically East German party since unification in 1990, Germany is given a "medium" score. No American party has an exclusively ethnic base, but the Democrats have been much more representative of and sensitive to the interests of ethnic and racial minorities than the Republicans, and when affirmative-action and other special minority programs have become controversial, Democrats have tended to support and Republicans to oppose them. And in Botswana, the ruling party "is perceived by the Bamangwato and the Bakwena tribes as representing their people" (Holm 1988, 191).

4. The urban-rural dimension. Differences between rural and urban areas and interests occur in all democracies, but they constitute the source of issue dimensions in the party systems of only a few and only with medium salience. Where agrarian parties are found, mainly in the Nordic countries, they have tended to become less exclusively rural and to appeal to urban electorates, too, prompted by the decline of the rural population. A clear sign of this shift is that the Swedish, Norwegian, and Finnish agrarian parties all changed their names to "Center Party" between 1957 and 1965. The Danish Liberals and the Icelandic Progressives also originated as agrarian parties but similarly try to portray themselves as center parties. The Swiss People's party and the Colombian Conservatives can also be regarded as parties that are to some extent representatives of rural interests. The Australian National party used to be called the "Country Party" and has been the traditional defender of rural and farming concerns. In deference to its classification as a "half" party, however, Australia is assigned only a "medium" score on the urban-rural dimension.

5. *The dimension of regime support.* This dimension may occur in democracies as a result of the presence of important parties that oppose the democratic regime. In our thirty-six democracies, it has occurred mainly in European and Asian countries with sizable Communist parties: France, Italy, Finland, Portugal, Greece, India, and Japan. However, the trend toward "Eurocommunism" has entailed basic changes in Communist attitudes toward both democracy and foreign policy, and the Indian and Japanese Communist parties have similarly become more moderate. For this reason, none of the party systems is given more than a "medium" rating on this dimension. The only other country with a sizable Communist party is Iceland, but the Icelandic Communists may be said to have been Eurocommunists since 1938. At that time, they joined with a Socialist faction to form a new party which, as the Icelandic political scientist Olafur R. Grimsson (1982, 145) states, "would acknowledge the parliamentary road to power, adhere to an Icelandic form of socialism, and resign the [party's] membership in the Comintern, a position which reflected more the European 1970s than the late 1930s." Colombia is assigned a "medium" score for a quite different reason: the prominent role of the AD-M19 party, which originated as a revolutionary movement but later participated in elections and even entered the cabinet in the early 1990s.

6. *The foreign policy dimension.* A great variety of foreign policy issues have divided the parties in twelve of our thirty-six democracies: the traditional, but declining pro-Soviet stance of the European Communist parties; opposition to NATO (North Atlantic Treaty Organization) membership in France and Iceland; opposition to membership in the European Union and its predecessors in Britain, Denmark, France, Ireland, and Malta; relationships with the United States in Japan and Jamaica; relationships with Australia in Papua New Guinea; relationships

with Libya in Malta; and different attitudes of the Irish parties toward the Northern Ireland problem. None of these was either prominent or durable enough, however, to merit more than a "medium" rating. The only country with a "high" score in Table 5.3 is Israel. Here the issue is a nationalist-territorial one, and the debate is, in the words of Israeli political scientist Ofira Seliktar (1982, 295) "between those who follow the maximalist territorial tradition of the Revisionists and those who adhere to the more moderate territorial demands of the Socialist-Zionist school." This issue dimension has been especially salient since the occupation of Arab territories in 1967.

7. *The materialist versus postmaterialist dimension.* This dimension revolves around the two issues of participatory democracy and environmentalism that both fit the cluster of values of what Ronald Inglehart (1977, 40–50; also Inglehart 1997, 108–30) has called "postmaterialism." Inglehart found that, especially among young middle-class people in Western democracies, a high priority is accorded to goals like "seeing that the people have more say in how things get decided at work and in their communities" and "giving the people more say in important government decisions." Moreover, in the richer nations the cluster of postmaterialist values also included the objective of "trying to make our cities and countryside more beautiful." As Table 5.3 shows, postmaterialism has become the source of a new dimension in only a few party systems. The explanation is that it has emerged only in the more developed countries and only recently, and that, as a result, the postmaterialist parties have remained small and generally without clear coalition potential. However, the Norwegian and Swedish Center parties have made a smooth transition from old-fashioned rural to modern environmentalist values, and two new Dutch parties, Democrats '66 and Radicals, espoused participationist proposals as early as the late 1960s and entered a coalition cabinet in 1973. Germany is also given a "medium" rating on this dimension

because of the prominence of the Green party; it has participated in several governments at the state level, and it was widely considered to have coalition potential at the national level as well, even before it actually entered a national cabinet, as the junior partner of the Socialists, in 1998.

Issue Dimensions and Party Systems

The last column of Table 5.3 shows the number of issue dimensions in each of the thirty-six democracies. This number could, in principle, range from 7 to 0 dimensions, but the actual range is only from 3.5 to 0.5. The countries with the same total scores are grouped in the table, and these groupings are listed in decreasing order of their number of issue dimensions. Within each category, countries that have the same pattern of issue dimensions are listed first. For instance, in the group with 2.5 issue dimensions, France, Japan, and Portugal have the same "high" socioeconomic dimension plus the same "medium" religious, regime support, and foreign policy dimensions. Costa Rica, Luxembourg, and Venezuela form a similar subgroup in the 2.0 category. Five countries with a British political heritage form two subgroups in the 1.5 category: one consists of Ireland, Jamaica, and the United Kingdom, and the other of Canada and Trinidad.

How are these numbers of issue dimensions related to the effective numbers of political parties? There are two reasons to expect a strong link. First, when there are several dimensions of political conflict in a society, one would expect that a relatively large number of parties are needed to express all of these dimensions, unless they happen to coincide. Second, issue dimensions have been defined in terms of differences between instead of within parties; this means that, for instance, two-party systems cannot easily accommodate as many issue dimensions as multiparty systems. The coefficient of correlation between the

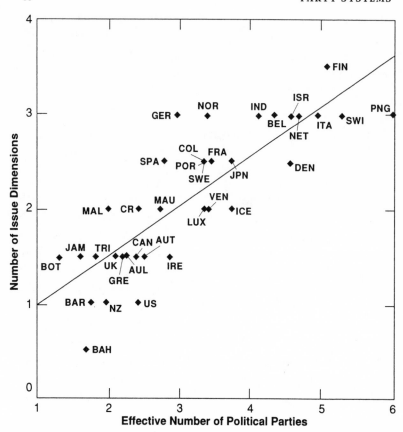

Fig. 5.1 The relationship between the effective number of parliamentary parties and the number of issue dimensions in thirty-six democracies, 1945–96

effective number of parties in the thirty-six democracies (Table 5.2) and the number of issue dimensions (Table 5.3) is indeed a very strong and statistically highly significant 0.84.

Figure 5.1 shows the shape of the relationship and the positions of each of the thirty-six countries graphically.[10] Rein

10. In Figure 5.1 and in similar figures in later chapters, the thirty-six democracies are identified by the first three characters of their English names,

Taagepera and Bernard Grofman (1985) have suggested that the relationship between the effective number of parties (N) and the number of issue dimensions (I) can be expressed as

$$N = I + 1.$$

The typical Westminster two-party system with typically one issue dimension fits this formula perfectly; then, with each increase in the number of parties, there will be exactly the same increase in the number of issue dimensions. The Taagepera-Grofman formula is an excellent estimate, although the actual regression line in Figure 5.1 is somewhat flatter than they would have predicted: at the bottom there are more and at the top fewer issue dimensions than predicted on the basis of their formula. However, the two numbers are very strongly linked. Germany, Norway, the United States, and the Bahamas are the farthest from the regression line, but even these four countries cannot be described as distant outliers.

Unlike the effective number of parties, and unlike the four variables discussed in the next four chapters, the number of issue dimensions is not an institutional variable and is therefore not used as one of the components of the overall executives-parties dimension. However, because it is so closely related to the number of parties, it would fit this dimension very closely and, if it were included, would barely affect the shape of this dimension.

---

except that AUL means Australia, AUT Austria, CR Costa Rica, JPN Japan, NZ New Zealand, PNG Papua New Guinea, UK United Kingdom, and US United States.

CHAPTER 6

Cabinets

Concentration Versus Sharing of Executive Power

The second of the ten basic variables that characterize the difference between majoritarian and consensus forms of democracy, to be discussed in this chapter, concerns the breadth of participation by the people's representatives in the executive branch of the government. As I stated at the beginning of Chapter 5, this variable can be regarded as the most typical variable in the majoritarian-consensus contrast: the difference between one-party majority governments and broad multiparty coalitions epitomizes the contrast between the majoritarian principle of concentrating power in the hands of the majority and the consensus principle of broad power-sharing.

Single-party majority cabinets and broad multiparty coalitions differ from each other in two respects: whether the cabinet is a one-party cabinet or a coalition cabinet and the kind of parliamentary support base that the cabinet has. As far as the support base is concerned, the standard threefold classification in coalition theory distinguishes among (1) minimal winning cabinets, which are "winning" in the sense that the party or parties in the cabinet control a majority of parliamentary seats but "minimal" in the sense that the cabinet does not include any party that is not necessary to reach a majority in parliament, (2) oversized cabinets, which do contain more parties than are necessary for majority support in the legislature, and (3) minority or "undersized" cabinets, which are not supported by a parliamentary majority. The most majoritarian type of cabinet is one that is single-party and minimal winning—that is, a one-party majority cabinet. The most consensual type of cabinet is multiparty and oversized. As I argue below, minority cabinets resemble oversized cabinets, and multiparty minority cabinets therefore also belong to the consensus end of the spectrum. This leaves two kinds of cabinets that are in an intermediate position: multiparty minimal winning cabinets and one-party minority cabinets.

In this chapter I review the major coalition theories and explain why they are such poor predictors of the kinds of cabinets that are actually formed in democracies. One important reason is that they are based almost entirely on majoritarian assumptions; another is that they tend to ignore institutional features that encourage the formation of minority and oversized cabinets. Next, after discussing the precise criteria for assigning cabinets to the different categories, I present the empirical findings concerning the types of cabinets found in thirty-six democracies in the period 1945–96; our democracies differ a great deal on this variable—from 100 percent cabinets that are one-party and minimal winning in five countries to 4.1 percent in Switzerland. Last, I analyze the relationship between types of cabinets and the effective numbers of parties in our set of thirty-six countries.

Coalition Theories

In parliamentary systems of government, cabinets have to be formed so that they will enjoy the confidence of—or will at least be tolerated by—a parliamentary majority. Can we predict which particular cabinet will form if we know the strengths of the different parties in parliament? If one party has a majority of the parliamentary seats, a prediction appears to be easy: the majority party is likely to form a one-party cabinet. This prediction is correct in most cases, but it is also possible that the majority party will form a coalition with one or more minority parties; for instance, the British Conservatives had a clear majority in the House of Commons during the Second World War, but Churchill's war cabinet was a broad coalition of the Conservative, Labour, and Liberal parties. If no party has a parliamentary majority, it is likely—barring the formation of a one-party minority cabinet—that a coalition cabinet will be formed, but which coalition is the most likely one? Several theories have been proposed to predict which coalitions will form in parliamentary systems. The six most important of these coalition theories predict the following kinds of coalitions:[1]

1. Minimal winning coalitions. William H. Riker's (1962, 32–46) "size principle" predicts that minimal winning coalitions will be formed: winning (majority) coalitions in which only those parties participate that are minimally necessary to give the cabinets majority status. Table 6.1 presents an example. Coalition ABC (a cabinet coalition of parties A, B, and C) is a winning coalition because A, B, and C control a majority of fifty-five out of one hundred parliamentary seats. It is minimal because all three parties are necessary to form a majority. The elimination of the smallest coalition partner, party A, would reduce the coalition's parliamentary support from a majority of the seats, fifty-five, to a minority of only forty-seven. The addition of party D to the coalition would make it larger than minimal, because in coalition ABCD either A or D could be eliminated without losing majority support.

The basic assumption of minimal winning coalition theory is both simple and quite plausible: political parties are interested in maximizing their power. In parliamentary systems, power means participation in the cabinet, and maximum power means holding as many of the cabinet positions as possible. To

1. The political science literature on the formation and durability of government coalitions is extensive. Useful summaries and critical reviews can be found in Laver and Schofield 1990, Strøm and Leipart 1993, Strøm 1995, and Grofman and van Roozendaal 1997.

Table 6.1 Cabinet coalitions predicted by six coalition
theories for a hypothetical distribution of parliamentary seats

Parties:	A (Left)	B	C	D	E (Right)
Seats:	8	21	26	12	33
Theories:					
Minimal winning coalition	ABC	ADE	BCD	BE	CE
Minimum size		ADE			
Bargaining proposition				BE	CE
Minimal range	ABC		BCD		CE
Minimal connected winning	ABC		BCD		CDE
Policy-viable coalition	ABC		BCD		CE

enter the cabinet, a minority party will have to team up with one
or more other parties, but it will resist the inclusion of unnecessary parties in the coalition because this would reduce its share
of ministers in the cabinet. For instance, in cabinet coalition CE
in Table 6.1, party C contributes almost half of the parliamentary
support, and hence it is likely to receive almost half of the ministerial appointments. If party B were added to the coalition, C's
share of cabinet positions would probably be only a third.

Only when there is a majority party in parliament can minimal winning coalition theory make a single specific prediction:
a one-party, noncoalition cabinet formed by the majority party.
When there is no majority party, the theory always predicts more
than one outcome. In the example of Table 6.1, five coalitions are
predicted. The next three coalition theories to be discussed attempt to improve minimal winning coalition theory by introducing additional criteria to arrive at more specific predictions.

2. Minimum size coalitions. Minimum size coalition theory
is based on the same assumption of power maximization as minimal winning coalition theory, but it follows this rationale to its
logical conclusion. If political parties want to exclude unnecessary partners from a coalition cabinet to maximize their share of

cabinet power, they should also be expected to prefer the cabinet to be based on the narrowest possible parliamentary majority. For instance, it is more advantageous for party E to form coalition ADE with fifty-three seats than CE with fifty-nine seats. In the former, E's thirty-three seats in parliament contribute 62 percent of the cabinet's parliamentary support, and in the latter only 56 percent. In a cabinet with twenty ministers, this difference is easily worth an additional ministerial appointment for party E. According to this reasoning, cabinets of minimum size are predicted. In the example of Table 6.1, coalition ADE with fifty-three parliamentary seats is predicted rather than the other four minimal winning coalitions whose sizes range from fifty-four to fifty-nine seats.

3. Coalitions with the smallest number of parties. A different criterion that may be used to choose among the many coalitions predicted by minimal winning coalition theory is Michael Leiserson's (1970, 90) "bargaining proposition." He argues that those minimal winning coalitions will tend to form that involve the smallest possible number of parties, because "negotiations and bargaining [about the formation of a coalition] are easier to complete, and a coalition is easier to hold together, other things being equal, with fewer parties." Of the five minimal winning coalitions in Table 6.1, the bargaining proposition predicts that coalitions BE or CE will form because they involve only two parties rather than one of the three-party coalitions.

4. Minimal range coalitions. The preceding theories base their predictions on the sizes and number of political parties but ignore their programs and policy preferences. Minimal range coalition theory makes the plausible assumption that it is easier to form and maintain coalitions among parties with similar policy preferences than among parties that are far apart in this respect. Of the several slightly different versions of this theory, Table 6.1 presents the most basic one: the parties are placed on a left-right scale, with party A at the extreme left and E at the extreme right, and the distance between them is measured in terms of the number of "spaces" separating them. The five minimal winning coalitions have ranges of two, three, and four "spaces." If parties seek to form a coalition with like-minded partners, coalition ABC, with a range of two "spaces," is much more likely than coalition ADE, with a range of four "spaces" covering the entire left-right spectrum. Minimal range theory also predicts coalitions BCD and CE, which have the same minimal range of two "spaces" as ABC.

5. *Minimal connected winning coalitions.* A closely related theory has been proposed by Robert Axelrod (1970, 165–87). He predicts that coalitions will form that are both "connected"— that is, composed of parties that are adjacent on the policy scale—and devoid of unnecessary partners. The underlying assumption of this theory is that parties will try to coalesce with their immediate neighbors and that other adjacent parties will be added until a majority coalition is formed. The example of Table 6.1 shows that minimal *connected* winning coalitions are not necessarily minimal winning coalitions. According to the latter theory, coalition CDE contains a superfluous partner— party D—but in Axelrod's theory, party D is necessary to make the coalition a connected one.

6. *Policy-viable coalitions.* The focus on the policy preferences of parties is taken to its ultimate conclusion by policy-viable coalition theory. If we assume that parties truly care only about policy instead of holding office, real power resides in the legislature, where major new policies have to be enacted, rather than in the cabinet. In the legislature, it is the "core" party that is of pivotal importance; the core party is the party that, on a one-dimensional policy scale like the left-right scale, contains the median member of parliament: party C in the example of Table 6.1. This pivotal party can virtually dictate policy because neither the party or parties on its left nor those on its right have the majorities necessary to enact any policy contrary to its wishes. This means that, in strict policy terms, it is completely irrelevant how many and which parties participate in the cabinet. In

fact, as Michael Laver and Norman Schofield (1990, 88) state, for the formation of policy-viable cabinets "it does not [even] matter whether or not the pivotal party" participates.

And yet, Laver and Schofield (1990, 55) concede that a distinction should be made between big policy questions and more detailed matters of policy. To influence detailed matters of policy, it can be quite important after all to be in the cabinet and at the head of a ministerial department, and this consideration "may provide a strong incentive for parties concerned not at all with the intrinsic rewards of office none the less to slug it out for a seat at the cabinet table." The importance of which party holds which cabinet portfolio is also emphasized in the recent work of Michael Laver and Kenneth A. Shepsle (1996). The implication is that parties are presumably also interested in "slugging it out" for as many cabinet seats and ministerial portfolios as possible— which takes us back to the logic of minimal winning coalitions, with the proviso that the pivotal party be included in such coalitions: coalitions ABC, BCD, and CE in Table 6.1. In the final analysis, policy-viable coalition theory either makes no prediction about the composition of cabinets or predicts minimal winning coalitions similar to those predicted by minimal range theory.[2]

Incentives for the Formation of Minority and Oversized Cabinets

Of the above six coalition theories, the policy-based ones have been able to predict actual cabinet coalitions more suc-

2. Two alternative interpretations of policy-viable coalition theory are that the core party should be able to govern by itself or that the coalition should include the core party (Strøm, Budge, and Laver 1994, 328). The first interpretation yields the prediction that a one-party minority cabinet will be formed—not a prediction that is likely to be successful because fewer than 20 percent of cabinets formed in minority situations are one-party minority cabinets (see Table 6.2 below). The problem with the second interpretation is that it produces a large number of predictions: in the situation of Table 6.1, fifteen coalitions can be formed that include party C. One of these may well be the cabinet that is formed; if so, the one correct prediction is still outweighed by fourteen incorrect ones.

cessfully than the policy-blind theories (de Swaan 1973). Some of this success has to be discounted because the assignment of parties to positions on the left-right scale may involve circular reasoning. Where a party stands on left-right issues may be inferred from its formal program, its votes in parliament, and so on, but is also likely to be influenced by whether the party is or has been a member of the government and with which other parties it has formed a coalition. In Germany, for instance, the Free Democratic party is usually assigned a center position on the policy scale—in contrast with the right-of-center position of other European Liberal parties—because it was in several cabinet coalitions with the leftist Social Democrats from 1969 to 1982. Explaining this coalition in terms of the two parties' adjacent policy positions, which are in turn derived from their coalition behavior, obviously does not explain very much.

The basic problem of all of the theories is that they predict minimal winning coalitions of one kind or another; Axelrod's theory is only a partial exception because few of his minimal connected winning coalitions are larger than minimal winning. The minimal winning prediction is based on a majoritarian assumption, and it conflicts with the large numbers of actual minority and oversized coalitions that are formed in parliamentary democracies. Laver and Schofield (1990, 70–71) classify 196 cabinets formed in "minority situations" (that is, where there is no majority party in parliament) in twelve European multiparty democracies from 1945 to 1987. Only 77 of these—39.3 percent—were minimal winning coalitions; 46 were oversized and 73 were minority cabinets.

Table 6.2 presents similar data on the cabinets in the thirty-two parliamentary systems investigated in this book (including Switzerland and the two short phases of parliamentary government in the French Fifth Republic). Several of these are countries that usually have majority parties in their parliaments; this accounts for the large proportion of one-party majority cabinets: 37.1 percent. As indicated earlier, when one party has a majority

Table 6.2   Proportions of time during which five types of
cabinets were in power in thirty-two parliamentary
democracies, 1945–96

Type of cabinet	All cabinets (%)	All cabinets except minimal winning, one-party cabinets (%)
Minimal winning, one-party	37.1	—
Minimal winning coalition	24.7	39.3
Minority, one-party	11.4	18.1
Minority coalition	5.8	9.2
Oversized coalition	21.0	33.4
Total	100.0	100.0

Source: Based on data in Woldendorp, Keman, and Budge 1998; Banks, Day,
and Muller 1997; Müller and Strøm 1997; Strøm 1990; von Beyme 1985; and
Keesing's Contemporary Archives

of the seats in parliament, it is easy, and almost always correct,
to predict the formation of a one-party majority cabinet. When
these cabinets are excluded, in the second column of Table 6.2,
the proportion of minimal winning coalitions is 39.3 percent—
which happens to be identical to the percentage found by Laver
and Schofield, in spite of the different countries, time periods,
and definitions of cabinets used in the two studies.[3] Oversized
coalitions comprise 33.4 percent of the total and minority cabinets 27.3 percent; together they outnumber minimal winning
cabinets by a margin of more than three to two.[4]

3. Laver and Schofield count each cabinet at the time of its formation and
regardless of how long it lasts, whereas I weight the cabinets by their duration.

4. The classification into minimal winning, oversized, and coalition cabinets is not exhaustive because it misses two borderline cases: so-called blocking
cabinets—composed of parties with exactly 50 percent of the seats in parliament—and cabinets that become blocking if the smallest cabinet partner leaves.
An example of the former is the 1989–93 Spanish cabinet under Prime Minister
Felipe González, whose Socialist party controlled 175 of the 350 seats in the
lower house of parliament. An example of the latter is the 1992–93 four-party
coalition of Prime Minister Giuliano Amati in Italy: together the four parties
controlled 331 of the 630 seats in the Chamber of Deputies, but without the

How can all of these oversized and minority cabinets be explained? The kind of rational incentives on which the above coalition theories are based can also account for the formation of other than minimal winning cabinets. One important consideration is the parties' time perspective. Even if it is correct to assume that parties seek power and that power means participation in the cabinet, it is not necessarily true that parties want to enter cabinets at all times; they may well believe that not carrying government responsibility for a while may be electorally advantageous and, hence, that a period in the opposition will offer the opportunity of both electoral gains and the possibility of enhanced cabinet participation in the future (Strøm 1990, 44–47). If this consideration is important for several parties, it creates a high probability that a minority cabinet will be formed.

Riker himself explicitly acknowledges a reason for the formation of larger than minimal winning cabinets. He calls it the "information effect": in the negotiations about the formation of a cabinet, there may be considerable uncertainty about how loyal one or more of the prospective coalition parties, or individual legislators belonging to these parties, will be to the proposed cabinet. Therefore, additional parties may be brought into the coalition as insurance against defections and as guarantee for the cabinet's winning status. In Riker's (1962, 88) words, "If coalition-makers do not know how much weight a specific uncommitted participant adds, then they may be expected to aim at more than a minimum winning coalition."

Second, the policy-based theories also take the size principle into account. They represent additions, instead of alternatives, to minimal winning theory: minimal range coalitions are also minimal winning coalitions, and minimal connected winning

---

smallest party only 315. For the classification of such cabinets, the best solution is to split the difference. Half of the time that blocking cabinets are in power can be credited to minimal winning and half to minority cabinets. Similarly, cabinets like the Amati cabinet can be counted half as oversized and half as minimal winning.

coalitions either equal or are only slightly larger than minimal winning size. In reality, however, the parties' policy preferences may exert strong pressures to enlarge instead of to minimize the size and range of coalitions. Each party naturally prefers to form a cabinet that will follow policies close to its own policy preferences; a cabinet in which it participates with parties of about equal weight on both its left and its right is ideal in this respect. In the example of Table 6.1 above, if B and C are inclined to participate in a coalition together, coalition ABC is more attractive to B because B occupies the center position in it, whereas for the same reason C prefers coalition BCD. In such a situation, it is not at all unlikely that the oversized coalition ABCD will be formed.

Third, policy considerations also lead to oversized coalitions if it is the overriding objective of all or most of the parties to work together to defend the country or the democratic regime against external or internal threats. Wars are the main external threats, and wartime grand coalitions, such as Churchill's war cabinet in Britain, have occurred frequently. Internal threats may be posed by anti-democratic parties and movements and by deep differences among prodemocratic parties in plural societies. Ian Budge and Valentine Herman (1978, 463) tested the following hypothesis in twenty-one countries during the period 1945–78: "Where the democratic system is immediately threatened (externally or internally), all significant pro-system parties will join the government, excluding anti-system parties." They found that of the cabinets formed under such crisis conditions, 72 percent were indeed such broad coalitions.

In addition, several institutional features may favor the formation of minority and oversized instead of minimal winning cabinets (Strøm, Budge, and Laver 1994). For instance, it is easier to form a minority cabinet in the absence of an investiture requirement—that is, if a new cabinet can take office without the need for a parliamentary vote formally electing or approving it; a minority cabinet is more likely to be formed when the parliamentary majority is allowed to tolerate it instead of having to give it explicit approval. There are many parliamentary democracies without investiture rules: examples are the United Kingdom and most former British colonies (but not Ireland and Papua New Guinea), the Scandinavian countries, and the Netherlands (Bergman 1995, 40–46).

The requirement of a "constructive" vote of no confidence— that is, the provision that a no-confidence motion must simultaneously propose an alternative cabinet—may have two different effects. A successful no-confidence vote, supported by a parliamentary majority, is akin to investiture and hence encourages the formation of majority cabinets. And yet, the constructive no-confidence requirement may also maintain a minority cabinet in power if the parliamentary majority opposing the cabinet is too divided to agree on an alternative. Germany was the first country to adopt the constructive vote of no confidence in its postwar constitution. It is now also used by Spain, Papua New Guinea, and, since 1993, by federal Belgium.

Minority cabinets are also encouraged by an innovative rule in the constitution of the French Fifth Republic. It gives the cabinet the right to make its legislative proposals matters of confidence and stipulates that such proposals be automatically adopted unless an absolute majority of the National Assembly votes to dismiss the cabinet: the government bill "shall be considered as adopted, unless a motion of censure . . . is voted under the conditions laid down in the previous paragraph." This previous paragraph prescribes that "the only votes counted shall be those favorable to the motion of censure, which may be adopted only by a majority of the members comprising the Assembly" (Article 49). Aided by this rule, the minority Socialist cabinets serving under President François Mitterrand managed not only to stay in power from 1988 to 1993 but also to pass much of their legislative program.

Probably the most important institutional feature favoring minority cabinets is the strength of parliamentary committees;

powerful committees with a great deal of influence on the general thrust as well as the details of proposed legislation give parties the ability to influence policy from their positions in the legislature—and decrease their incentives to try to enter the cabinet (Strøm 1990, 70–72). The strength of legislative committees is one aspect of the general question of the balance of power between executives and legislatures (the subject of the next chapter): all other factors being equal, the incentives to participate in cabinets decrease, and the probability of minority cabinets increases, when legislatures are relatively strong vis-à-vis executives.

Oversized cabinets may also be encouraged by particular institutional provisions. An unusually clear example can be found in the National Front agreement between the Liberal and Conservative parties that ended the violent civil war of the late 1940s and 1950s in Colombia. Equal representation of both parties in the cabinet, as well as alternation in the presidency, were constitutionally prescribed from 1958 to 1974. The requirement of broad coalition cabinets was extended for four more years, but even after 1978 the second largest party had to be offered "adequate and equitable" representation in the cabinet (Hartlyn 1989, 292). This led to the continuation of two-party coalitions until 1986, when the Conservatives refused to participate in the cabinet of Liberal president Virgilio Barco.

A different example of a constitutional provision concerning the composition of the cabinet is the prescription of linguistic balance in Belgium. It has indirectly tended to enlarge the cabinet. If, for instance, the Flemish Socialists are invited into the cabinet, the requirement of linguistic balance increases the probability that the Francophone Socialists will be included, too, even if they are not needed to give the cabinet a parliamentary majority.

Finally, special majorities necessary for the adoption of constitutional amendments or regular legislation may be strong reasons for forming oversized cabinets. If the policy agenda of a new cabinet includes one or more important amendments to the constitution, any special majorities required for this purpose are likely to broaden the composition of the cabinet. The two-thirds majority rule for constitutional amendments in Belgium was one of the reasons for its many oversized cabinets during the long process of constitutional reform that led to the establishment of a federal state in 1993. Belgium is also an example of other important laws that require not just two-thirds majorities but concurrent majorities within each of the linguistic groups (see Chapter 3). Until the early 1990s, Finland's tendency to have oversized cabinets was similarly reinforced by the requirement of two-thirds and even five-sixths majorities for certain types of economic legislation. Moreover, "even ordinary laws passed by simple majority could be deferred until after the next election by a vote of one-third of the members, a striking provision for a temporary minority veto. These procedures rewarded consensual behavior and made a minimum-majority coalition less valuable than a broader one" (McRae 1997, 290). In Colombia, most legislative measures required two-thirds majorities for passage during the first ten years of the National Front.

Minority Cabinets

The threefold classification into minimal winning, oversized, and minority cabinets and the twofold classification into one-party and coalition cabinets appear simple and straightforward, but they raise a number of problems that need to be resolved before they can be used to measure the degree of concentration of executive power. The most important of these problems are the treatment of minority cabinets and presidential cabinets.

It is clear that minimal winning and one-party cabinets represent majoritarian characteristics and that oversized and coalition cabinets express consensus traits. But where do minority cabinets fit? In principle, there can be two kinds of minority cabinets. One is a genuine minority cabinet that has to negotiate continually with one or more noncabinet parties both to stay in office and to solicit support for its legislative proposals; this bargaining relationship, typically with different noncabinet parties for different purposes, makes such minority cabinets resemble oversized coalitions. The other kind is described by Strøm (1997, 56) as "majority governments in disguise"—minority cabinets that are more like majority cabinets because they have received a firm commitment of support from one or more specific parties in the legislature, although these have opted not to take portfolios in the cabinet.

In his earlier study, Strøm (1990, 95) found that only 11 percent of the many minority cabinets he analyzed could be regarded as such disguised majorities—allowing him to conclude that, by a large margin, most minority cabinets are *not* "simply majority governments in disguise.... Instead, the typical minority cabinet is a single-party government ... which may have to look for legislative support from issue to issue on an *ad hoc* basis." On the basis of Strøm's findings as well as two additional considerations—that the commitment of a support party is never as solid as that of a party actually in the cabinet and that it is often difficult to determine whether a party qualifies as a support party—it makes the most sense, both theoretically and practically, to treat minority cabinets like oversized cabinets. Accordingly, the contrast will be between minimal winning cabinets on one hand and oversized and minority cabinets on the other.

Presidential Cabinets

The classifications into one-party versus coalition cabinets and minimal winning versus oversized versus minority cabinets have been applied mainly to cabinets in parliamentary systems of government, which has been the almost exclusive focus of coalition theorists. Can they also be applied to presidential cabinets? Two crucial adjustments are needed for this purpose. The differences between parliamentary and presidential systems are more fully and systematically discussed in the next chapter, but one major difference is that the executive (cabinet) in parliamentary systems depends on majority support in the legislature both to stay in office and to get its legislative proposals approved, whereas the executive in presidential systems needs legislative majority support only for the president's legislative proposals; presidents are elected for a fixed term of office, and neither they nor the cabinets they appoint are dependent on the confidence of the legislature for their survival in office. Therefore, in one respect—staying in office—presidents and presidential cabinets are minimal winning by definition; in the other respect—legislative support for proposed laws—presidential cabinets may be minimal winning, oversized, or minority cabinets depending on the party affiliations of the presidents and of their cabinet members and the sizes of the respective parties in the legislature. This means that whereas cabinets in parliamentary systems can vary between 0 and 100 percent minimal winning, the variation for presidential cabinets is only between 50 and 100 percent.

The other difference between parliamentary and presidential systems that is of critical relevance here is that parliamentary executives are collegial cabinets, whereas presidential executives are one-person executives; in presidential systems, executive power is concentrated in the president, and his or her cabinet consists of advisers to the president instead of more or less coequal participants. For the distinction between one-party and coalition executives, this means that in one respect presidential cabinets are one-party cabinets by definition—the one party being the president's party because of the president's dominant status in the cabinet. On the other hand, it does make a substantial difference whether a president appoints only members of his or her own party to the cabinet or whether members of one or more other parties are also included. On the assumption that these two aspects can be weighted equally, presidential

cabinets can vary between 50 and 100 percent one-party cabinets in contrast with parliamentary cabinets where the range of
variation is the full 0 to 100 percent. As is explained more fully
in the next chapter, the five presidential systems are the United
States, France (except in the two short parliamentary phases),
Costa Rica, Colombia, and Venezuela.[5] So-called semipresidential systems other than France can be treated like parliamentary
systems. Switzerland is an intermediate case, but for the purpose of classifying the composition of its executive, it can be
treated as a parliamentary system.

Unusual Cabinets in Austria, the United States, and Japan

The great variety of forms that cabinets can assume can be
illustrated further by three of our democracies: Austria, the
United States, and Japan. Even these unusual cabinets, however, can still be classified in terms of the basic criteria distinguishing one-party cabinets from coalitions and minimal winning from oversized and minority cabinets.

The so-called grand coalition cabinets in Austria from 1949
to 1966 exemplify the rather frequent occurrence of very broad
coalitions, composed of a country's two largest parties—which
are, however, minimal winning cabinets in purely technical
terms. These Austrian coalitions were composed of the Socialists and the conservative People's party, which together controlled on average more than 92 percent of the parliamentary
seats during this period. Since each of the parties had fewer than
half of the seats, however, their cabinets were technically minimal winning because the defection of either would have turned
the cabinet into a minority cabinet. In substantive terms, such
broad coalitions should obviously be regarded as oversized. Accordingly, I classified as oversized any coalition cabinet based

5. In addition, Israel's brief experience—only about one month at the end of
the period under analysis—under the "directly elected prime minister" should
also be treated like a presidential phase (see Chapter 7).

on a large supermajority of four-fifths—80 percent—or more of the seats in the legislature.[6]

American cabinets provide the main examples of partisan cabinets with one or two "token" members drawn from a different party; token participation in cabinets means a share of cabinet seats that is much lower than what a party could expect on the basis of proportionality. For instance, Republicans C. Douglas Dillon and Robert S. McNamara served in President John F. Kennedy's cabinet, and Democrat John B. Connally served in President Richard M. Nixon's cabinet; the example of Connally is especially striking because he had been an active Democratic politician and had served as Democratic governor of Texas (Jones 1984, 107–8). A similar more recent example is the appointment of former Republican senator William Cohen as secretary of defense in the second Clinton administration. Richard F. Fenno's (1959, 68) conclusion is still valid: "Typically, the entire Cabinet is of the same political party as the President. . . . The few exceptions serve only to prove the rule. Many deviations from this norm are more apparent than real, involving men whose ideas and sympathies obviously do not coincide with their partisan labels." It is worth noting that Connally later switched parties and became a candidate for the Republican presidential nomination in 1980. One important general finding concerning coalition cabinets is that approximate proportionality in the division of cabinet positions tends to be adhered to scrupulously (Browne and Frendreis 1980). It is

6. The other cases of substantively oversized cabinets are a later Austrian cabinet (1987–90), the 1961–65 Belgian cabinet, the National Front cabinets in Colombia with equal representation of Liberals and Conservatives from 1958 to 1978, the well-known "grand coalition" of Christian Democrats and Social Democrats in Germany from 1966 to 1969, the 1954–59 cabinet in Luxembourg, and the three-month coalition of the two main Venezuelan parties in 1992. However, I deviate from my own 80 percent rule in the case of the French Gaullist-Republican cabinet that took office in 1993, because its huge parliamentary majority (81.8 percent) was manufactured from a mere 39.9 percent of first-ballot votes. Technically—according to the 80 percent rule—this was an oversized cabinet, but substantively it can be regarded only as minimal winning.

therefore not at all difficult to distinguish tokenism from genuine coalitions, and token ministers—just like nonpartisan ministers in otherwise partisan cabinets[7]—can be ignored in the classification of cabinets.

The Liberal Democratic (LDP) cabinets in Japan from 1976 to 1993 present the unusual case of a numerically minimal winning cabinet behaving like a minority cabinet. T. J. Pempel (1992, 11) writes that the LDP, instead of using "its parliamentary majority to ram through controversial legislation," tended to follow "the norm of cross-party consensus building. Usually the LDP [tried] to ensure support for its proposals by at least one, and often more, opposition parties." In Japan, this was called the strategy of "partial coalition" with the parliamentary opposition (Krauss 1984, 263). Especially because experts on Japanese politics link this behavior to strong consensual norms "that operate against what the Japanese usually refer to as 'tyranny of the majority' " (Pempel 1992, 11), these LDP cabinets should be counted as minority rather than minimal winning.[8]

7. Because all of the classifications of cabinets are based on their partisan composition, cabinets that are entirely "nonparty" or "business" cabinets have to be disregarded, but fortunately these do not occur frequently: the only cases in our thirty-six democracies are three short-lived cabinets, serving less than two years altogether, in Finland, the 1995–96 caretaker cabinet of Prime Minister Lamberto Dini in Italy, and the 1993–94 nonpartisan administration of President Ramón Velásquez after the forced resignation of President Carlos Andrés Pérez in Venezuela.

8. Two final issues of classification need to be mentioned briefly. First, the logical consequence of the treatment of factionalized and closely linked parties as one-and-a-half parties, explained in Chapter 5, is that cabinets composed of such parties have to be classified as half one-party cabinets and half two-party coalition cabinets. For instance, all of the Liberal-National cabinets in Australia have to be counted as in between one-party and coalition cabinets; moreover, when the Liberals have had a majority of seats in parliament, such cabinets are halfway between minimal winning and oversized cabinets. Second, any major interelection changes in the legislative seats controlled by cabinet parties must be taken into consideration. For instance, the British Labour cabinet began as a minimal winning cabinet in October 1974 but became a minority cabinet in the middle of 1976 (see Chapter 2). A reverse example is the Indian Congress cabinet that started off as a minority cabinet in 1991 but became a minimal winning

Cabinets in Thirty-Six Democracies

The first and second columns of Table 6.3 present the types of cabinets in thirty-six democracies in terms of the time that minimal winning and one-party cabinets were in power. The values in the third column are the averages of those in the first two; they measure the overall degree of majoritarianism in the formation of cabinets. The countries are listed in ascending order of the majoritarian nature of their cabinets.

The scores in the first two columns are strongly correlated (r=0.62, significant at the 1 percent level), mainly because at the top of the table both scores tend to be low and at the bottom they tend to be high. Most one-party cabinets are also minimal winning, and oversized cabinets are coalitions by definition. In the middle of the table, however, are several countries in which the two elements are unequally combined: some that have mainly minimal winning cabinets but few one-party cabinets—especially Belgium, Germany, Iceland, and Luxembourg—and some with relatively few minimal winning but many one-party cabinets—especially Spain and Sweden. The range of variation on both variables is wide: from 8.2 to 100 percent on minimal winning cabinets and from 0 to 100 percent on one-party cabinets. Six countries always had minimal winning cabinets without exception, and nine countries always had one-party cabinets; by contrast, five countries never had one-party cabinets. The tendency to have minimal winning cabinets is slightly stronger than the tendency toward one-party cabinets: the mean and median of the values in the first column are 64.0 and 65.4 percent, compared with 55.2 and 53.5 percent in the second column. The third column ranges from 4.1 to 100 percent with a mean of 59.6 and a median of 57.3 percent.

As expected, Switzerland turns up at the top of the table; its only minimal winning coalition occurred from 1955 to 1959

---

cabinet in December 1993 when several defectors from other parties were welcomed into the Congress party.

Table 6.3 Proportions of time during which minimal winning
cabinets and one-party cabinets were in power in thirty-six
democracies, 1945–96

	Minimal winning cabinets (%)	One-party cabinets (%)	Mean (%)
Switzerland	8.2	0.0	4.1
Israel	21.6	0.1	10.8
Italy	11.4	10.3	10.9
Finland	14.6	10.9	12.8
Mauritius	28.0	0.0	14.0
Papua New Guinea	46.0	0.0	23.0
Netherlands	50.5	0.0	25.3
Denmark	17.4	42.9	30.2
Germany	70.8	1.7	36.2
Belgium	66.7	8.3	37.5
Portugal	37.4	43.0	40.2
Austria	49.1	33.8	41.4
Luxembourg	88.3	0.0	44.1
Iceland	88.2	3.0	45.6
Sweden	24.6	70.4	47.5
Japan	49.9	46.2	48.1
India	63.6	41.4	52.5
Colombia	58.5	52.9	55.7
Ireland	64.0	53.9	58.9

when there was a three-party executive without the Social Democrats instead of the usual four-party executive. Belgium is farther down in the table but would have had a higher position had
only more recent decades been analyzed. Toward the majoritarian end at the bottom of the table, we find, also as expected,
the United Kingdom, New Zealand, and Barbados. More generally, there are two groups of countries on the majoritarian side:
democracies with a British political heritage—in fact, the seven
countries at the bottom are all former British colonies—and
presidential democracies. Part of the majoritarian character of
the presidential democracies, as discussed earlier, is due to the

Table 6.3   *continued*

	Minimal winning cabinets (%)	One-party cabinets (%)	Mean (%)
France	71.9	53.1	62.5
Norway	46.9	79.4	63.1
Spain	46.0	100.0	73.0
Venezuela	63.6	83.1	73.4
United States	73.2	89.1	81.2
Australia	94.6	69.2	81.9
Costa Rica	78.7	100.0	89.4
Canada	82.0	100.0	91.0
United Kingdom	93.3	100.0	96.7
Greece	97.3	96.4	96.9
Trinidad	100.0	98.1	99.1
New Zealand	99.2	99.7	99.5
Bahamas	100.0	100.0	100.0
Barbados	100.0	100.0	100.0
Botswana	100.0	100.0	100.0
Jamaica	100.0	100.0	100.0
Malta	100.0	100.0	100.0

Source: Based on data in Woldendorp, Keman, and Budge 1998; Banks, Day, and Muller 1997; Müller and Strøm 1997; Strøm 1990; von Beyme 1985; *Keesing's Contemporary Archives*; and data provided by Octavio Amorim Neto

constitutional position and power of presidents in presidential systems. There are also notable exceptions to this concentration of British-heritage and presidential democracies at the majoritarian end, however. Presidential Colombia, with its many broad coalition cabinets, is roughly in the middle of the table. So are India and Ireland, both former British colonies. And two other British colonies, both deeply plural societies like India, are in fifth and sixth place at the consensual top of the table: Mauritius and Papua New Guinea. Greece, in contrast, is a rather surprising presence among the British-heritage countries at the majoritarian end.

Cabinets and Party Systems

There is an extremely strong relationship between party systems and types of cabinets, as Figure 6.1 shows. As the effective number of parliamentary parties increases, the incidence of one-party minimal winning cabinets decreases; every increase in the effective number of parties by one party is associated with

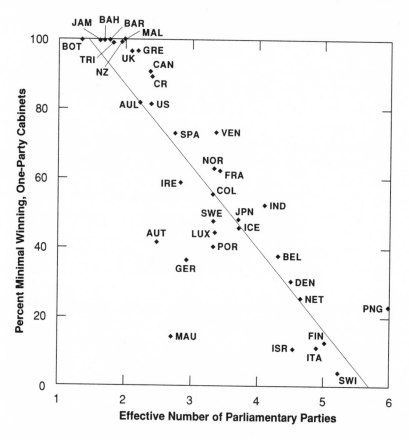

Fig. 6.1 The relationship between the effective number of parliamentary parties and type of cabinet in thirty-six democracies, 1945–96

a 23.5 percent decrease in one-party majority cabinets. The correlation coefficient is −0.87 (significant at the 1 percent level). Most countries are located very close to the regression line, and there are no extreme outliers. The most deviant case is Mauritius, where the plurality system of elections has reduced the effective number of parties but not to the extent of creating a two-party system, and where moderate multipartism and coalition cabinets have gone hand in hand; moreover, the usual inclusion in the cabinet of the party representing the distant island of Rodrigues has tended to make the coalitions oversized. Two other relatively deviant cases are Austria and Germany, both countries with two large parties but usually not majority parties—resulting in moderate multipartism but frequent coalition cabinets.

The strong relationship between party systems and cabinet types is part of the cluster of five closely related variables that comprise the executives-parties dimension of the contrast between majoritarian and consensus democracy, described in the first three chapters of this book. The next three chapters will analyze the other three variables in this cluster: executive-legislative relations, electoral systems, and interest groups. This analysis will again show strong empirical relationships, although not quite as strong and significant as the strikingly close link between party systems and cabinets.

Addendum: Prime Ministerial Power

What is the strength of the head of a cabinet within his or her cabinet? In presidential systems, the cabinet is the president's cabinet and the president's constitutional position makes him or her preeminent. This position can be called, in Giovanni Sartori's (1994b, 109) words, "a *primus solus,* as in the case of the American president (whose government is only his private cabinet)." In parliamentary systems, the power of the prime minister who heads the cabinet can vary greatly from—again using Sartori's terminology—a strong "first *above unequals*" to a medium "first *among unequals*" to a relatively weak "first *among equals*."

In this chapter, I have measured the concentration of power and the degree of majoritarianism in the cabinet in terms of the breadth of representation and the numbers of parties included in the cabinet. A logical corollary would be to expect the degree of prime ministerial power to be related to the concentration of power in the cabinet. Anthony King's (1994, 153) threefold classification of the within-cabinet power of prime ministers in thirteen European countries—similar to Sartori's trichotomous scheme—allows a test of this hypothesis. King classifies six prime ministers as having a high degree of influence within their cabinets: those in Germany, Greece, Ireland, Portugal, Spain, and the United Kingdom. The Austrian, Belgian, Danish, and Swedish prime ministers are placed in a medium position. Those in Italy, the Netherlands, and Norway have a relatively low degree of influence.[9]

A comparison of King's ranking with the scores in the third column of Table 6.1 shows that prime ministers indeed appear to have greater power in countries with majoritarian than in those with consensual cabinets. Only three prime ministers deviate markedly from the general pattern: the Norwegian prime minister has less power and the German and Portuguese prime ministers have more power than predicted on the basis of the type of cabinet. The correlation coefficient is 0.58 (significant at the 5 percent level). The correlation would be stronger still if Switzerland had been included. The Swiss cabinet (Federal Council) is an extremely egalitarian body with a chair rotating

9. King (1994, 152) omits the French and Finnish prime ministers because they "share power in somewhat idiosyncratic ways" with their respective presidents. He also omits the chair of the Swiss executive (presumably because Switzerland is not a parliamentary system), the prime ministers of the two small European countries of Iceland and Luxembourg, and all non-European prime ministers.

annually among all of its seven members—possibly even necessitating the addition of a fourth type of prime minister to Sartori's three categories: that of an "equal among equals"! And Switzerland also has the highest incidence of oversized coalition cabinets.

CHAPTER 7

Executive-Legislative Relations

Patterns of Dominance and Balance of Power

The third difference between the majoritarian and consensus models of democracy concerns the relationship between the executive and legislative branches of government. The majoritarian model is one of executive dominance, whereas the consensus model is characterized by a more balanced executive-legislative relationship. In real political life, a variety of patterns between complete balance and severe imbalance can occur.

In this chapter I first contrast the two most prevalent formal arrangements of executive-legislative relations in democratic regimes: parliamentary government and presidential government. I propose a classificatory scheme based on the three major differences between these types of government and show that almost all of the thirty-six democracies included in this study fit either the pure parliamentary or the pure presidential type. The next topic is the question of how to measure degrees of executive dominance. I propose an index that is mainly, but not entirely, based on the durability of cabinets; several important adjustments are required, especially for presidential systems. After presenting the empirical findings concerning the different levels of executive dominance in thirty-six democracies between 1945 and 1996, I explore two relationships: the link between the five basic types of cabinets and the durability of these cabinets in parliamentary systems and the relationship between the incidence of one-party majority government and the degree of executive dominance in the thirty-six democracies. I close with a brief discussion of the power exercised by heads of state—monarchs and presidents—and some of the problems associated with monarchical and presidential power.

Parliamentary and Presidential Forms of Government

Parliamentary and presidential systems of government have three crucial differences. First, in a parliamentary system, the head of government—who may have such different official titles as prime minister, premier, chancellor, minister-president, *taoiseach* (in Ireland), or, rather confusingly, even "president" (in Botswana), but whom I generically term the prime minister—and his or her cabinet are responsible to the legislature in the sense that they are dependent on the legislature's confidence and can be dismissed from office by a legislative vote of no confidence or censure. In a presidential system, the head of government—always called president—is elected for a constitutionally prescribed period and in normal circumstances cannot be forced to resign by a legislative vote of no confidence (although it may be possible to remove a president for criminal wrongdoing by the process of impeachment).[1]

The second difference between presidential and parliamentary governments is that presidents are popularly elected, either directly or via a popularly elected presidential electoral college, and that prime ministers are selected by legislatures. The process of selection may take a variety of forms. For instance, the German chancellor is formally elected by the Bundestag, the Irish taoiseach by the Dáil, the Japanese prime minister by the House of Representatives, the Botswanan "president" by the

---

1. In addition, as I argue below, we can still speak of presidential government if the legislature can dismiss the president, but only if two conditions apply: first, that the president also has the right to dissolve the legislature, and second, that in either event new elections of both the president and the legislature take place.

National Assembly, and the Papua New Guinean prime minister by the House of Assembly. In Italy and Belgium, cabinets emerge from negotiations among the parties in parliament and especially among party leaders, but they also require a formal parliamentary vote of investiture. In the United Kingdom, the king or queen normally appoints the leader of the majority party to the prime ministership, and in many multiparty systems, too, the cabinets that emerge from interparty bargaining are appointed by the heads of state without formal election or investiture; these cabinets are assumed to have the legislature's confidence unless and until it expresses its lack of confidence.

The third fundamental difference is that parliamentary systems have collective or collegial executives whereas presidential systems have one-person, noncollegial executives. As I indicated at the end of the previous chapter, the prime minister's position in the cabinet can vary from preeminence to virtual equality with the other ministers, but there is always a relatively high degree of collegiality in decision-making; in contrast, the members of presidential cabinets are mere advisers and subordinates of the president. The most important decisions in parliamentary systems have to be made by the cabinet as a whole, not just by the prime minister; the most important decisions in presidential systems can be made by the president with or without, and even against, the advice of the cabinet.

Because parliamentary and presidential governments are defined in terms of three dichotomous criteria, their joint application yields the eight possible combinations shown in the typology of Figure 7.1. In addition to the pure parliamentary and presidential types, there are six hybrid forms of government, labeled I through VI in the typology. Thirty-five of our thirty-six democracies fit the criteria of the two pure types, although France and Israel have to be classified differently in different periods. Five countries have been mainly or wholly presidential—the United States, France, Costa Rica, Colombia, and Venezuela—and thirty have been mainly or wholly parliamentary.

	Collegial executive		One-person executive	
	Dependent on legislative confidence	Not dependent on legislative confidence	Dependent on legislative confidence	Not dependent on legislative confidence
	Parliamentary	Hybrid I	Hybrid II	Hybrid III
Executive selected by legislature	Australia * Austria Bahamas Barbados Belgium Botswana Canada Denmark * Finland * France (1986–88, 1993–95) Germany Greece * Iceland India * Ireland Israel (1949–96) Italy Jamaica Japan Luxembourg Malta Mauritius Netherlands New Zealand Norway Papua New Guinea * Portugal Spain Sweden Trinidad United Kingdom	Switzerland		
	Hybrid IV	Hybrid V	Hybrid VI	Presidential
Executive selected by voters				Colombia Costa Rica * France (1958–86, 1988–93, 1995–97) Israel (1996–) United States Venezuela

* Semipresidential systems

Fig. 7.1 Parliamentary, presidential, and hybrid forms of government in thirty-six democracies, 1945–96: a typology

Switzerland fits hybrid form I, and it is the only example among our thirty-six democracies that can be classified in any of the hybrid categories. This hybrid is parliamentary in two respects and presidential in one: the Swiss "cabinet," the collegial Federal Council, is elected by parliament, but the seven councillors stay in office for a fixed four-year term and cannot be dismissed by a legislative vote of no confidence.

Hybrid types III and V are presidential in two respects and parliamentary in one. The United States would have provided an example of type III if the Constitutional Convention of 1787 had not changed its mind at the last moment. The Virginia plan included the election of the president by the national legislature, and the Constitutional Convention voted three times in favor of this plan before finally settling on the electoral college solution. It should also be noted that if no presidential candidate wins a majority in the electoral college, the U.S. Constitution prescribes hybrid III as the next step: election by the House of Representatives. An interesting example of type V is the Uruguayan political system, which had a collegial presidency from 1952 to 1967: a Swiss-inspired nine-member body, collegial and serving for a fixed term, like the Swiss Federal Council, but popularly elected.

There are no empirical examples of hybrid types II, IV, and VI—which is not surprising because the logic of legislative confidence militates against them. Type II would be a parliamentary system except that the prime minister's relationship to the cabinet would resemble that of a president to his or her cabinet. On paper, the German constitution appears to call for such a system, but because the chancellor needs the Bundestag's confidence, the negotiation of a collegial coalition cabinet takes place before the formal election of the chancellor by the Bundestag. Types IV and VI are problematic because a legislative vote of no confidence in a popularly elected executive would be seen as defiance of the popular will and of democratic legitimacy. The only democratically acceptable form of these two types would be one in which a legislative vote of no confidence in the executive would be matched by the executive's right to dissolve the legislature, and where either action would trigger new elections of both legislature and executive. Such an amended type VI system appears to be what the Committee on the Constitutional System proposed for the United States in 1987, but, as I argue below, this proposal entailed a special form of presidential government rather than a hybrid type.

The only serious problem of classifying democracies according to the eightfold typology is raised by systems that have both a popularly elected president and a parliamentary prime minister, usually referred to as "semipresidential" (Duverger 1980) or "premier-presidential" systems (Shugart and Carey 1992). Among our thirty-six democracies, there are six of these semipresidential systems: Austria, Finland, France, Iceland, Ireland, and Portugal. These cases can be resolved by asking the question: who is the *real* head of government—the president or the prime minister? The Austrian, Icelandic, and Irish presidents are weak though popularly elected, and these three democracies operate much like ordinary parliamentary systems. The same applies to Portugal, especially after the president's powers were severely reduced in the constitutional revision of 1982.

The French case is more problematic. Until 1986, the French president, popularly elected for a fixed seven-year term, was clearly the head of the government and not the prime minister. Presidential power, however, was based more on the support by strong parliamentary majorities than on constitutional prerogatives, and in the early 1980s two well-known French political scientists predicted that, if the president were to lose this majority support, the presidential system would change to a parliamentary one. Raymond Aron (1982, 8) wrote: "The President of the Republic is the supreme authority as long as he has a majority in the National Assembly; but he must abandon the reality of power to the prime minister if ever a party other than his own has a majority in the Assembly." Based on the same logic, Maurice Duverger (1980, 186) predicted that the French Fifth Republic would develop a pattern of alternation between presidential and parliamentary phases. This is exactly what happened when the Gaullists and Republicans won a legislative victory in 1986 and Jacques Chirac became prime minister: "Except for some issues concerning foreign relations and defense . . . [Socialist president] Mitterrand stood on the legislative sidelines while Chirac functioned as France's political executive" (Huber 1996, 28). The situation repeated itself from 1993 to 1995 when Gaullist premier Edouard Balladur replaced President Mitterrand as the real head of government, and Socialist premier Lionel Jospin inaugurated the third parliamentary phase under President Chirac in 1997.

The Finnish semipresidential system is the most difficult case. Finland has an elected president—until recently elected indirectly via an electoral college—with less power than the French president usually has but more than that of the presidents in the other semipresidential systems. Yet there is a close resemblance to the French system in its parliamentary phase during which the prime minister is head of government and the president's power is limited to a special role in foreign affairs. If this phase in the French system can be regarded as parliamentary, the similar situation in Finland should be considered parliamentary, too. This classification may be somewhat debatable for the long period from 1956 to 1981 during which the formidable Urho Kekkonen served as president, but it clearly fits the period since his departure from the political scene.[2] A constitutional amendment in 1991 reduced presidential power by removing the president's right to dissolve parliament—a right that the French president does have—but at the same time increased presidential prestige by abolishing the presidential electoral college and instituting direct popular election. On balance, Finnish democracy can be classified as a parliamentary system in

2. G. Bingham Powell (1982, 56) classified Finland as a parliamentary system even during the Kekkonen era.

the typology of Figure 7.1; it is certainly much closer to a parliamentary than a presidential system.

Finally, Israel shifted from a system that was unambiguously parliamentary in every respect to the direct popular election of the prime minister in 1996—presenting another intriguing puzzle of classification. The basic rules are that the prime minister is elected directly by the voters, that parliament is elected simultaneously, that parliament retains the right to dismiss the prime minister, that the prime minister also has the right to dissolve parliament, and that either action results in new elections of both prime minister and parliament (Hazan 1997). The Israelis entered uncharted territory with this innovation, but it resembles one of the solutions proposed by the Committee on the Constitutional System (1987, 16) for the problem of executive-legislative deadlock in the United States: "If it were possible for a President to call new elections, or for Congress to do so, we would have a mechanism for resolving deadlocks over fundamental policy issues." Such a mutual right to call new elections, both presidential and congressional, would be a change *in* rather than a change *of* the presidential system—that is, the United States would still be a presidential system according to all three basic criteria.

The new Israeli system is very similar to this special form of presidentialism except that the president is called "prime minister." The prime minister is (1) popularly elected instead of being selected by parliament, (2) elected for a fixed period of four years, except if the special rule of mutual dismissal and new elections becomes operative, and (3) predominates over the cabinet by virtue of his or her popular election and hence democratic legitimation. As far as the third point is concerned, the Israeli rule that the other members of the cabinet need a parliamentary vote of investiture before taking office sounds like the retention of one aspect of the old parliamentarism, but remember that in the United States, too, the president can appoint the members of his or her cabinet only with the "advice and con-

sent" of the Senate. The directly elected prime minister is therefore much more like a president in a presidential system than
like a prime minister in a parliamentary system.[3]

The only uncertainty about this classification concerns the
likelihood of frequent new elections. The Committee on the
Constitutional System (1987, 16) predicted that such new elections would be rare in the United States because neither side
would want to shorten its own tenure in office; in fact, the committee hoped that the very existence of the kind of mechanism it
proposed "would be an inducement to avoid a deadlock that
could trigger new elections." For Israel, some commentators
have made the opposite prediction—that the main effect of the
new system will be extremely frequent elections; for instance,
Giovanni Sartori (1994a, 115) warns of the danger of "incessant
elections." If this prediction turns out to be correct, the Israeli
system will, at least in this respect, look quite different from
other presidential systems with their fixed and often long terms
of office.

Additional Parliamentary-Presidential Contrasts

A few eminent political scientists have argued that in addition to the three crucial differences between parliamentary and
presidential systems discussed above, there are three other important differences (esp. Verney 1959, 17–56). On closer examination, these contrasts turn out to have serious empirical exceptions and not to be essential for the distinction between the
two major forms of government.

3. According to Matthew Soberg Shugart and Scott Mainwaring (1997, 15),
presidentialism can be defined in terms of two basic characteristics: "separate
origin" (separate popular elections), and "separate survival" (fixed terms of office for both president and legislature). According to the second criterion, the
proposal of the Committee on the Constitutional System and the new Israeli
system would clearly not qualify as presidential, but neither would the French
Fifth Republic because the National Assembly can be dissolved prematurely.
Moreover, a fixed term of office for the legislature can also be a characteristic of
parliamentary systems, as in the case of Norway.

First, separation of powers in presidential systems is usually taken to mean not only the mutual independence of the executive and legislative branches but also the rule that the same person cannot simultaneously serve in both. In contrast, the nonseparation of powers in parliamentary systems means not only that the executive is dependent on the legislature's confidence but also that the same persons can be members of both parliament and the cabinet. With regard to the latter, however, there is great deal of variation within the parliamentary type of government. On one end of the spectrum, many parliamentary systems—especially those in the United Kingdom and the former British colonies—make it an almost absolute requirement that cabinet members be members of the legislature, too. On the other end, there are three countries—the Netherlands, Norway, and Luxembourg—in which membership in the cabinet cannot be combined with membership in parliament; in all three, however, cabinet members can and do participate in parliamentary debates. Because the incompatibility rule emphasizes the separate status of the cabinet, it tends to strengthen the cabinet's authority vis-à-vis parliament, but it cannot be considered more than a minor variation within the parliamentary type. It would certainly be incorrect to argue that these three countries fit or even approximate the presidential form of government in this respect.

Second, it is often claimed that a key difference between presidentialism and parliamentarism is that presidents do not have the right to dissolve the legislature whereas prime ministers and their cabinets do have this right. One exception on the presidential side is that the French president does have the power to dissolve the National Assembly; another exception is the Israeli example of mutual dismissal and new elections for both, discussed earlier. In parliamentary systems, there is again a wide range of variation. In the British and many British-inspired systems, the power to dissolve is virtually unlimited and it is a specifically prime ministerial prerogative. In Germany and several other countries, parliament can be dissolved only under special circumstances and not at the sole discretion of the executive. In Norway, parliament is elected for a four-year term and cannot be dissolved at all. Executive authority is obviously affected by whether the executive does or does not have such power over the legislature, but this factor cannot be considered an essential distinction between the parliamentary and presidential forms of government.

Third, parliamentary systems usually have dual executives: a symbolic and ceremonial head of state (a monarch or president) who has little power and a prime minister who is the head of the government and who, together with the cabinet, exercises most executive power. The normal rule in presidential systems is that the president is simultaneously the head of state and the head of the government. However, there are major exceptions on both sides. Botswana has a prime minister, elected by and subject to the confidence of the legislature, who is the head of the government but who also serves as head of state—and who therefore has the formal title "president." Another example is democratic South Africa, whose first head of the government was President Nelson Mandela—not a president in a presidential system but a combined head of government and head of state in a parliamentary system.

If the new directly elected Israeli prime minister can indeed be seen as a president in a presidential system, Israel provides an example of a presidential system with a dual instead of a single executive: in addition to the presidential prime minister there is a president who is the head of state. Another example that shows that a dual executive is, in principle, compatible with a presidential form of government is the proposal for a directly elected prime minister in the Netherlands (Andeweg 1997, 235). This plan, widely debated in the late 1960s and early 1970s, entailed the popular election of the prime minister for a fixed four-year term and not subject to parliamentary confidence—but not to change the monarchy. In effect, such a "prime minister" would be the head of the government in a presidential system—but not the head of state, because the monarch would continue in that position. The prestige of being head of state obviously enhances the influence of most presidents and is an advantage that most prime ministers lack, but it is not an essential distinction between the two forms of government.

Separation of Power and Balance of Power

The distinction between parliamentary and presidential systems is of great importance in several respects. For instance, as discussed in the previous chapter, presidential cabinets are fundamentally different, and have to be classified differently, from cabinets in parliamentary systems; moreover, both later on in this chapter and in the next chapter, presidential systems are again treated differently from parliamentary systems in the measurement of key variables. However, the parliamentary-presidential distinction does not bear directly on the distribution of power in executive-legislative relationships. In parliamentary systems, one can find a rough balance of power between cabinet and parliament, as in Belgium, but one can also find clear executive dominance, as in the United Kingdom, New Zealand, and Barbados (see Chapters 2 and 3). The same range of variation occurs in presidential systems. In the United States, separation of powers also means a balance of power between president and Congress; the same applies to Costa Rica as well as to Switzerland, the one separation-of-powers system that is not a presidential system. The French presidential system is at the opposite end; in Anthony King's (1976, 21) words, "The French legislature has . . . become even more subordinate to the executive than the British." Colombia and Venezuela are in intermediate positions.

Presidential powers derive from three sources. One is the power of presidents defined in constitutions, consisting of "reactive powers," especially presidential veto power, and "proactive powers," especially the ability to legislate by decree in certain areas (Shugart and Mainwaring 1997, 41). The second source of power is the strength and cohesion of presidents' parties in the legislature. Third, presidents derive considerable strength from their direct popular election and the fact that they can claim that they (and their vice presidents, if any) are the only public officials elected by the people as a whole. The French, Venezuelan, and Costa Rican presidents are constitutionally fairly weak but have considerable partisan powers.[4] The American and Colombian presidents depend much more on constitutional power: the strong veto power in the American case, and both decree and veto powers in Colombia.

The frequent dependence of presidents on their partisan powers means that the relative power of presidents and legislatures can and often does change abruptly and that it is generally less stable than in parliamentary systems. This is especially true in Venezuela, with its "partyarchy" of extremely strong parties that can give presidents a very firm support base when their parties control legislative majorities but can cause stalemate when executive and legislative power is divided (Coppedge 1994). Constitutional powers are more stable; the one example of major changes in this respect among our five presidential systems is the substantial enhancement of presidential power that occurred in Colombia as a result of the constitutional revision of 1968, followed by a slight reduction in 1991. The democratic legitimacy derived from popular election can vary according to the magnitude of the president's electoral victory. It helps to be elected by 64.7 percent of the voters, as President José Figueres of Costa Rica was in 1953, and it is not helpful to win with 30.5 percent of the vote as President Rafael Caldera of Venezuela did in 1993. Nor is it helpful to be an unelected president like Gerald R. Ford in the United States from 1974 to 1977.

4. In France, as discussed earlier, not just presidential power but the presidential system itself depends on the president having majority or near-majority support in the National Assembly.

Substantial changes have occurred in the historical experience of the United States. Woodrow Wilson (1885) decried the predominance of Congress and stated that the American "presidential" system should more realistically be called, as the title of his famous book indicates, *Congressional Government*. More recent critics have charged that, especially under Presidents Lyndon B. Johnson and Richard M. Nixon, an "imperial presidency" tended to overshadow Congress. In the much shorter history of the French presidential system, John T. S. Keeler and Martin A. Schain (1997, 95–100) see four alternations between "hyperpresidential" and "tempered presidential" phases in the period 1962–93.

Measuring Degrees of Dominance and Balance of Power

How can the relative power of the executive and legislative branches of government be measured? For parliamentary systems, the best indicator is cabinet durability. A cabinet that stays in power for a long time is likely to be dominant vis-à-vis the legislature, and a short-lived cabinet is likely to be relatively weak.[5] Coalition theorists have paid great attention to the duration of cabinets, but they usually assume—either explicitly or, more often, implicitly—that cabinet durability is an indicator not just of the cabinet's strength compared with that of the legislature but also of regime stability. The argument is that short-lived cabinets do not have sufficient time to develop sound and coherent policies and that ineffective policy-making will endanger the viability of democracy: cabinet instability is assumed to lead to, and is therefore taken as an indicator of, regime instability. An explicit statement to this effect is Paul V. Warwick's (1994, 139): "a parliamentary system that does not

5. This interpretation is supported by the contrast between democracies in general and nondemocratic systems. In the latter we find the strongest executives and the most subservient legislatures or no legislatures at all—and we also find, "not surprisingly," as Henry Bienen and Nicolas van de Walle (1991, 103) state, the greatest incidence of "long-lasting leaders."

produce durable governments is unlikely to provide effective policy making, to attract widespread popular allegiance, or perhaps even to survive over the longer run."

This view is as wrong as it is prevalent. Even the proverbially short-lived cabinets of the Fourth French Republic were far from completely ineffective policy-makers. Many members of each defunct cabinet served again in the new one, and their average life as ministers was considerably longer than that of the cabinets as whole. The contemporary French observer André Siegfried (1956, 399) explained this "paradox of stable policy with unstable cabinets" as follows: "Actually the disadvantages are not as serious as they appear. . . . When there is a cabinet crisis, certain ministers change or the same ministers are merely shifted around; but no civil servant is displaced, and the day-to-day administration continues without interruption. Furthermore, as the same ministers hold over from one cabinet to another, they form as it were teams of government."[6] Mattei Dogan (1989) attacks the equation of cabinet stability with regime stability head-on and argues emphatically that cabinet stability is *not* a valid indicator of the health and viability of the democratic system; the major reason is that in most systems with seemingly unstable cabinets, there is a highly stable "core" of ministerial personnel—similar to the situation in the Fourth Republic described by Siegfried.

What should be added to Dogan's argument is that, in relatively short-lived cabinets, there tends to be continuity not only of personnel but also of participating parties. One-party cab-

6. In their comparative nineteen-nation analysis of cabinet durability, Michael Taylor and Valentine M. Herman (1971, 29) state: "A considerable empirical study would be necessary before it could be said that [cabinet durability] was an indicator of *anything*." They argue that their article does not make any assumption about the broader significance of cabinet durability, but they also state that their "results would be of greater interest if Siegfried's observation that the instability of the Fourth Republic made no difference to public policy-making were found to be untrue of instability generally." Their unspoken assumption, of course, is that the significance of studying cabinet durability has much to do with its putative link with regime viability.

inets tend to be more durable than coalition cabinets, but a change from a one-party cabinet to another is a wholesale partisan turnover, whereas a change from one coalition cabinet to another usually entails only a piecemeal change in the party composition of the cabinet. I return to the general issue of the effectiveness of policy-making in Chapter 15; there the question is whether majoritarian democracies with their typically more dominant and durable executives are better policy-makers than consensus democracies with their usually shorter-lived and less dominant executives—and the answer is that there is simply not much of a difference.

The next step—after having decided that cabinet duration can be used as an indicator of executive dominance—is to decide how to measure it. This question concerns the events that are considered to end the life of one cabinet and to herald the beginning of a new one. There are two major alternatives. One is to focus exclusively on the partisan composition of cabinets and to count a cabinet as one cabinet if its party composition does not change; one pioneering study of cabinet duration took this approach (Dodd 1976). It is much more common, however, to regard several additional events as marking the end of one and the beginning of the next cabinet: a parliamentary election, a change in the prime ministership, and a change in the minimal winning, oversized, or minority status of the cabinet.[7] An ad-

7. Such interelection changes in coalitional status occurred in Britain in 1976 and in India in 1993 (see Chapter 6, note 8). Instead of this criterion, Warwick (1994) uses formal cabinet resignation as one of the events that signifies the end of a cabinet. This criterion is not satisfactory, because it depends too much on particular rules and customs in different parliamentary systems: under otherwise similar circumstances, cabinets in some countries take the step of tendering their resignations much more quickly than in other countries. Moreover, if a cabinet resignation actually leads to the formation of a new cabinet with a different party composition or a different prime minister, or if it leads to new elections, the cabinet will be regarded as having terminated anyway; if, however, a cabinet resigns but is reappointed under the same prime minister and with the same partisan make-up, it is hard to make a convincing case that the cabinet has "changed" in any significant way.

Table 7.1   Average cabinet duration according to two criteria (in years), the mean of these two measures, and the index of executive dominance in thirty-six democracies, 1945–96

	Average cabinet life I	Average cabinet life II	Mean of measures I and II	Index of executive dominance
Costa Rica	4.74	3.88	4.31	1.00*
United States	7.07	1.83	4.45	1.00*
Switzerland	16.19	0.99	8.59	1.00*
Italy	1.28	0.99	1.14	1.14
Finland	1.31	1.18	1.24	1.24
Papua New Guinea	1.57	1.57	1.57	1.57
Israel	1.69	1.48	1.58	1.58
Mauritius	1.95	1.63	1.79	1.79
Belgium	2.29	1.68	1.98	1.98
Venezuela	2.82	2.62	2.72	2.00*
India	2.41	1.75	2.08	2.08
Portugal	2.32	1.86	2.09	2.09
Denmark	2.81	1.75	2.28	2.28
Iceland	2.78	2.17	2.48	2.48
Japan	3.85	1.28	2.57	2.57
Netherlands	2.94	2.50	2.72	2.72
Germany	3.60	2.03	2.82	2.82
Greece	3.60	2.16	2.88	2.88
Colombia	4.74	2.23	3.48	3.00*
Ireland	3.72	2.42	3.07	3.07
Norway	4.22	2.11	3.17	3.17

vantage of Dodd's broad definition is that it measures cabinet durations that can be interpreted very well as indicators of extecutive dominance. In particular, cabinets that win several successive elections—and which Dodd therefore counts as the same cabinet—are less and less likely to meet serious challenges from their parliaments. In deference to the more common usage of the narrower definition, however, I combine both approaches in Table 7.1. The second column of the table is based on the narrow definition of cabinet duration that uses four criteria for the termination of a cabinet—changes in party composition, prime

Table 7.1 *Continued*

	Average cabinet life I	Average cabinet life II	Mean of measures I and II	Index of executive dominance
Sweden	4.77	2.07	3.42	3.42
New Zealand	6.19	2.15	4.17	4.17
Spain	6.35	2.38	4.36	4.36
Luxembourg	5.62	3.16	4.39	4.39
Canada	7.26	2.54	4.90	4.90
Australia	8.28	1.84	5.06	5.06
Austria	8.42	2.53	5.47	5.47
Barbados	7.58	3.37	5.48	5.48
France	2.88	2.08	2.48	5.52*
United Kingdom	8.49	2.55	5.52	5.52
Jamaica	8.56	3.42	5.99	5.52*
Trinidad	8.66	3.85	6.26	5.52*
Malta	10.09	4.32	7.21	5.52*
Bahamas	11.89	4.76	8.32	5.52*
Botswana	31.33	3.92	17.63	5.52*

*These values of the index of executive dominance (for the five presidential systems, Switzerland, and five former British colonies) differ from the values of the mean of measures I and II

Source: Based on data in Woldendorp, Keman, and Budge 1998; Banks, Day, and Muller 1997; Müller and Strøm 1997; Strøm 1990; von Beyme 1985; *Keesing's Contemporary Archives;* and data provided by Octavio Amorim Neto

ministership, and coalitional status, as well as new elections; the first column is based solely on the party-composition criterion. The third column presents the averages of the first two.

Two important adjustments are required to translate the averages in the third column of Table 7.1 into a satisfactory index of executive dominance. First, some of these averages assume extreme values. Botswana, which had one-party cabinets made up of the Botswana Democratic party from 1965 to 1996, is the most glaring example. Its four-year election cycle reduces the average duration in the third column to 17.63 years, but this is still more than three times as long as the average of 5.52 years for Britain—

and there is no good reason to believe that the Botswana cabinet is three times as dominant as the British cabinet. In fact, there is no good reason to judge any cabinets to be more dominant than the British cabinet, which is the exemplar of cabinet dominance in the Westminster model. Accordingly, any values higher than 5.52 years in the third column are truncated at this level in the fourth column. This entails a major reduction for Botswana but much less substantial adjustments for four other countries.

A much greater adjustment is necessary for the presidential systems and for the Swiss separation-of-powers system. In four of the six cases, cabinet duration gives a completely wrong impression of the degree of executive dominance. The Swiss average of 8.59 years—based on only three different party compositions from 1947 to 1996 but a change in the chairmanship of the Federal Council every year—is obviously completely wrong as a measure of executive dominance because Switzerland is a prime example of executive-legislative balance. Hence, I impressionistically assign it a value of 1.00 year. The same is appropriate for the United States and Costa Rica. On the other end of the scale, France must be assigned the highest value for executive dominance—the same as Britain's. The degree of presidential dominance has fluctuated considerably in Colombia and Venezuela; on average, I judge the degree of dominance to be higher in Colombia, but even in Colombia presidents have not been as powerful as strong cabinets in parliamentary systems tend to be. As Mainwaring and Shugart (1997, 6) state, "Although Colombian presidents have been portrayed as dominant due to their substantial formal powers, they have regularly had problems garnering enough support even within their own parties to make lasting policy changes."

Executive-Legislative Relations in Thirty-Six Democracies

Table 7.1 lists the thirty-six democracies in ascending order of executive dominance. The index ranges from the arbitrarily assigned value of 1.00 year for Costa Rica, the United States, and Switzerland to the truncated value of 5.52 years for seven countries at the bottom of the table. The mean value is 3.32 and the median is 2.94 years. The six countries at the majoritarian end are the United Kingdom and five former British colonies. Barbados has only a slightly lower value: 5.48 compared with the maximum of 5.52 years. New Zealand's index of executive dominance is considerably lower—4.17 years—mainly due to its short three-year parliamentary term, which makes it impossible for its cabinets, according to the narrow definition, to last longer than three years. Former British possessions Australia, Canada, and Ireland are also in the bottom half of the table. But several British-heritage countries turn up at the consensual end at the top of the table—most strikingly, of course, the United States. Papua New Guinea and Mauritius are also among the more consensual systems toward the top of the table—as they were in Table 6.3 in the previous chapter. India is also in the top half.

Of the two prototypes of consensus democracy, Switzerland and Belgium, Switzerland was assigned to the top of the table, together with the United States and Costa Rica, and Belgium is farther down but still in ninth place. Of the six separation-of-power systems—the presidential democracies and Switzerland—only the French executive is clearly dominant. Colombia is roughly in the middle and the other four are all in higher positions— suggesting that constitutional separation of powers between executive and legislature does correspond to a considerable extent with a greater balance of power between the two branches.[8]

Cabinet Types and Cabinet Durability

How are the different cabinet types, analyzed in the previous chapter, related to the degree of executive dominance? There are

8. Note, however, that these six systems are the successful separation-of-powers systems and that our set of thirty-six long-term democracies excludes the many failed presidential democracies—which tend to be the ones in which the difficult act of balancing executives and legislatures has *not* been achieved.

three reasons to expect a positive relationship between minimal winning and one-party cabinets on one hand and executive dominance on the other. First, as discussed in Chapter 1, both variables belong the same cluster of variables that make up the executives-parties dimension of the majoritarian-consensus contrast. Second, minority cabinets are by their nature at the mercy of the legislature in parliamentary systems and can therefore not be expected to dominate their legislatures. Third, studies of the independence shown by individual legislators in voting against their own cabinet in Britain have found that this kind of independent parliamentary behavior has tended to vary directly with the size of the cabinet's majority in the House of Commons: bare-majority cabinets have generally received solid support from their partisans in parliament, whereas cabinets with ample majorities have frequently found their parliamentary party to be more rebellious (Crowe 1980). Analogizing from this tendency in the British House of Commons to the other parliamentary systems, we can expect greater legislative independence when cabinets are oversized rather than minimal winning.

Table 7.2 and Figure 7.2 show the strength of these relationships. Table 7.2 classifies the cabinets that have been in power in thirty-one parliamentary systems—including the two parliamentary phases in France but excluding the other presidential democracies and Switzerland—according to the five basic types of cabinet, and it presents the average duration of these cabinets according to the broad and narrow definitions of cabinet duration (measures I and II, respectively).[9] As expected, we find fewer and longer-lasting cabinets in the first two columns,

9. Table 7.2 includes all cabinets that fall clearly into one of the five categories—which means that cabinets that have to be counted as, for instance, halfway between minimal winning and oversized or halfway between one-party and coalition cabinets had to be disregarded; moreover, cabinets that the broad definition of cabinet duration counts as the same cabinet but that changed their coalitional status during the life of the cabinet also had to be put aside.

Table 7.2 Frequency and average cabinet duration according to two criteria (in years) of five types of cabinets in thirty-one parliamentary democracies, 1945–96

Type of cabinet	Measure I		Measure II	
	Number of cabinets	Average cabinet duration (years)	Number of cabinets	Average cabinet duration (years)
Minimal winning, one-party	45	8.01	142	3.00
Minimal winning coalition	71	3.28	107	2.41
Minority, one-party	38	2.24	76	1.64
Minority coalition	52	1.01	59	0.91
Oversized coalition	91	2.07	120	1.71
All cabinets	297	3.09	504	2.12

Source: Based on data in Woldendorp, Keman, and Budge 1998; Banks, Day, and Muller 1997; Müller and Strøm 1997; Strøm 1990; von Beyme 1985; and *Keesing's Contemporary Archives*

which are based on the broad measure, than in the third and fourth columns.

The overall pattern is very similar regardless of which definition of cabinet duration is used. Minimal winning one-party cabinets have the longest average life span. And both types of minimal winning cabinets last longer than minority and oversized cabinets. Oversized coalitions and one-party minority cabinets—which in terms of their parliamentary support appear to be at a maximum distance from each other—actually have very similar durations: the oversized cabinets last slightly less long according to the first measure but slightly longer according to the second. Minority coalitions have the shortest life. An important explanation is that in multiparty systems such coalitions are often temporary caretakers after a cabinet has fallen and while awaiting a new election. In countries where they are more like regular cabinets, as in the Scandinavian countries, minority coalition cabinets last longer. For instance, Denmark

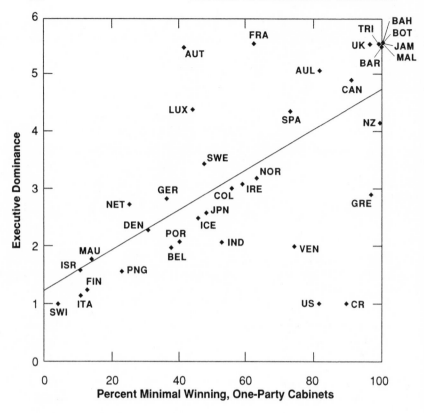

Fig. 7.2 The relationship between type of cabinet and executive dominance in thirty-six democracies, 1945–96

had seven minority coalition cabinets (eleven cabinets according to the narrower definition) that lasted an average of 2.87 years (1.83 years according to the narrower definition).

Figure 7.2 shows the relationship between types of cabinet and executive dominance in terms of the combination of the two characteristics in each of our thirty-six democracies (based on the data in the third column of Table 6.3 and the fourth column of Table 7.1). The pattern is clear: the countries with more minimal winning single-party cabinets also tend to be the countries with greater executive dominance. The correlation coefficient is 0.68 (statistically significant at the 1 percent level). A 10 percent increase in the frequency of minimal winning one-party cabinets is associated with an increase of 0.35 unit in the index of executive dominance.

Most of the countries are near the regression line. The main outliers are four of the presidential systems. The United States, Costa Rica, and Venezuela have a much lower level of executive dominance than expected on the basis of their frequent majoritarian-type cabinets; France exhibits the opposite combination of characteristics. The explanation for the first three appears to be an intrinsic feature of presidentialism: their cabinets are partly majoritarian—minimal winning and one-party—by definition, as argued in the previous chapter, but their separation of powers contributes to the consensual trait of executive-legislative balance. Because, however, there are only five presidential systems among our thirty-six democracies (disregarding the short period of presidentialism in Israel), this observation must be regarded as tentative.

Of the parliamentary democracies, only two are in clearly deviant positions: Austria and Greece. Austria has had many oversized coalitions that were unusually long-lived: one stretch of these—counted as one cabinet according to the broad definition—lasted from 1947 to 1966. In Greece, the turmoil caused by two indecisive parliamentary elections and three elections in less than ten months in 1990–91, is especially responsible for shortening the average cabinet duration.

Addendum: Monarchs and Presidents

The position of head of state has been mentioned repeatedly in this chapter, but the different kinds of heads of state and their relative powers have not been treated systematically. The most striking difference in this respect in our set of thirty-six democracies is that almost half are monarchies: Australia, the Bahamas, Barbados, Belgium, Canada, Denmark, Jamaica, Japan, Luxembourg, the Netherlands, New Zealand, Norway, Papua New Guinea, Spain, Sweden, and the United Kingdom. The monarchs are mainly kings or queens—represented by a governor-general in Australia, the Bahamas, Barbados, Canada, Jamaica, New Zealand, and Papua New Guinea—but Japan has an emperor and Luxembourg has a grand duke as head of state. The exact number of monarchies as of the middle of 1996 was sixteen; in the early 1970s, a majority of nineteen were monarchies, but three Commonwealth countries later became republics: Malta in 1974, Trinidad in 1976, and Mauritius in 1992. It is rather surprising that so many of our democracies are or were monarchies, a constitutional form that appears to be less democratic than republican government. The explanation is that they are constitutional monarchies in which the power of the monarch is severely limited. As Richard Rose and Dennis Kavanagh (1976, 568) write, "Monarchs have remained in power where the reigning family has been willing to withdraw from a politically active role. Reciprocally, monarchies have fallen when the monarch has sought to continue to assert political power."

The advantage that the monarchy is frequently claimed to have for a democratic regime is that it provides a head of state who is an apolitical and impartial symbol of unity. This is generally true, although it is also possible for monarchs to become a divisive force. For instance, the behavior of King Leopold III during the Second World War became a major political issue in postwar Belgium. In the 1950 referendum on whether the king should be retained, a majority of Flemings and Catholics supported the king, and most Walloons, Socialists, and Liberals wanted him removed. Leopold III won the referendum with an overall majority of 58 percent—not a landslide victory for a king!—but he soon abdicated in favor of his son Baudouin.

In terms of basic democratic principles, a disadvantage is that monarchs are not entirely powerless. In parliamentary systems, they generally retain the right to appoint the prime minister. This is not a significant function when there is a unanimous preference for a prime ministerial candidate, but when there is a sudden death or resignation, or when the parties in a multiparty parliament are unable to reach an agreement, the monarch's influence on the eventual choice of a prime minister may be far from negligible. In order to reduce the monarch's role to a purely ceremonial one, Sweden's constitution of 1974 transferred the function of appointing a prime minister from the monarch to the speaker of parliament.

Even though monarchs may have residual powers, the general assumption, accepted by the monarch himself or herself, is that the monarch is purely a head of state and not a head of government. The temptation to intrude on the powers of the head of government and of the cabinet is greater when parliamentary democracies have a president as head of state—generally someone who has had a former political career. One method that parliamentary systems use to minimize this risk is to not allow the president the democratic prestige and implicit power of being popularly elected. Instead, the usual procedure is to have parliament (or a special electoral college of members of national and state parliaments, as in Germany and India) elect the president. Another solution is not to have a separate president at all but to give the title and function of the president to the prime minister, as in Botswana. Switzerland uses a similar method by having the head of government—the rotating chair of the Federal Council—serve simultaneously as president. However, the special characteristic of semipresidential democracies that function mainly as parliamentary systems—Austria, Finland, Iceland, Ireland, and Portugal—is that they do have a popularly elected president. The danger here is that popular election may provide the head of state with a democratically legitimate justification to encroach upon or take over leadership of the government, thereby changing the nature of the parliamentary system.

Finally, for those who consider parliamentary systems to be

preferable to presidential systems, an important advantage of a constitutional monarchy is that it is generally regarded as incompatible with presidentialism. As I argued earlier in this chapter, this view is not correct: in theory, it is quite possible to institute a presidential system with a president who serves as head of government and a monarch who is head of state. But there are no empirical examples of such a system, and the view that presidentialism and monarchy cannot be combined, however mistaken, may save democratizing countries with a monarch as head of state, like Spain in the late 1970s, from seriously considering the adoption of a presidential form of government.

CHAPTER 8

Electoral Systems
Majority and Plurality Methods
Versus Proportional Representation

The fourth difference between the majoritarian and consensus models of democracy is clear-cut. The typical electoral system of majoritarian democracy is the single-member district plurality or majority system; consensus democracy typically uses proportional representation (PR). The plurality and majority single-member district methods are winner-take-all methods—the candidate supported by the largest number of voters wins, and all other voters remain unrepresented—and hence a perfect reflection of majoritarian philosophy. Moreover, the party gaining a nationwide majority or plurality of the votes will tend to be overrepresented in terms of parliamentary seats. In sharp contrast, the basic aim of proportional representation is to represent both majorities and minorities and, instead of overrepresenting or underrepresenting any parties, to translate votes into seats proportionally.

The gap between the two types of electoral systems is also wide in the sense that changes within each type are common but that very few democracies change from PR to plurality or majority methods or vice versa (Nohlen 1984). Each group of countries appears to be strongly attached to its own electoral system. In a comment on his withdrawal of the nomination of Lani Guinier to the position of assistant attorney general for civil rights in 1993, President Bill Clinton—the head of a country that uses mainly plurality elections—stated that he objected to her advocacy of PR, which he called "very difficult to defend" and even "antidemocratic" (*New York Times*, June 4, 1993, A18).

In this chapter I present a more detailed classification of the electoral systems used in our thirty-six democracies in terms of seven basic aspects of these systems, emphasizing the electoral formula, district magnitude, and electoral thresholds. The scholarly literature on electoral systems focuses on the degree of proportionality or disproportionality in their translation of votes into seats and on their effects on the numbers of parties in party systems. This is the focus of the remainder of this chapter. After discussing the question of how degrees of disproportionality can be most accurately measured, I show that, although there is a great deal of variation within the PR family and although no PR system is perfectly proportional, PR systems do tend to be considerably less disproportional than plurality and majority systems, except in presidential democracies. Electoral systems are also a crucial determinant, though by no means the sole determinant, of party systems. Last, I explore the relationship between electoral disproportionality and the effective number of parliamentary parties in the thirty-six democracies.

Electoral Formulas

Although the dichotomy of PR versus single-member district plurality and majority systems is the most fundamental dividing line in the classification of electoral systems, it is necessary to make some additional important distinctions and to develop a more refined typology.[1] Electoral systems may be described in terms of seven attributes: electoral formula, district magnitude, electoral threshold, the total membership of the body to be

1. For thorough treatments of electoral systems, see Rae (1967), Nohlen (1978), Katz (1980), Taagepera and Shugart (1989), Lijphart (1994), Cox (1997), and Reynolds and Reilly (1997).

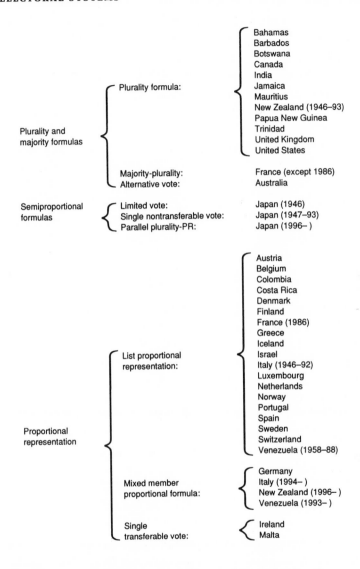

Fig 8.1   A classification of the electoral formulas for the
election of the first or only chambers of legislatures in thirty-six
democracies, 1945–96

elected, the influence of presidential elections on legislative elections, malapportionment, and interparty electoral links.

Figure 8.1 presents a classification according to the first of these dimensions, the electoral formula, and it shows to which categories the thirty-six democracies or, in a few cases, particular periods in these countries belong. The first category of plurality and majority formulas can be subdivided into three more specific classes. The plurality rule—usually termed "first past the post" in Britain—is by far the simplest one: the candidate who receives the most votes, whether a majority or a plurality, is elected. It is obviously a popular formula: twelve of the thirty-six democracies used it in the period 1945–96. It is also used for presidential elections in Venezuela, Iceland, Costa Rica (in slightly modified form),[2] and in Colombia (until 1990).

Majority formulas require an absolute majority for election. One way to fulfill this requirement is to conduct a run-off second ballot between the top two candidates if none of the candidates in the first round of voting has received a majority of the votes. This method is frequently used for presidential elections—in France, Austria, Portugal, and, since 1994, in Colombia and Finland, as well as in the direct election of the Israeli prime minister—but not for legislative elections. A closely related method, however, is used in France for elections to the legislature. The National Assembly is elected by a mixed majority-plurality formula in single-member districts: on the first ballot an absolute majority is required for election, but if no candidate wins a majority, a plurality suffices on the second ballot; candidates failing to win a minimum percentage of the vote on the first ballot— 12.5 percent of the registered voters since 1976—are barred from the second ballot. The second-ballot contest is usually be-

---

2. In Costa Rica, the rule is that a president is elected by plurality as long as this plurality is at least 40 percent of the total vote; if it is less than 40 percent, a run-off election has to be held, but no such run-offs have been necessary in any of the elections from 1953 to 1994. On presidential electoral systems generally, see Blais, Massicotte, and Dobrzynska (1997).

tween two principal candidates so that, in practice, there is no big difference between the majority-plurality formula and the majority-runoff.

The alternative vote, used in Australia, is a true majority formula. The voters are asked to indicate their first preference, second preference, and so on among the candidates. If a candidate receives an absolute majority of the first preferences, he or she is elected. If there is no such majority, the candidate with the lowest number of first preferences is dropped, and the ballots with this candidate as the first preference are transferred to the second preferences. This procedure is repeated by excluding the weakest candidate and redistributing the ballots in question to the next highest preferences in each stage of the counting, until a majority winner emerges. The alternative vote is also used for presidential elections in Ireland.

Three main types of PR must be distinguished. The most common form is the list PR system, used in half—eighteen out of thirty-six—of our democracies during most of the period 1945–96. There are minor variations in list formulas, but they all basically entail that the parties nominate lists of candidates in multimember districts, that the voters cast their ballots for one party list or another (although they are sometimes allowed to split their votes among several lists), and that the seats are allocated to the party lists in proportion to the numbers of votes they have collected. List PR systems may be subdivided further according to the mathematical formula used to translate votes into seats. The most frequently applied method is the d'Hondt formula, which has a slight bias in favor of large parties and against small parties compared with several other methods (see Lijphart 1994, 153–59, for a more detailed description).[3]

3. Another difference among list PR formulas is whether their lists are open, partly open, or closed. In closed-list systems, voters can only vote for the list as a whole and cannot express a preference for any specific candidates on the list; candidates are elected strictly according to the order in which the party has nominated them. Examples are Costa Rica, Israel, and Spain. In a completely

The second form of PR is the "mixed member proportional" (MMP) formula—a term coined in New Zealand for its version of the system but now generally applied to the entire category. About half of the legislators in Germany, New Zealand, and Venezuela and about three-quarters in Italy are elected by plurality in single-member districts and the others are elected by list PR. Each voter has two votes, one for a district candidate and one for a party list. The reason why this combination of methods qualifies as a PR system is that the list PR seats compensate for any disproportionality produced by the district seat results. The exact degree of the overall results depends on how many list PR seats are available for the purpose of compensation; the Italian results have been considerably less proportional than those in the other three countries.

The third main type of PR is the single transferable vote (STV). It differs from list PR in that the voters vote for individual candidates instead of for party lists. The ballot is similar to that of the alternative vote system: it contains the names of the candidates, and the voters are asked to rank-order these. The procedure for determining the winning candidates is slightly more complicated than in the alternative vote method. Two kinds of transfers take place: first, any surplus votes not needed by candidates who already have the minimum quota of votes required for election are transferred to the next most preferred candidates on the ballots in question; second, the weakest candidate is eliminated and his or her ballots are transferred in the same way. If necessary, these steps are repeated until all of the available seats are filled. STV is often praised because it combines the advantages of permitting votes for individual candidates and of yield-

---

open-list system, of which Finland is the best example, the voters vote for individual candidates on the list, and the order in which the candidates are elected is determined by the votes they individually receive. In Belgium, the Netherlands, and several other countries, the lists are partly open: although voters can express preferences for individual candidates, the list order as presented by the parties tends to prevail.

ing proportional results, but it is not used very frequently. The only instances in Figure 8.1 are Ireland and Malta. The other major example of its use is for Senate elections in Australia.

Most electoral formulas fit the two large categories of PR and plurality-majority, but a few fall in between. These semiproportional formulas are rarely used, and the only examples in our set of countries are the three systems that have been used in Japan. The limited vote, used in the 1946 election, and the single nontransferable vote (SNTV), used in all subsequent elections until 1996, are closely related. Voters cast their votes for individual candidates and, as in plurality systems, the candidates with the most votes win. However, unlike in plurality systems, the voters do not have as many votes as there are seats in the district and districts have to have at least two seats. The more limited the number of votes each voter has, and the larger the number of seats at stake, the more the limited vote tends to deviate from plurality and the more it resembles PR. In the 1946 election, each voter had two or three votes in districts ranging from four to fourteen seats. SNTV is the special case of the limited vote where the number of votes cast by each voter is reduced to one. In the Japanese version of it, it was applied in districts with an average of about four seats.

In the parallel plurality–PR system, introduced by the Japanese in 1996, three hundred legislators are elected by plurality in single-member districts and two hundred are elected by list PR; each voter has both a district vote and a PR vote. These features make it resemble MMP, but the crucial difference is that the PR seats are not compensatory. The plurality and PR components of the election are kept entirely separate. Hence, unlike MMP, this system is only partly proportional instead of a form of PR.

Most countries did not change their electoral formulas during the period 1945–96. The one-time use of the limited vote in Japan in 1946 and of list PR in France in 1986 are minor exceptions. The more important changes that did occur all took place in the 1990s—in New Zealand, Italy, Japan, and Venezuela—and three of these four countries switched to MMP. Note, however, that the first elections according to the new formulas in Japan and New Zealand were held in the second half of 1996, after the mid-1996 cut-off date for this study.

District Magnitude

The magnitude of an electoral district denotes the number of candidates to be elected in the district. It should not be confused with the geographical size of the district or with the number of voters in it. Plurality and majority formulas may be applied in both single-member and multimember districts. PR and SNTV require multimember districts, ranging from two-member districts to a single nationwide district from which all members of parliament are elected. That district magnitude has a strong effect on the degree of disproportionality and on the number of parties has been known for a long time. George Horwill (1925, 53) already called it "the all-important factor," and in Rein Taagepera and Matthew S. Shugart's (1989, 112) analysis, it was again found to be "the decisive factor."

District magnitude is of great importance in two respects. First, it has a strong influence in both plurality-majority systems and PR (and SNTV) systems, but in opposite directions: increasing the district magnitude in plurality and majority systems entails greater disproportionality and greater advantages for large parties, whereas under PR it results in greater proportionality and more favorable conditions for small parties. With regard to plurality, assume, for instance, that the election contest is between parties A and B and that party A is slightly stronger in a particular area. If this area is a three-member district, party A is likely to win all three seats; however, if the area is divided into three single-member districts, party B may well be able to win in one of the districts and hence one of the three seats. When the district magnitude is increased further, disproportionality also increases; in the hypothetical case of a nationwide plurality district, and assuming that all voters cast strictly partisan votes, the party winning a nationwide plurality of the votes would win all of the seats.

In the Australian alternative vote system and in the French majority-plurality system, only single-member districts have been used. In plurality systems, there are quite a few instances of the use of two-member and even larger districts, but larger than single-member districts are increasingly rare. The United Kingdom used several two-member districts in 1945, and both the United States and Canada had a few in the period 1945–68. In the 1952 and 1957 Indian elections, about a third of the legislators were elected from two-member districts, and Barbados elected its entire legislature from two-member districts in 1966. By 1970, however, all these two-member districts had been abolished.[4]

The only plurality country in which larger than single-member districts survive is Mauritius, where sixty-two legislators are elected from twenty three-member districts and one two-member district. An intermediate case is Papua New Guinea, where each voter has two votes, one to be cast in one of the eighty-nine relatively small single-member districts and the other in one of the twenty larger provincial single-member districts.[5] An important reason why multimember districts have become rare is that, as explained above, they lead to even greater disproportionality than the already highly disproportional single-member districts. In the case of Mauritius, it should be noted, however, that the three-member districts have facilitated a different kind

4. Other minor exceptions are the one-time use of an eight-member district (the state of Alabama) in the 1962 U.S. congressional election, the use of majority-runoff systems in Louisiana (where the first stage of the election is termed the "nonpartisan primary") and, until recently, in Georgia, and the use of four STV districts in the 1945 British election.

5. Large multimember districts also survive in the American system for electing the presidential electoral college in which the fifty states and the District of Columbia serve as the election districts: the average magnitude is 10.5 seats per district.

of proportionality: they encourage the parties and party alliances to nominate ethnically and religiously balanced slates, which has resulted in better ethnic and religious minority representation than would have been achieved through single-member district elections. Moreover, in addition to the sixty-two elected legislators, eight seats are allocated to the so-called best losers to further ensure fair minority representation (Mathur 1991, 54–71; 1997). Three other plurality countries have made special provisions for ethnic and communal minority representation by earmarking specific districts for this purpose: the Maori districts in New Zealand, discussed in Chapter 2; about a fifth of the districts in India that are set aside for the "scheduled castes" (untouchables) and "scheduled tribes"; and "affirmatively" gerrymandered districts in the United States.

The second reason why district magnitude is so important is that—unlike in plurality and majority systems—it varies greatly in PR systems and, hence, that it has a strong impact on the degree of proportionality that the different PR systems attain. For instance, a party representing a 10 percent minority is unlikely to win a seat in a five-member district but will be successful in a ten-member district. Two-member districts can therefore hardly be regarded as compatible with the principle of proportionality; conversely, a nationwide district is, all other factors being equal, optimal for a proportional translation of votes into seats. Israel and the Netherlands are examples of PR systems with such nationwide districts.

Many list PR countries use two levels of districts in order to combine the advantage of closer voter-representative contact in small districts and the higher proportionality of large, especially nationwide districts. As in MMP systems, the larger district compensates for any disproportionalities in the smaller districts, although these are likely to be much less pronounced in the small multimember list PR districts than in the MMP single-member districts. Examples of two-tiered list PR systems with a nationwide district at the higher level are Denmark, Sweden since 1970, and Norway since 1989.

Electoral Thresholds

High-magnitude PR districts tend to maximize proportionality and to facilitate the representation of even very small parties. This is especially true for the Dutch and Israeli nationwide districts as well as for all systems that use upper-level nationwide districts. In order not to make it too easy for small parties to win election, all countries that use large or nationwide districts have instituted minimum thresholds for representation, defined in terms of a minimum number of seats won in the lower-tier districts and/or a minimum percentage of the total national vote. These percentages may be relatively low and hence innocuous, as the 0.67 percent threshold in the Netherlands since 1956 and the 1 percent threshold in Israel (increased to 1.5 percent in 1992). But when they reach 4 percent, as in Sweden and Norway, or 5 percent, as in the German and post-1996 New Zealand MMP systems, they constitute significant barriers to small parties.

District magnitudes and electoral thresholds can be seen as two sides of the same coin: the *explicit* barrier against small parties imposed by a threshold has essentially the same function as the barrier *implied* by district magnitude. A reasonable approximation of their relationship is

$$T = \frac{75\%}{M+1}$$

in which T is the threshold and M the average district magnitude. According to this equation, the median four-member district in Ireland (which uses districts with three, four, and five seats) has an implied threshold of 15 percent, and the average district with a magnitude of 6.7 seats in the Spanish single-tier list PR system has an implied threshold of 9.7 percent. Con-

versely, the German 5 percent and Swedish 4 percent thresholds
have roughly the same effect as district magnitudes of 14.0 and
17.8 seats.

Other Electoral System Attributes

Another factor that can affect the proportionality of election
outcomes and the number of parties is the size of the body to be
elected. At first glance, this may appear to a property that is not
really part of the electoral system; however, because electoral
systems are methods for translating votes into seats, the number
of seats available for this translation is clearly an integral part of
the system of translation. This number is important for two reasons. First, assume that three parties win 43, 31, and 26 percent
of the national vote in a PR election. If the election is to a mini-
legislature with only five seats, there is obviously no way in
which the allocation of seats can be handled with a high degree
of proportionality; the chances of a proportional allocation improve considerably for a ten-member legislature; and perfect
proportionality could be achieved, at least in principle, for a
hundred-member legislative body. For legislatures with a hundred or more members, size becomes relatively unimportant,
but it is far from negligible for the lower or only legislative
chambers of Mauritius (70 members in the last election held
before mid-1996), Malta (65), Iceland (63), Jamaica and Luxembourg (60 each), Costa Rica (57), the Bahamas (49), Botswana
(44), Trinidad (36), and Barbados (28).

Second, the general pattern is that populous countries have
large legislatures, that countries with small populations have
smaller legislatures, and that the size of the legislature tends to
be roughly the cube root of the population. Plurality elections
always tend to be disproportional, but this tendency is reinforced when the membership of the legislature is significantly
below the cube root of the population (Taagepera and Shugart

1989, 156–67).[6] Barbados is a case in point: on the basis of its population of 266,000 (see Table 4.3), its House of Assembly "should" have 64 instead of 28 members. Similarly, Trinidad should have a lower house with 109 instead of 36 members, and the Bahamas, Botswana, Jamaica, and Mauritius are also well below the number predicted by the cube root law—and can therefore be expected, all other factors being equal, to have abnormally high disproportionality in their election results. Small legislative size is not a characteristic of all plurality systems: for instance, the British House of Commons is quite a bit larger than predicted by the cube root law.

Presidential systems can have an indirect but strong effect on the effective number of parliamentary parties. Because the presidency is the biggest political prize to be won and because only the largest parties have a chance to win it, these large parties have a considerable advantage over smaller parties that tends to carry over into legislative elections, even when these are PR elections as in Costa Rica, Colombia, and Venezuela. This tendency is especially strong when the presidential election is decided by plurality instead of majority-runoff (where small parties may want to try their luck in the first round) and when the legislative elections are held at the same time or shortly after the presidential elections (Shugart and Carey 1992, 206–58, Jones 1995, 88–118). Even in France, where presidential and legislative elections usually do not coincide and where presidential elections are by majority-runoff, presidentialism has reduced multipartism. Maurice Duverger (1986, 81–82) compares the presidential Fifth Republic with the parliamentary Third Re-

---

6. The cube law holds that if, in two-party systems and plurality single-member district elections, the votes received by the two parties are divided in a ratio of a:b, the seats that they win will be in the ratio of $a^3:b^3$. However, the exponent of 3 applies only when the size of the legislative body is in accordance with the cube root law, and the exponent goes up—and hence disproportionality also increases—as the size of the legislature decreases and/or the population increases (Taagepera and Shugart 1989, 158–67).

public, both of which used the two-ballot system for legislative elections, and asks "why the same electoral system coincided with a dozen parties in the Third Republic but ended up with only four [parties in a two-bloc format] in the Fifth Republic." His main explanation is "the direct popular election of the president, which has transformed the political regime."

Malapportionment may also contribute to electoral disproportionality. In single-member districts, malapportionment means that the districts have substantially unequal voting populations; malapportioned multimember districts have magnitudes that are not commensurate with their voting populations. It is especially hard to avoid in plurality and majority systems with single-member districts, because equal apportionment requires that relatively many small districts be drawn with exactly equal electorates or populations. It is much less of a problem in PR systems that use relatively large districts of varying magnitudes, because seats can be proportionally allocated to preexisting geographical units like provinces or cantons. And malapportionment is entirely eliminated as a problem when elections are conducted in one large nationwide district as in Israel and the Netherlands or with a nationwide upper tier as in Germany and Sweden.

The main cases of malapportionment have had to do with rural overrepresentation: for instance, the United States (until the reapportionment revolution of the 1960s), Australia and France (until about 1980), Japan under the SNTV system, Norway until 1985, Iceland from 1946 to 1959, and Spain. However, malapportionment in favor of rural areas only leads to increased disproportionality in partisan representation if the larger parties benefit from it; this has clearly been the case for the Liberal Democrats in Japan, the Progressive party in Iceland, and the National party (formerly the Country party) in Australia to the extent that this relatively small party can be treated as part of the larger party formation with the Liberals.

Finally, some list PR systems allow parties to have separate lists on the ballot but to formally "link" these lists, which means that their combined vote total will be used in the initial allocation of seats; the next step is the proportional distribution of the seats won by the linked parties to each of the parties. A set of such interparty connected lists is usually referred to by the French term *apparentement*. Examples of list PR systems with this special feature are Switzerland, Israel, and, since 1977, the Netherlands. Because apparentement helps the smaller parties, which tend to be underrepresented, it tends to reduce disproportionality and to increase the effective number of parties. Moreover, the formation of mutually beneficial interparty electoral links is allowed not only by apparentement in some list PR systems but also as a logical consequence of three other electoral systems. Both the alternative vote and STV permit parties to link up for maximum electoral gain by simply agreeing to ask their respective voters to cast first preferences for their own candidates but the next preferences for the candidates of the linked party—an advantage of which Australian and Irish parties, but not the Maltese, often avail themselves. Similarly, the French two-ballot system implies the possibility for parties to link for the purpose of reciprocal withdrawal from the second ballot in different districts; both the parties of the left and those of the right regularly use this opportunity.

Degrees of Disproportionality

As we have seen, many attributes of electoral systems influence the degree of disproportionality and indirectly the number of parties in the party system. How can the overall disproportionality of elections be measured? It is easy to determine the disproportionality for each party in a particular election: this is simply the difference between its vote share and its seat share. The more difficult question is how to aggregate the vote-seat share deviations of all of the parties. Summing the (absolute) differences is not satisfactory because it does not distinguish between a few large and serious deviations and a lot of small and relatively insignificant deviations.[7] The index of disproportionality proposed by Michael Gallagher (1991), which is used in this study, solves this problem by weighting the deviations by their own values—thus making large deviations account for a great deal more in the summary index than small ones. The computation of the Gallagher index (G) is as follows: the differences between the vote percentages (v_i) and seat percentages (s_i) for each party are squared and then added; this total is divided by 2; and finally the square root of this value is taken:[8]

$$G = \sqrt{\frac{1}{2} \sum (v_i - s_i)^2}$$

In a few electoral systems, two sets of votes can be used for the purpose of calculating vote-seat share differences; which of the two should be used? In MMP systems, the choice is between the party list votes and the district votes, and the scholarly consensus is that the party list votes express the party preferences of the electorate most accurately. In alternative vote and STV systems, the choice is between first preference votes and final-count votes—that is, the votes after the transfer of preferences has been completed; only first preference votes are usually reported, and scholars agree that the differences between the two are of minor importance. The one case where the difference is substantial is between the first and second ballot results in France. On the first ballot, the votes tend to be divided among many candidates, and the real choice is made on the second

7. One of the consequences of this problem is that the Loosemore-Hanby (1971) index, which uses the additive approach, tends to understate the proportionality of PR systems. An obvious alternative, offered by the Rae (1967) index, is to average the absolute vote-seat share differences. It errs in the other direction by overstating the proportionality of PR systems (see Lijphart 1994, 58–60).

8. In the calculation of the Gallagher index, any small parties that are lumped together as "other" parties in election statistics have to be disregarded.

ballot. The best solution is to count the *decisive* votes: mainly second-ballot votes, but first-ballot votes in districts where candidates were elected on the first ballot (Goldey and Williams 1983, 79).[9]

Electoral Disproportionality in Presidential Democracies

The discussion of electoral systems has focused so far almost entirely on legislative elections. In presidential democracies, however, the election of the president is at least as important as the legislative election: of roughly the same importance in systems with executive-legislative balance and of greater importance in systems with executive dominance. In fact, even in balanced executive-legislative systems, the voters consider the presidential election to be the more important one, as indicated by their lower turnout levels in legislative elections when these are not held simultaneously with presidential elections; for instance, voter turnout in off-year congressional elections in the United States tends to be only about two-thirds of turnout in presidential election years.

Presidential elections are inherently disproportional as a result of two of the electoral system properties discussed above: the electoral formula, which for the election of a single official is necessarily one of the plurality or majority formulas (or the majoritarian election by an electoral college), and the "size of the

9. Several smaller methodological issues concerning the calculation of the index of disproportionality also need to be clarified. First, as in the calculation of the effective number of parliamentary parties, the seats are those in the lower or only houses of parliaments. Second, unlike in the calculation of the effective number of parties, the seats won by parties in the election are used and not those gained from legislators who join parties after the election, as in Japan and Papua New Guinea. Third, any uncontested seats, mainly occurring but increasingly rare in plurality systems, are excluded (if it is possible to do so). Fourth, the two boycotted elections in Trinidad in 1971 and Jamaica in 1983 are disregarded. Fifth, factionalized and closely allied parties are again counted as one-and-a-half parties—a procedure that, however, has only a minimal impact on the index of disproportionality.

Table 8.1 Average disproportionalities in legislative and in presidential elections, the numbers of elections on which these averages are based, and the geometric means of the two disproportionalities in six presidential systems, 1946–96

	Legislative disproportionality (%)	Legislative elections (N)	Presidential disproportionality (%)	Presidential elections (N)	Geometric mean (%)
Israel[a]	1.65	1	49.51	1	9.05
Colombia	2.96	14	38.04	10	10.62
Costa Rica	4.13	11	45.11	11	13.65
Venezuela	4.28	8	48.49	8	14.41
United States	4.90	25	45.38	12	14.91
France[b]	11.34	8	46.23	6	22.90

Notes: [a]Only the 1996 election, in which the prime minister was directly elected
[b]Not including the 1986 and 1993 elections, which led to parliamentary phases

Source: Based on data in Mackie and Rose 1991; Mackie and Rose 1997; Nohlen 1993; Goldey and Williams 1983; and data provided by Michael Coppedge, Brian F. Crisp, Gary Hoskin, Mark P. Jones, and J. Ray Kennedy

body to be elected," which is the absolute minimum of one. The party that wins the presidency wins "all" of the seats—that is, the one seat that is available—and the losing parties win no seats at all. This is also another respect in which presidential systems tend to be inherently majoritarian, in addition to their inherent tendency to have majoritarian cabinets and their reductive effects on the number of parties.

Table 8.1 presents the indexes of disproportionality for legislative and presidential elections in six presidential systems. As expected, the disproportionality in presidential elections is higher than in legislative elections: on average, between 38 and 50 percent in the six countries. If there are only two candidates, the index of disproportionality equals the vote percentage of the losing candidate. For instance, in the 1996 direct election of the Israeli prime minister, the only candidates were Benjamin Netanyahu, who won with 50.49 percent of the vote, and Shimon Peres, who lost with 49.51 percent of the vote, yielding a disproportionality index of 49.51 percent.[10] Moreover, the disproportionality in presidential elections is not just higher than in legislative elections, but a great deal higher: five of the six presidential systems have average indexes of legislative disproportionality that are below 5 percent. If both disproportionalities are relevant and should be counted, how can we best combine them? If the arithmetic average were used, the disproportionality in presidential elections would overwhelm that in legislative elections. It is therefore better to use the geometric mean—which is also generally more appropriate when values of greatly different magnitudes are averaged.[11] These geometric means are shown in the last column of Table 8.1.

10. For prime ministerial elections, Israel uses the majority-runoff system, but when only two candidates compete, a runoff is obviously not necessary. In all presidential elections decided by a runoff, the runoff votes, necessarily shared by only two candidates, were used to calculate the index of disproportionality.

11. The geometric mean of two numbers, like the two percentages in Table 8.1, is simply the square root of the product of these two numbers.

Table 8.2 Average electoral disproportionality and type of electoral system (used in legislative elections) in thirty-six democracies, 1945–96

	Disproportionality (%)	Electoral System		Disproportionality (%)	Electoral system
Netherlands	1.30	PR	Spain	8.15	PR
Denmark	1.83	PR	Australia	9.26	Maj.
Sweden	2.09	PR	Papua New Guinea	10.06	Plur.
Israel	2.27	PR	United Kingdom	10.33	Plur.
Malta	2.36	PR-STV	Colombia	10.62	PR*
Austria	2.47	PR	New Zealand	11.11	Plur.
Germany	2.52	PR	India	11.38	Plur.
Switzerland	2.53	PR	Canada	11.72	Plur.
Finland	2.93	PR	Botswana	11.74	Plur.
Belgium	3.24	PR	Costa Rica	13.65	PR*
Italy	3.25	PR	Trinidad	13.66	Plur.
Luxembourg	3.26	PR	Venezuela	14.41	PR*
Ireland	3.45	PR-STV	United States	14.91	Plur.*
Portugal	4.04	PR	Bahamas	15.47	Plur.
Iceland	4.25	PR	Barbados	15.75	Plur.
Norway	4.93	PR	Mauritius	16.43	Plur.
Japan	5.03	SNTV	Jamaica	17.75	Plur.
Greece	8.08	PR	France	21.08	Maj.*

*Presidential systems

Note: The number of elections on which these averages are based may be found in Table 5.2

Source: Based on data in Mackie and Rose 1991; Mackie and Rose 1997; Nohlen 1993; Singh 1994; Lijphart 1994; and data provided by Pradeep K. Chhibber, Michael Coppedge, Brian F. Crisp, Gary Hoskin, Mark P. Jones, J. Ray Kennedy, Hansraj Mathur, Shaheen Mozaffar, Ben Reilly, and Andrew S. Reynolds

Degrees of Disproportionality in Thirty-Six Democracies

The average electoral disproportionalities in all thirty-six countries are presented in ascending order in Table 8.2 together with the main type of electoral system used in their legislative elections—PR (including the STV systems of Ireland and Malta), SNTV, plurality, and majority (Australia and France)—and an asterisk indicating whether the country is presidential or usually presidential (that is, including France but not Israel). The indexes span a wide range from 1.30 percent in the Netherlands to 21.08 percent in France; the mean is 8.26 and the median 8.11 percent.

There is a strikingly clear line dividing the PR parliamentary systems from the plurality and majority systems. Even the two PR countries that are often regarded as only barely belonging to the PR family—Greece and Spain—are still situated on the PR side of the dividing line. Spain's PR system is not very proportional mainly because of its low district magnitude. The Greek PR system has changed frequently, but the usual system is "reinforced PR"—a deceptive label because what is being reinforced is the large parties rather than proportionality. Nevertheless, even these two impure PR systems have lower disproportionalities than any of the plurality and majority systems. It is also worth noting that Japan's SNTV system—a semiproportional rather than PR system and one with a low district magnitude—is also clearly on the PR side of the dividing line. In fact, its average disproportionality of 5.03 percent is well below that of Greece and Spain. Most of the PR countries have average disproportionalities between 1 and 5 percent; the exemplar cases of Belgium and Switzerland are approximately in the middle of this range.

On the plurality and majority side of the dividing line, Australia is the only country with a disproportionality below 10 percent. Most of these countries have disproportionalities between 10 and 20 percent. The four parliamentary systems with the highest disproportionalities—the Bahamas, Barbados, Mauritius, and Jamaica—are all small countries with plurality systems and unusually small legislatures; moreover, Mauritius uses mainly three-member districts. The United Kingdom and New Zealand are actually among the least disproportional of the plurality systems. The only exceptional cases of PR systems that are highly disproportional are three presidential democracies: Colombia, Costa Rica, and Venezuela. A glance back at Table 8.1 reveals, however, that their legislative disproportionalities range from only 2.96 to 4.28 percent—entirely normal for PR systems—and that it is the presidentialism of these countries that gives them high overall disproportionality.

Legislative disproportionality is also relatively low in the United States in spite of the plurality method for congressional elections. The main explanation of this unusual phenomenon is the existence of primary elections in the United States. In most plurality systems, a major portion of the disproportionality of elections is caused by small parties that remain unrepresented or are severely underrepresented; there are very few of these in the United States because primary elections give strong incentives for dissidents to try their luck in one of the major party primaries instead of establishing separate small parties; in addition, state laws tend to discriminate against small parties. Yet the presidential elections give the United States a high overall level of disproportionality after all. France is the most disproportional system in Table 8.2 as a result of its disproportional legislative election system in combination with presidentialism. Its index is slightly lower in Table 8.2 than the geometric mean shown in Table 8.1 because for the two elections in 1986 and 1993, which inaugurated parliamentary phases, only legislative disproportionality was counted. Israel's one presidential (prime ministerial) election in 1996 raised the overall level of disproportionality only slightly because it was preceded by thirteen purely parliamentary elections in which the average disproportionality was only 1.75 percent.

Electoral Systems and Party Systems

A well-known proposition in comparative politics is that the plurality method favors two-party systems; Maurice Duverger (1964, 217, 226) calls this proposition one that approximates "a true sociological law." Conversely, PR and two-ballot systems (like the French majority-plurality method) encourage multipartism. Duverger explains the differential effects of the electoral system in terms of "mechanical" and "psychological" factors. The mechanical effect of the plurality rule is that all but the two strongest parties are severely underrepresented because they tend to lose in each district; the British Liberals, continually the disadvantaged third party in the postwar era, are a good example. The psychological factor reinforces the mechanical one: "the electors soon realize that their votes are wasted if they continue to give them to the third party: whence their natural tendency to transfer their vote to the less evil of its two adversaries." In addition, the psychological factor operates at the level of the politicians, whose natural tendency is not to waste their energy by running as third-party candidates but instead to join one of the large parties.

Douglas W. Rae (1967, 67–129) has contributed a number of significant refinements to the study of the links between electoral and party systems. Different electoral systems have varying impacts on party systems, but, Rae emphasizes, they also have important effects in common. In particular, all electoral systems, not just the plurality and majority ones, tend to overrepresent the larger parties and underrepresent the smaller ones. Three important aspects of this tendency must be distinguished: (1) all electoral systems tend to yield disproportional results; (2) all electoral systems tend to reduce the effective number of parliamentary parties compared with the effective number of electoral parties; and (3) all electoral systems can manufacture a parliamentary majority for parties that have not received majority support from the voters. On the other hand, all

Table 8.3 Manufactured majorities, earned majorities, and natural minorities in three types of electoral systems, 1945–96

	Manufactured majority (%)	Earned majority (%)	Natural minority (%)	Total (%)	Elections (N)
Plurality and majority systems (14 countries)	43.7	39.1	17.2	100.0	151
Semiproportional systems (Japan)	42.1	15.8	42.1	100.0	19
Proportional representation (22 countries)	9.4	8.3	82.3	100.0	265
All legislative elections in 36 democracies	22.8	19.3	57.9	100.0	435

Source: Based on data in Mackie and Rose 1991; Mackie and Rose 1997; Nohlen 1993; Singh 1994; Lijphart 1994; and data provided by Pradeep K. Chhibber, Michael Coppedge, Brian F. Crisp, Gary Hoskin, Mark P. Jones, J. Ray Kennedy, Hansraj Mathur, Shaheen Mozaffar, Ben Reilly, and Andrew S. Reynolds

three tendencies are much stronger in plurality and majority than in PR systems.

Rae's first proposition is clearly shown in Table 8.2: even the most proportional system, that of the Netherlands, still has a disproportionality of 1.30 percent instead of zero percent. But, as highlighted earlier, the disproportionality of PR systems is much lower than that of plurality and majority systems. Rae's second and third propositions are based on the fact that the disproportionalities of electoral systems are not random but systematic: they systematically advantage the larger parties and disadvantage the smaller parties—and again especially so in plurality and majority systems. That is why elections generally, but plurality and majority elections in particular, reduce the effective number of parties.

The systematic advantage that electoral systems give to large parties becomes especially important when parties that fail to get a majority of the votes are awarded a majority of the seats. This makes it possible to form single-party majority cabinets— one of the hallmarks of majoritarian democracy. Rae (1967, 74– 77) calls such majorities "manufactured"—that is, artificially created by the electoral system. Manufactured majorities may be contrasted with earned majorities, when a party wins majorities of both votes and seats, and natural minorities, when no party wins a majority of either votes or seats. Table 8.3 presents the average incidence of manufactured and earned majorities and of natural minorities in the three main types of electoral systems.[12] All three are capable of creating majorities where none are created by the voters, but this capacity is especially strong in the plurality and majority systems—closely followed by the Japa-

---

12. For the purpose of constructing Table 8.3, closely allied parties and factionalized parties were counted as one party. The seven Colombian legislative elections from 1958 to 1970 were excluded because the Liberal and Conservative parties were each awarded half of the legislative seats according to the National Front prearrangement.

nese semiproportional system, which has frequently manufactured majorities for the Liberal Democrats.

The clearest examples of manufactured majorities can be found in our prototypical cases of Great Britain and New Zealand, but many such majorities have also occurred in Australia and Canada. Earned majorities are common in plurality systems with strict two-party competition: the Bahamas, Botswana, Jamaica, Trinidad, and the United States. In fact, as a result of the frequency of congressional elections, the United States contributes a large proportion of the total of earned majorities in plurality and majority systems: twenty-three of the fifty-nine earned-majority elections. In contrast, PR rarely produces either manufactured or earned majorities. These results have occurred mainly in countries that, in spite of PR, have relatively few parties (Austria and Malta), in countries with relatively impure PR (Spain and Greece), and in presidential systems that use PR for legislative elections (Colombia, Costa Rica, and Venezuela). The most salient feature of Table 8.3 is that more than 80 percent of plurality and majority elections lead to manufactured or earned majorities and that more than 80 percent of PR elections yield natural minorities.

We can also expect a strong negative relationship between the disproportionality of the electoral system and the effective number of parliamentary parties. Figure 8.2 shows this relationship in our thirty-six democracies. The correlation coefficient is −0.50, which is statistically significant at the 1 percent level. As disproportionality increases, the effective number of parties decreases. A 5 percent increase in disproportionality is associated with a reduction of about half a party (0.52 to be exact) in the effective number of parties.

The figure shows considerable scattering and quite a few outliers, however. Other factors clearly also strongly affect the number of parties. One is the degree of pluralism and the number of groups into which a society is divided, which can explain the multipartism of Papua New Guinea and India in spite of the

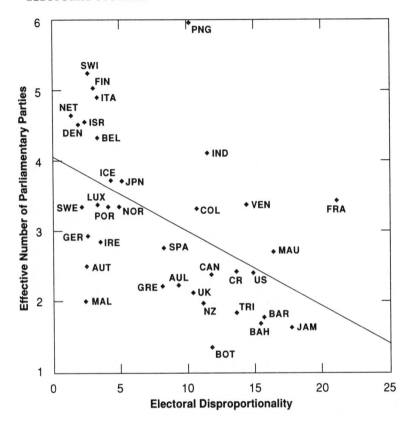

Fig. 8.2   The relationship between electoral disproportionality and the effective number of parliamentary parties in thirty-six democracies, 1945–96

reductive effects of their disproportional electoral systems. Another plural society, Switzerland, has even more multipartism than could be expected from its proportional election system. The opposite effect can be seen in Austria, whose plural and later semiplural society consists mainly of two large "camps," and in Malta where the electorate has long tended to line up in two groups of almost equal size: in these two countries, two-party and two-and-a-half party systems have coexisted with highly proportional PR systems. Two of the presidential systems—France and Venezuela—are also relatively deviant, with considerably more parties than expected on the basis of the disproportionalities of these systems.

Another way of looking at Figure 8.2 is to note the gap in degrees of disproportionality that occurs between about 5 and 8 percent. On the more disproportional side of this gap, there is considerable scatter, but if the deviant cases of Papua New Guinea and India are excluded, the average effective number of parties is 2.32; with India and Papua New Guinea it is 2.61. On the more proportional side of the gap, the number of parties ranges widely and there is no discernible pattern at all, but the average is a considerably higher 3.78 parties. The overall relationship between the two variables depends to a large extent on this sizable difference between two groups of countries, largely but not entirely coinciding with the difference between PR and plurality systems: most of the PR countries plus Japan on one hand, and the plurality and majority countries, the impure PR systems of Greece and Spain, and the presidential democracies on the other.

CHAPTER 9

Interest Groups
Pluralism Versus Corporatism

The fifth difference between majoritarian and consensus democracy—and the last of the five that together constitute the executives-parties dimension—concerns the interest group system. The typical interest group system of majoritarian democracy is a competitive and uncoordinated pluralism of independent groups in contrast with the coordinated and compromise-oriented system of corporatism that is typical of the consensus model. Corporatism is often also termed "democratic corporatism," "societal corporatism," or "neocorporatism" to distinguish it from authoritarian forms of corporatism in which interest groups are entirely controlled by the state. I shall use the short term "corporatism" but always as a synonym of democratic corporatism.

Corporatism has two conceptually distinct meanings. The first refers to an interest group system in which groups are organized into national, specialized, hierarchical, and monopolistic peak organizations. The second refers to the incorporation of interest groups into the process of policy formation. Philippe C. Schmitter (1982, 263–64) argues that the second type of corporatism ought to be labeled "concertation." Empirically, however, the two tend to occur together because corporatism in the narrow sense is almost a necessary condition for concertation. As

Schmitter states, there appears to be a "structural compatibility . . . between corporatism and concertation," and he suggests that "elements of centralization, monopoly representation, etc., have historically emerged first and have, so to speak, prepared the way for initial policy concertation, which in turn encouraged further corporatization of interest associations."

Each of the two elements can be subdivided to arrive at the four key components by which corporatism can be readily recognized. Corporatism in Schmitter's narrow sense means that (1) interest groups are relatively large in size and relatively small in number, and (2) they are further coordinated into national peak organizations. Concertation means (3) regular consultation by the leaders of these peak organizations, especially those representing labor and management, both with each other and with government representatives to (4) arrive at comprehensive agreements that are binding on all three partners in the negotiations—so-called tripartite pacts. Interest group pluralism can be recognized by the opposite characteristics: a multiplicity of small interest groups, the absence or weakness of peak organizations, little or no tripartite consultation, and the absence of tripartite pacts. Katzenstein (1985, 32, 157) adds another distinctive trait of corporatism: "an ideology of social partnership" and the absence of "a winner-take-all mentality"—a characteristic that links corporatism to the other characteristics of consensus democracy. Of course, pure pluralism and pure corporatism are rare, and most democracies can be found somewhere on the continuum between the pure types.

In this chapter I discuss the continuing relevance of the pluralist-corporatist distinction for the description and analysis of interest groups and then turn to the question of how degrees of pluralism and corporatism can be measured, both in the industrialized and in the developing countries. After presenting the index of interest group pluralism for all thirty-six democracies, I analyze the relationship of this variable with the types of cabinets in the thirty-six countries and with their effective number of parliamentary parties.

The Decline of Corporatism?

Since the 1970s the subject of corporatism and its contrast with pluralism have been the major focus in the scholarly study of interest groups (Almond 1983, Wilson 1990). The general verdict of this literature has tended to be highly favorable to corporatism. In particular, its macroeconomic performance measured in terms of high growth, low unemployment, and low inflation rates was found to be superior to that of pluralist interest group systems: it appeared to produce "a superior economic system" (Pekkarinen, Pohjala, and Rowthorn 1992). More recently, however, scholars have begun to dissent from this sanguine interpretation, and it is now often claimed that corporatism is "in decline" (Gobeyn 1993), even in the once most strongly corporatist countries such as Austria (Gerlich 1992) and Sweden (Lewin 1994).

These judgments, however, must not be taken to mean that the distinction between corporatist and pluralist interest group systems should be abandoned. First of all, what the "decline of corporatism" usually means is that the efficacy of corporatist structures and the frequency of their use have decreased, not that these structures themselves have disappeared or are being dismantled. Second, to the extent that there has been a decline in some countries, it has been merely a matter of degree. For instance, when Peter Gerlich (1992, 145) says "farewell to corporatism" in Austria—to cite the title of his article—his main point is that Austria is no longer the exceptionally pure example of corporatism it was for several decades, not that it is turning into its pluralist opposite; instead, he predicts that Austria will simply become more like "other European nations," which tend to be more moderately corporatist.

Third, in Alan Siaroff's (1998) painstaking quantitative study of changes in corporatism from the 1960s to the 1980s in twenty-one democracies, no overall decline turns up at all. Only two countries experienced a change of more than 10 percent on the spectrum from pure pluralism to pure corporatism in their interest group systems: Finland became more and Israel less corporatist. Eleven other countries underwent smaller changes, but also in opposite directions: six became slightly more pluralist and five slightly more corporatist.

Fourth, Howard J. Wiarda (1997, 175) argues that corporatism, instead of declining, is simply developing into new areas: "it is not so much corporatism that is under attack or disappearing [but] just one particular arena (labor-management relationships) that is now being restructured and taking new directions." He speculates that although the "*industrial* phase of corporatist tripartite relationships is fading, new *postindustrial* issues (education, health care, welfare, the environment, others) are coming to the fore," and that these new issues are frequently negotiated in the familiar corporatist manner among the relevant interest groups—representing teachers, doctors, nurses, retired persons, and environmentalists—and the government. He concludes that "the policy process is still corporatist."

Fifth, a major and often used explanation for the decline of traditional corporatism is economic globalization, which "limits governmental capacity to act effectively in economic policy, in particular in macro-economic steering of the economy" (Armingeon 1997, 165). What should be noted here is that Katzenstein (1985, 9) uses precisely the same factor to explain not the decline but the *growth* of corporatism, and why it developed especially in the smaller European countries: "because of their open economies," these small countries "have been vulnerable to shifts in the world economy during the twentieth century," and they adopted corporatism as a protective device. Katzenstein's analysis suggests that the negative influence of globalization on corporatism is not inescapable and that, in the longer run, it may well reverse course.

Sixth, another reason for the decline of corporatism is the "eroding . . . level of integration of individuals with interest organizations and political parties" (Armingeon 1997, 165). In particular, this development weakens the ability of labor unions to act on behalf of large numbers of workers and hence also weakens their influence in tripartite negotiations. Katzenstein's (1985, 104–23) distinction between liberal corporatism, in which business is the stronger force, and social corporatism, in which labor dominates, is relevant here. It suggests that the decline in the strength of labor unions does not necessarily mean an overall decline in corporatism but merely a shift from social to liberal corporatism.

Schmitter's (1989, 72) long-term view—stated in his provocatively titled article "Corporatism Is Dead! Long Live Corporatism!"—is eminently sensible: interest group corporatism has a kind of "dynastic continuity punctuated by periodic demise and subsequent resurrection." The clamor about the decline of corporatism in the late 1980s and 1990s is reminiscent of the concern about what Alfred Grosser (1964, 242) called "the indisputable decline of . . . legislatures," which were "definitely in a state of crisis" in the 1960s. Contrary to Grosser's dire prediction, legislatures are still a sufficiently important institution in the 1990s for me to devote a chapter to them (Chapter 11) as well as one on executive-legislative relations in which one of the forms of this relationship is a balance of power between the two branches of government (Chapter 7)!

Degrees of Pluralism and Corporatism in Thirty-Six Democracies

Although many comparative analyses of interest groups have attempted to measure the degree of pluralism or corporatism in relatively large numbers of countries, these measurements are of limited utility for the purposes of this study. For one thing, they tend to focus on different aspects of corporatism: some are based more on the presence and strength of peak organizations, whereas others emphasize the process of concertation; some studies focus on how centralized wage bargaining tends to be; others emphasize the strength and historical orientation—reformist versus revolutionary—of labor unions; yet others try to measure the success, or rather the failure, of concertation in terms of the levels of strikes and lockouts in different countries. These different emphases account for the fact that, although the measures used in different studies are in reasonable agreement with one another, there is far from perfect agreement (Lane and Ersson 1997, Lijphart and Crepaz 1991). Other weaknesses of these measures are that most of them are rough trichotomous classifications—high versus medium versus low pluralism or corporatism—that they usually cover short periods and only from fifteen to eighteen countries, and that their focus is entirely on the industrialized democracies.

Most of these problems are solved by Siaroff's (1998) recent comparative study of as many as twenty-four industrialized democracies. Siaroff takes eight basic aspects of the pluralism-corporatism contrast—aggregating the foci of previous studies, mentioned in the previous paragraph—and rates his twenty-four democracies on each of these, using a five-point scale. He then averages these ratings to arrive at a comprehensive score for each country. Moreover, he does so for two periods: 1963–70 for twenty-one countries and 1983–90 for the same twenty-one countries plus Spain, Portugal, and Greece. These two periods may be considered representative for the long time span from the late 1940s to 1996 used for the analysis of twenty countries in this study and for France in the period 1958–96. Similarly, the years 1983–90 are a good representative sample of the period from the democratization of Spain, Portugal, and Greece in

Table 9.1   Interest group pluralism in thirty-six democracies
in the 1960s and 1980s

	Index of interest group pluralism		Index of interest group pluralism
Norway	0.44	Costa Rica	2.50
Sweden	0.50	Botswana	2.60
Austria	0.62	Australia	2.66
Denmark	1.00	Barbados	2.80
Switzerland	1.00	France	2.84
Israel	1.12	Ireland	2.94
Netherlands	1.19	New Zealand	3.00
Belgium	1.25	Portugal	3.00
Japan	1.25	Italy	3.12
Finland	1.31	Spain	3.25
Germany	1.38	Bahamas	3.30
Luxembourg	1.38	Jamaica	3.30
Mauritius	1.60	Malta	3.30
Venezuela	1.90	Trinidad	3.30
Papua New Guinea	2.10	United States	3.31
Iceland	2.25	United Kingdom	3.38
India	2.30	Greece	3.50
Colombia	2.50	Canada	3.56

Source: Based on data in Siaroff 1998 for the 24 industrial democracies and the
author's estimates for the other 12 democracies

the mid-1970s until 1996. Two-thirds of Table 9.1 is based on
Siaroff's figures.[1]

The only remaining problem is that the twelve developing
countries are included neither in Siaroff's study nor in any of
the earlier comparative studies. One reason for this neglect is

1. An earlier attempt to arrive at a comprehensive score, by Markus Crepaz
and myself, relied on the combined wisdom of twelve eminent scholars of interest group corporatism by averaging their ratings. This could be done for eighteen
industrialized countries for which at least six scholarly judgments were available (Lijphart and Crepaz 1991). All of these countries are also included in
Siaroff's set of twenty-four countries. These "combined wisdom" scores are

that the necessary data are often not available for the less developed countries. Another is that scholars of interest group systems have been particularly interested in corporatist instead of pluralist systems and that, broadly speaking, the developing countries tend to be more pluralist than corporatist. Stephan Haggard and Robert R. Kaufman (1995, 341) point out that the most important reason for this is "the organizational weakness of the relevant players, including both interest groups and parties," which makes tripartite concertation very difficult. Nevertheless, the interest group systems of the developing countries are not uniformly and purely pluralist, and the degree to which they are pluralist or, to some extent, corporatist is measurable on the basis of judgments expressed by country and area experts.

Of the twelve developing democracies included in this study, the country with the most corporatist interest group system is Mauritius. Deborah Bräutigam (1997, 54–55) writes that Mauritius cannot be called highly corporatist but that it does have "institutional mechanisms [that] ensure that labor, business, and government meet periodically to negotiate wage rates and other economic parameters." Mauritian political scientist Hansraj Mathur (personal communication, March 31, 1997) adds the following more detailed description: "Most of the trade unions are members of federations which are in turn members of large confederations. These large confederations, along with the Mauritius Employers Federation (a strong group uniting all the employers) and the government hold tripartite meetings to discuss the annual quantum of compensation to be paid to meet any rise in the cost of living. The quantum once decided is applied to all the workers of the various industries. Thus, although sectoral negotiations continue to exist, the quantum of compen-

---

strongly correlated with the scores in Table 9.1: the correlation coefficient is an overwhelmingly strong 0.95 (statistically significant at the 1 percent level).

sation decided by the tripartite must be respected by all the economic sectors."

John A. Peeler (1985, 104) calls the interest group systems of Colombia, Costa Rica, and Venezuela "broadly corporatist, with varying overlays of pluralism." Venezuela is generally regarded as the most corporatist of the three. Michael Coppedge (1993, 260) describes its institutional structure as "virtually identical to that of two societal corporatist states, Germany and Austria," although he qualifies this statement by pointing out that the process is less well institutionalized and that Venezuelan labor is less autonomous than in the European cases. Corporatist representation is mainly channeled through many advisory commissions. Brian Crisp (1994, 1492–93) counts 330 of these commissions, created between 1959 and 1989, "with participants named to represent interest groups or entire socioeconomic sectors." Crisp adds that these "advisory" commissions actually give the interest groups "formal access to government decision making" and that their great influence and the fact that they are appointed by the president "help explain why the Venezuelan president has been so dominant relative to congress."

In Papua New Guinea and Botswana, the interest group systems are not highly developed and labor unions are weak. Nevertheless, in the opinion of Botswana expert John D. Holm and the two Botswanan social scientists Patrick P. Molutsi and Gloria Somolekae (1996, 58), "Botswana is developing toward the democratic corporatism so evident in Western Europe. . . . Groups organize on a bottom up basis and work with government officials to formulate a comprehensive policy regarding a particular sector of society or the economy." This description also fits—in fact somewhat more strongly—the interest group system of Papua New Guinea. The other small Commonwealth democracies—the Caribbean countries and Malta—have remained mainly pluralist, although Barbados has developed corporatist practices to some extent in recent years, as noted in Chapter 3. The ruling party in Trinidad and Tobago organized a tripartite conference in 1964, shortly after independence, which led to the appointment of several tripartite committees to study and make recommendations on labor utilization and economic development. This incipient corporatism failed mainly because of the hostility of the labor unions, who saw it as a ploy by the government and the employers to weaken labor (MacDonald 1986, 150).

The Indian interest group system, finally, has traditionally been largely pluralist. The field of agriculture is the one exception—but a significant one because India is still mainly a rural and agricultural country. The "institutional centerpiece of agricultural policy" is the Commission on Agricultural Costs and Prices, composed of technocrats representing the government and farmers' representatives (Varshney 1995, 147).[2]

The scores in Table 9.1 are pluralism scores ranging from a theoretical high of 4.00 to a theoretical low of zero, but having a somewhat narrower empirical range from 3.56 for the most pluralist country—Canada—to 0.44 for the most corporatist country—Norway. The countries are listed in ascending order of pluralism. The mean score is 2.24 and the median 2.50, considerably higher than the theoretical midpoint of 2.00 between pluralism and corporatism—indicating that the thirty-six democracies as a group are more pluralist than corporatist. An important reason for this is the presence of the twelve developing countries, only two of which, Mauritius and Venezuela, are on the corporatist side of the midpoint. The United Kingdom and Switzerland are respectively near the pluralist and corporatist ends of the spectrum; the other three prototypical democracies are clearly in the expected halves of the table but not in extreme positions.

2. The pluralism scores for the twelve developing countries are based on my reading of the descriptions of their interest group systems by the various country experts cited in the text, on additional advice from almost all of them, and on my reading of the criteria used by Siaroff. They remain largely impressionistic, however, and clearly lack the precision of the scores for the twenty-four industrialized countries.

Interest Group Systems, Party Systems, and Cabinet Types

The interest group system differs from the other basic variables of the executives-parties dimension in that there is no clear causal connection that links it to the other four variables, whereas these other four do have such causal links: electoral systems shape party systems, which in turn have a strong causal effect on the formation of cabinets, and types of cabinets are further causally related to cabinet duration. Therefore, the hypothesis that interest group systems are related to these other variables rests entirely on the conceptual correspondence between the corporatism-pluralism distinction and the broad consensus-majoritarian difference.

Figures 9.1 and 9.2 show the relationships between the interest group systems in the thirty-six democracies and their types of cabinets and party systems. As hypothesized, democracies that have more minimal winning one-party cabinets are also the countries that have more pluralist interest group systems; countries with greater multipartism tend to be less pluralist. The correlation coefficient is stronger for the link between cabinets and interest groups than for the link between parties and interest groups (0.68 and −0.55, respectively) but both are statistically significant at the 1 percent level. The main deviant cases in Figure 9.1 are the three most corporatist systems—Austria, Norway, and Sweden—which are much more consensus-oriented in this respect than with regard to their usual cabinets. Italy and Portugal, by contrast, are considerably less corporatist than expected on the basis of their infrequent minimal winning one-party cabinets.

Figure 9.2 shows a roughly similar pattern: corporatist Austria, Norway, and Sweden are outliers again, and so is Italy. Papua New Guinea's corporatism is much weaker than its extreme multipartism, but not as weak as its relatively low level of development would lead us to expect. Joseph LaPalombara

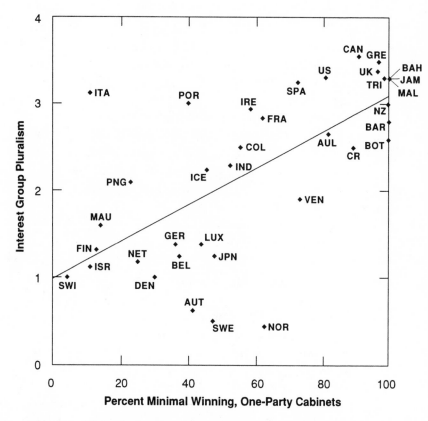

Fig. 9.1 The relationship between type of cabinet and interest group pluralism in thirty-six democracies, 1945–96

(1987, 213, 220) offers an intriguing explanation for Italy's unusual position. He describes Italy, before the reforms of 1994, as a *partitocrazia* with broad participation of all parties in policymaking and a strong inclination to seek consensus: the party leaders had "a deep psychological aversion to divisive confrontations." The consensus produced by partitocrazia was so strong, in LaPalombara's opinion, that there was simply no need for any further consensus to be produced by corporatism. This

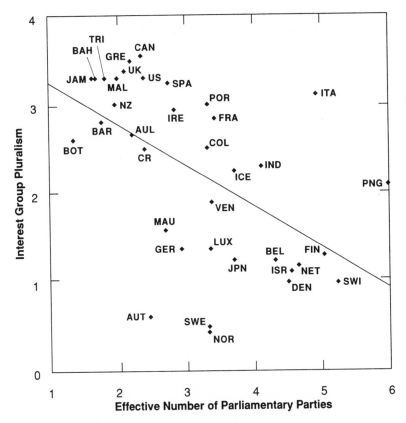

Fig. 9.2 The relationship between the effective number of parliamentary parties and interest group pluralism in thirty-six democracies, 1945–96

view is certainly plausible: broad political coalitions and interest group corporatism are both methods of achieving consensus and, in principle, can be seen as alternative methods. Strong interparty cooperation can therefore compensate for weaknesses in interest group coordination. This appears to have been the case in Italy, but it is clearly not a general pattern in most democracies; if it were, we would find a negative relationship between multipartism and broad coalition cabinets on one hand and corporatism on the other—instead of the strong positive relationships that are shown in Figures 9.1 and 9.2.

The type of interest group system is also correlated with the electoral system and, though less strongly, with executive dominance. The correlations among all five variables involved in the executives-parties dimension are presented in Chapter 14. First, however, I turn in the next four chapters to a discussion of the variables belonging to the federal-unitary dimension.

CHAPTER 10

Division of Power

The Federal-Unitary and
Centralized-Decentralized Contrasts

The prime characteristic of the majoritarian model of democracy, as I have emphasized in previous chapters, is concentration of power in the hands of the majority. The consensus model is characterized by *non*-concentration of power, which can take the two basic forms of sharing of power and division of power. These two forms provide the theoretical underpinnings of the two dimensions of the majoritarian-consensus contrast. The crucial distinction is whether in consensus democracy power is dispersed to political actors operating together *within* the same political institutions or dispersed to *separate* political institutions (see Chapter 1). In the previous five chapters I discussed the five variables of the executives-parties (joint-power) dimension; in this chapter I deal with the first variable of the federal-unitary (divided-power) dimension: federalism and decentralization versus unitary and centralized government. It is appropriate to give this first-place honor to the subject of federalism because it can be considered the most typical and drastic method of dividing power: it divides power between entire levels of government. In fact, as a term in political science, "division of power" is normally used as a synonym for federalism.

In all democracies, power is necessarily divided to some extent between central and noncentral governments, but it is a highly one-sided division in majoritarian democracy. To maintain majority rule in the pure majoritarian model, the central government must control not only the central government apparatus but also all noncentral, potentially competing, governments. Majoritarian government is therefore both unitary (nonfederal) and centralized. The consensus model is inspired by the opposite aim. Its methods are federalism and decentralization—that is, not only a guaranteed division of power between the central and noncentral levels of government but also, in practice, strong noncentral governments that exercise a substantial portion of the total power available at both levels.

In this chapter I discuss the concept of federalism and its primary and secondary characteristics. On the basis of the primary traits, I develop a five-point scale of federalism and decentralization and assign each of the thirty-six democracies a place on this scale. This scale will be compared with two alternative methods of measuring division of power. Last, I discuss the potential advantages of federalism for two purposes: providing autonomy for minority groups in plural societies and permitting institutional experimentation.

Federalism and Decentralization

A variety of definitions of federalism may be found in the literature on this subject, but there is broad agreement on its most basic characteristic: a guaranteed division of power between central and regional governments. William H. Riker's (1975, 101) authoritative definition reads as follows: "Federalism is a political organization in which the activities of government are divided between regional governments and a central government in such a way that each kind of government has some activities on which it makes final decisions." One aspect of this definition that deserves emphasis and to which I return later in this chapter, is that the component units are called "regional" governments. This is in accordance with the conventional view: federalism is usually described as a spatial or territorial division of power in which the component units are geographically defined. These units are variously called states (in the United States, India, Australia, and Venezuela), provinces (Canada), *Länder* (Germany and Austria), cantons (Switzerland), and regions (Belgium).

Instead of Riker's definition in terms of a guaranteed division of power, the description preferred by Daniel J. Elazar (1997, 239) focuses on "noncentralization" of power: he sees federalism as "the fundamental distribution of power among multiple centers . . . , not the devolution of powers from a single center or down a pyramid." None of these multiple centers in the federal system "is 'higher' or 'lower' in importance than any other, unlike in an organizational pyramid where levels are distinguished as higher or lower as a matter of constitutional design."

Both Elazar's and Riker's definitions allow for a wide range of actual power exercised by the different levels of government. Riker (1975, 101) states that each level "has some activities on which it makes final decisions" but does not specify any particular ratio of such activities between the central and regional governments. Likewise, Elazar (1997, 239) states that "the powers assigned to each [of the] multiple centers" in federalism may be large or small. Both of these federalism experts assume, however, that the fundamental purpose of guaranteeing a division of power is to ensure that a substantial portion of power will be exercised at the regional level or, to put it more succinctly, that the purpose of noncentralization of power is decentralization of power. These two elements are conceptually distinct, but they should both be regarded as primary characteristics of federalism.

In addition to these primary characteristics, federalist theorists often identify several secondary characteristics of federalism: in particular, a bicameral legislature with a strong federal chamber to represent the constituent regions, a written constitution that is difficult to amend, and a supreme court or special constitutional court that can protect the constitution by means of its power of judicial review. These are among the most important of what Ivo D. Duchacek (1970, 188–275) calls the "yardsticks of federalism." Their connection with federalism is that they can all serve to ensure that the basic federal division of power will be preserved. Unlike the primary characteristics, they are guarantors of federalism rather than components of federalism itself. I discuss these variables in more detail in the next two chapters.

The primary federal characteristics of noncentralization and decentralization are the building blocks for the construction of the fivefold classification in Table 10.1. The first criterion is whether states have formally federal constitutions. As Elazar (1987, 42) argues, "The first test of the existence of federalism is the desire or will to be federal on the part of the polity involved. Adopting and maintaining a federal constitution is . . . the first and foremost means of expressing that will." This criterion yields an initial distinction between federal and unitary systems. Each of these categories can then be divided into centralized and decentralized subclasses; centralization and decentralization are obviously matters of degree, but it is not difficult in practice to classify most countries according to the simple centralized-decentralized dichotomy. Finally, an intermediate category of semifederal systems is needed for a few democracies that cannot be unambiguously classified as either federal or unitary.

Table 10.1 also assigns a score to each category so that the classification can serve as a quantitative index of federalism, and it shows in which category—or, in some cases, between which categories—each of the thirty-six democracies belongs. The table is organized so that the easy cases that clearly fit a particular category are listed in the left and middle columns and the column to the right contains the more complex cases that fall between categories or changed their status during the period under consideration. The same convention is used for similar tables in the next few chapters.

Two striking features of the classification in Table 10.1 are, first, that federalism is relatively rare: there are more than twice

Table 10.1 Degrees of federalism and decentralization in
thirty-six democracies, 1945–96

Federal and decentralized [5.0]		
Australia	Switzerland	(Belgium after 1993)
Canada	United States	
Germany		
Federal and centralized [4.0]		
Venezuela		Austria [4.5]
		India [4.5]
Semi-federal [3.0]		
Israel	Papua New Guinea	Belgium [3.1]
Netherlands	Spain	(Belgium before 1993)
Unitary and decentralized [2.0]		
Denmark	Norway	
Finland	Sweden	
Japan		
Unitary and centralized [1.0]		
Bahamas	Jamaica	France [1.2]
Barbados	Luxembourg	Italy [1.3]
Botswana	Malta	Trinidad [1.2]
Colombia	Mauritius	
Costa Rica	New Zealand	
Greece	Portugal	
Iceland	United Kingdom	
Ireland		

Note: The indexes of federalism are in square brackets

as many unitary as federal states. Second, the federal-unitary
and centralized-decentralized differences are closely related:
most federal systems are decentralized and most unitary systems are centralized. As a result, more than half of the democracies can be classified in one of the two extreme categories. The
mean score is 2.3 and the median is 1.6—both much closer to the
1.0 score of the most unitary and centralized countries than to
the 5.0 score at the other end of the scale.

Six of the nine federal systems—Australia, Canada, Germany, Switzerland, the United States, and, from 1993 on, Belgium—are also clearly decentralized systems of government. Only one—Venezuela—is clearly centralized; its "federalist terminology," Daniel H. Levine (1989, 273) writes, "should not obscure what is in practice a highly centralized system of government and public administration." Austria and India are roughly in between these two types of federalism: not as decentralized as, for instance, Australia, but considerably more so than Venezuela. Instead of shoehorning them into one or the other category, therefore, it is more realistic to give them an intermediate position and the intermediate score of 4.5. K. C. Wheare's (1964, 28) conclusion that both the constitution of India and its governmental practices are only "quasi-federal" instead of fully federal is often cited. In particular, the frequent use of so-called President's Rule for partisan purposes detracts from strong federalism: the constitution gives the central government the right to dismiss state governments and to replace them with direct rule from the center for the purpose of dealing with grave emergencies, but in practice President's Rule has been used mainly by the central government to remove state governments controlled by other parties and to call new state elections in the hope of winning these (Tummala 1996, 378–82).

Of the many unitary democracies, only the four Nordic countries and Japan can be classified as decentralized. Many of the others are very small countries, which hardly need a great deal of decentralization, but the unitary and centralized category also includes several larger countries like the United Kingdom, France, Italy, and Colombia. France, Italy, and Trinidad are given a slightly higher score than the minimum of 1.0 because they became slightly less centralized—to a point roughly halfway between the centralized and decentralized categories—during the period under consideration. This process started in Italy around 1970 and in France after the election of President Mitterrand in 1981 (Loughlin and Mazey 1995). In Trinidad and

Tobago, the smaller island of Tobago was granted a measure of self-government and its own House of Assembly in 1980 (MacDonald 1986, 196, Payne 1993, 61). The scores of these three countries represent averages for the entire period.

The semifederal category includes three democracies that Robert A. Dahl has called "sociologically federal" (cited in Verba 1967, 126): Belgium, the Netherlands, and Israel. The central governments of these countries have long recognized, heavily subsidized, and delegated power to private associations with important semipublic functions, especially in the fields of education, culture, and health care, established by the major religious and ideological groups in these societies. Because these groups are not geographically concentrated, sociological federalism deviates from Riker's criterion that the component units of a federation be *regional* in nature. Belgium moved from this sociological federalism to a more formal semifederalism from 1970 on and finally to full federalism in 1993—which, however, still includes the nongeographically defined cultural communities among the constituent units of the federation. Belgium's score of 3.1 is the average over the whole 1946–96 period. Spain and Papua New Guinea must be placed in the same semifederal category. Spain has granted extensive autonomy, first to Catalonia, the Basque Country, and Galicia, but later to other regions as well without, however, becoming a formally federal state; Luís Moreno (1994) calls the Spanish system one of "imperfect federalism." Papua New Guinea had a highly decentralized system of government, often called "quasi-federal," during almost the entire democratic period covered in this study; it was adopted in 1977 but was abolished by a constitutional amendment in 1995.

Other Indicators of Federalism and Decentralization

Does the index of federalism express the properties of federalism and decentralization accurately and reliably? Confidence in the index can be strengthened by comparing it with two other indicators: the central government's share of a country's total tax receipts and Jan-Erik Lane and Svante Ersson's (1994b, 224) institutional autonomy index. Unfortunately, these indicators cannot be used as alternative measures themselves in this study because they are available for only about half of the thirty-six democracies.

The tax-share measure is based on the reasonable assumption that the scope of the activities of the central and noncentral governments can be measured in terms of their expenditures and revenues. Because expenditures and revenues are, if not in balance, at least in rough correspondence with each other, they can be used interchangeably. However, if we are interested in the noncentral governments' strength vis-à-vis the central government, it is theoretically more attractive to focus on their respective resources, especially tax revenues. Noncentral taxes are the taxes collected by the noncentral governments for themselves plus those shares of taxes collected by the central government that accrue automatically to noncentral governments.[1] Government centralization can then be measured as the central government's share of total central and noncentral tax receipts. Sufficiently accurate data exist for only twenty-one countries: those belonging to the Organization for Economic Cooperation and Development (OECD), except New Zealand and Luxembourg (Lane, McKay, and Newton 1997, 86). In the period 1980–92—chosen because 1992 is the most recent year for which the tax data are available and because starting in 1980 permits the inclusion of Spain, Portugal, and Greece—the central govern-

1. All transfers, whether conditional or unrestricted, from the central government to noncentral governments must be excluded. Conditional or restricted transfers are spent for purposes mandated by the central government, but even unrestricted grants do not necessarily mean that the noncentral government is given a free hand. As Douglas E. Ashford (1979, 82) points out, they are frequently "not functions of the strength of local governments, but a measure of the central governments' ability to predict how the funds will be used." All social security taxes must also be excluded.

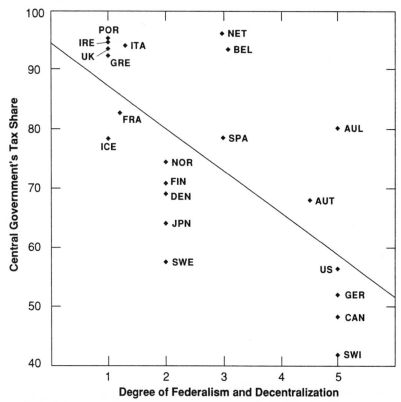

Fig. 10.1 The relationship between the degree of federalism-decentralization and the central government's share of total central and noncentral tax receipts in twenty-one democracies, 1980–1992

ment's tax share ranges from a high of 96.1 percent in the Netherlands to a low of 41.9 percent in Switzerland.

Figure 10.1 shows the relationship between the index of federalism and the central government's tax share: as the index of federalism assumes higher values, the lower the central government's tax share becomes. The difference between the unitary-

centralized countries, with a score of or close to 1.0 on the index
of federalism, and the federal-decentralized countries with
scores of 5.0, is especially striking. The correlation coefficient is
−0.66 (which is significant at the 1 percent level). For three
deviant cases, the scattergram suggests that the index of federalism overestimates or underestimates the degree of centralization: Australia is the only federal and decentralized federal system that does not have a low central government tax share, and
Japan and Sweden are already classified as decentralized among
the unitary countries but appear to be even more decentralized
according to their central governments' tax shares. Remember,
however, that the index of federalism explicitly aims at including the federal-unitary distinction, whereas the tax-share indicator solely measures the degree of centralization. Belgium
and the Netherlands are also outliers; here the explanation is
that the tax-share measure fails to take the element of sociological federalism into consideration.

The Lane-Ersson institutional autonomy index does take
both federalism and sociological federalism into account—the
authors call sociological federalism "functional autonomy"—as
well as territorial autonomy for particular regions and the degree of "regional and local government discretion." Cumula-
tively, the scores on these four variables, all based on the authors' impressionistic but plausible judgments, yield a six-point
scale with a high of five points in the case of Switzerland and a
low of zero points for Greece and Ireland.[2] Lane and Ersson
propose their index in a comparative study of West European
democracies and supply specific figures for only sixteen large
and medium-size European countries—fewer than half of the
countries covered in this book. For these sixteen democracies,

2. The scores for all sixteen countries are as follows: 5 for Switzerland, 4 for
Belgium and Germany, 3 for Austria, Denmark, and the Netherlands, 2 for Finland, Norway, Sweden, and the United Kingdom, 1 for France, Italy, Portugal,
and Spain, and 0 for Greece and Ireland. Of these sixteen scores, only the rather
low Spanish and rather high British scores appear questionable.

however, the Lane-Ersson index correlates strongly with the index of federalism: the correlation coefficient is a statistically highly significant 0.82.

The comparisons with the above two alternative measures provide strong validation for the index of federalism. In the next several chapters I show that this index is also strongly correlated with the other variables of the second dimension.

Federalism and Ethnic Autonomy

Federalism tends to be used in two kinds of countries: relatively large countries and plural societies. The largest countries in terms of population included in this study, India and the United States, are both federations; the least populous federation is Switzerland, which is approximately in the middle of our thirty-six democracies ranked by population. Four of the nine federal systems are plural societies: Belgium, Canada, India, and Switzerland. These are also the largest of the nine plural societies listed in Table 4.3. In these plural societies, federalism performs the special function of giving autonomy to ethnic minorities.

To analyze this function of federalism it is useful to distinguish between congruent and incongruent federalism, as suggested by Charles D. Tarlton (1965, 868). Congruent federations are composed of territorial units with a social and cultural character that is similar in each of the units and in the federation as a whole. In a perfectly congruent federal system, the component units are "miniature reflections of the important aspects of the whole federal system." Conversely, incongruent federations have units with social and cultural compositions that differ from one another and from the country as a whole.[3]

3. Tarlton uses the terms "symmetry" and "asymmetry" instead of "congruence" and "incongruence." Because the former pair of terms is most often used to describe different distributions of power—for instance, between the two chambers of bicameral legislatures—it is less confusing to use the latter pair of

Another way of expressing this difference is to compare the political boundaries between the component units of the federation and the social boundaries among groups like ethnic minorities. In incongruent federations these boundaries tend to coincide, but they tend to cut across each other in congruent federal systems.

If the political boundaries are drawn so as to approximate the social boundaries, the heterogeneity in the federation as a whole is transformed into a high degree of homogeneity at the level of the component units. In other words, incongruent federalism can make a plural society less plural by creating relatively homogeneous smaller areas. This is the pattern in all four of the federal systems that are also plural societies, although their political and ethnic boundaries generally do not coincide perfectly. In Switzerland, there is considerably less linguistic diversity in the cantons than at the national level. The Swiss federation has four official languages, but twenty-two of the twenty-six cantons (and half-cantons) are officially unilingual; only three—Bern, Fribourg, and Valais—are bilingual, and just one—Graubünden— has three official languages (McRae 1983, 172–79). In Canada, the Francophone minority is concentrated mainly in Quebec, and the Quebec government has served as the principal mouthpiece for the interests of the French-speaking community in Canada, but Ontario and New Brunswick also contain relatively large numbers of French-speakers.

The British colonial rulers of India drew the administrative divisions of the country without much regard for linguistic differences; the imposition of federalism on these divisions led to a mainly congruent type of federalism in the early years of independent India. However, a complete transformation to an incongruent federal system based on linguistic divisions took place in

terms to characterize different compositions of two or more entities. Congruence and incongruence in federalism have a meaning that is analogous to congruence and incongruence in bicameralism (see Chapter 11).

the 1950s. After the state of Madras was divided into the separate Tamil-speaking and Telugu-speaking states of Tamil Nadu and Andhra Pradesh in 1953, the States Reorganization Commission embraced the linguistic principle and recommended drastic revisions in state boundaries along linguistic lines in 1955. These were quickly implemented in 1956, and several additional linguistic states were created in later years (Brass 1990, 146–56). Because of India's extreme linguistic diversity, this incongruent linguistic federalism has not managed to accommodate all of the smaller minorities, but on the whole it has, in Indian political scientist Rajni Kothari's (1970, 115) words, succeeded in making language "a cementing and integrating influence" instead of a "force for division."

Finally, the new Belgian federalism is the result of a determined effort to set up a federation that is as incongruent as possible. The three geographically defined regions are already highly incongruent: the two largest, Flanders and Wallonia, are unilingual, and only Brussels is bilingual. In order to perfect this linguistic incongruence, three nongeographically defined cultural communities are superimposed on the regions; here the political and linguistic boundaries coincide completely—making the federal system a purely incongruent one (see Chapter 3).

Federalism and Institutional Experimentation

One aspect of the autonomy of the constituent units of federations is that they have their own constitutions, which they can amend freely within certain limits set by the federal constitution. In theory, this gives them the opportunity to experiment with different forms of government. Such experimentation, if successful, can be beneficial both for the other members of the federation and for the central government. In practice, however, we find almost complete isomorphism both between the central and component units' governmental forms and between those of the component units in each country.

With regard to the choice of presidential or parliamentary systems, for instance, the United States is solidly presidential, with governors serving as "presidents" at the state level. However, there has been more experimentation with the electoral system in the United States than in other federations. The principal example at the state level is Illinois, which used a semi-proportional system—cumulative voting—for electing its lower house from 1870 to 1980. Moreover, as was mentioned in Chapter 8, a few states have used the majority-runoff instead of the plurality rule for electing their members of the U.S. House of Representatives. More far-reaching experimentation would be encouraged under the Voters' Choice Act, introduced by Representative Cynthia McKinney in 1997 (but not acted on by the end of 1998): it would allow states to use multimember instead of single-member districts for House elections if they applied PR or semiproportional systems in these districts.

The Australian House of Representatives and the lower houses of the Australian states are all elected by the alternative vote, except one: Tasmania uses the STV form of PR. PR is the norm both at the national and cantonal levels in Switzerland, but a few, mainly small, cantons use majority methods. The other federations are even more isomorphic with regard to their electoral systems: Canada and India are solidly wedded to the plurality rule, and Austria, Belgium, Germany, and Venezuela to PR. The same isomorphism is apparent with regard to the choice of presidential and parliamentary systems, as already noted for the American case. The only slight exceptions can be found in Germany and Switzerland. All of the German Länder have parliamentary systems, but in Bavaria the prime minister cannot be dismissed by a vote of no confidence. In Switzerland, the cantons deviate in one respect from the hybrid parliamentary-presidential system at the federal level—their collegial executives are popularly elected—but they are similar to each other in this respect. It is symptomatic that the drafters of the constitution of the new canton of Jura, which formally came into being in 1979, discussed the British and German examples of parliamentary systems but that in the end they stuck to "accepted Swiss norms" (Tschaeni 1982, 116).

CHAPTER 11

Parliaments and Congresses
Concentration Versus Division of Legislative Power

The second component of the federal-unitary dimension is the distribution—concentration versus division—of power in the legislature. The pure majoritarian model calls for the concentration of legislative power in a single chamber; the pure consensus model is characterized by a bicameral legislature in which power is divided equally between two differently constituted chambers. In practice, we find a variety of intermediate arrangements. In Chapters 2 and 3 we saw that the New Zealand parliament (after 1950) and the Swiss parliament are, in this respect, perfect prototypes of majoritarian and consensus democracy, respectively, but that the other three main examples deviate from the pure models to some extent. The British parliament is bicameral, but because the House of Lords has little power, it can be described as asymmetrically bicameral. The same description fits the Barbadian legislature because its appointed Senate has delaying but no veto power. The prefederal bicameral Belgian parliament was characterized by a balance of power between the two chambers, but these chambers hardly differed in composition; in the new federal legislature, elected for the first time in 1995, the Senate is still not very differently composed from the Chamber of Representatives, and it has also lost some of its former powers.

The first topic of this chapter is the simple dichotomous

classification of parliaments as bicameral or unicameral. Next, I discuss the differences between the two chambers of bicameral legislatures, especially with regard to their respective powers and composition. On the basis of these two key differences, I develop a quantitative index of bicameralism. Last I explore the relationship between the strength of bicameralism, as measured by this index, and the degree of federalism and decentralization discussed in the previous chapter.

Two additional introductory comments are in order. First, legislative chambers have a variety of proper names (among them House of Commons, House of Representatives, Chamber of Deputies, Bundestag, and Senate), and in order to avoid confusion the following generic terms will be used in the discussion of bicameral parliaments: first chamber (or lower house) and second chamber (or upper house). The first chamber is always the more important one or, in federal systems, the house that is elected on the basis of population.[1] Second, the bicameral legislature as a whole is usually called Congress in presidential systems—but not, of course, in France, where the term "parliament" originated—and Parliament in parliamentary systems of government. However, the term "parliament" is also often used generically as a synonym for "legislature," and I shall follow this conventional usage here.

Unicameralism and Bicameralism

A dichotomous classification of parliaments as unicameral or bicameral appears to be simple and straightforward, but two legislatures do not fit either category: those of Norway and, until 1991, Iceland. Norwegian legislators are elected as one body, but after the election they divide themselves into two chambers by

1. The only potential difficulty of this terminology is that the first chamber of the Dutch parliament is formally called the Second Chamber, and the second chamber is called the First Chamber. Similarly, the first and second chambers of the pre-1970 bicameral legislature of Sweden were called the Second and First Chamber, respectively.

choosing one-fourth of their members to form a second chamber. The two chambers, however, have joint legislative committees, and any disagreements between the chambers are resolved by a plenary session of all members of the legislature. Roughly the same description fits the Icelandic case as well, except that the second chamber in Iceland was formed from one-third of the elected legislators. These legislatures therefore have some features of unicameralism and some of bicameralism; the resolution of disagreements by means of a joint session does not necessarily point to unicameralism because it is not an uncommon method for unambiguously bicameral legislatures either. If one were forced to make a purely dichotomous choice, these legislatures should probably be regarded as somewhat closer to unicameralism than to bicameralism. But there is no need for such a difficult choice, and the classification of all legislatures presented later in this chapter simply places these two cases in a special one-and-a-half chambers category.

In their broad comparative study of bicameralism, George Tsebelis and Jeannette Money (1997, 1) report that about one-third of the countries in the world have bicameral and about two-thirds have unicameral legislatures. The ratio for our thirty-six democracies is quite different: bicameralism is much more common than unicameralism. In 1996, only thirteen of the thirty-six democracies, slightly more than one-third, had unicameral parliaments. Four countries shifted to unicameralism during the period under consideration: New Zealand in 1950, Denmark in 1953, Sweden in 1970, and Iceland in 1991 (Longley and Olson 1991). At the beginning of the period in which each of the thirty-six democracies is covered, only nine—exactly one-fourth—had unicameral legislatures: Costa Rica, Finland, Greece, Israel, Luxembourg, Malta, Mauritius, Papua New Guinea, and Portugal. There were no shifts in the opposite direction, from a unicameral to a bicameral parliament.

The thirteen countries with unicameral parliaments listed in the previous paragraph tend to be the smaller countries; Greece, with a population of slightly more than ten million, is the largest. An even more striking characteristic is that none of them is a federal system. To put it slightly differently, the nine formally federal systems among the thirty-six democracies all have bicameral legislatures, whereas, as of 1996, the twenty-seven formally unitary systems (including those labeled semifederal in the previous chapter) are evenly divided between unicameralism and bicameralism: thirteen have unicameral legislatures; thirteen have bicameral legislatures; and Norway has a one-and-a-half chamber system. This is already a strong indicator of the relationship between cameral structure and the federal-unitary distinction. This relationship is analyzed in more detail at the end of this chapter, after the discussion of the different forms that bicameralism can assume.

Varieties of Bicameralism

The two chambers of bicameral legislatures tend to differ in several ways. Originally, the most important function of second chambers, or "upper" houses, elected on the basis of a limited franchise, was to serve as a conservative brake on the more democratically elected "lower" houses. With the advent of universal franchise for all elections in our set of fully democratic regimes, this function has become obsolete. However, the British House of Lords and the House of Chiefs in Botswana are borderline cases: membership in the House of Lords is still based mainly on hereditary principles, and in Botswana, although the chiefs are now subject to formal election, heredity still prevails in practice. As a result, these two bodies are firmly conservative in outlook; the House of Lords, for instance, has a permanent Conservative majority. Of the remaining six differences between first and second chambers, three are especially important in the sense that they determine whether bicameralism is a significant institution. Let us first take a brief look at the three less important differences:

First, second chambers tend to be smaller than first chambers. In fact, this would be an absolute rule for the bicameral legislatures in our set of democracies if it were not for the British House of Lords, which has approximately 1,200 members, almost twice as many as the 659 members of the House of Commons following the 1997 election. However, the exception is more apparent than real: if we exclude the members who rarely attend, especially many of the hereditary peers, the number is reduced to about 300. Among all of the other second chambers that are smaller than the first chambers, there is still a great variety in how much smaller they are. A few second chambers are relatively close to the sizes of the respective first chambers: for instance, in Trinidad the respective numbers are 31 and 36, and in Spain 257 and 350. At the other extreme, Germany has the world's largest democratic first chamber with 672 members after the 1994 election (to be reduced, according to a parliamentary vote in early 1998, to about 600 for the election in the year 2002) and one of the smaller second chambers consisting of just 69 members.

Second, legislative terms of office tend to be longer in second than in first chambers. The first chamber terms range from two to five years compared with a second chamber range of four to nine years (and, in Britain and Canada, respectively, life membership and membership until retirement). Switzerland is the only, relatively minor, exception: a few of its second-chamber members are elected for terms that are shorter than the four-year term of the first chamber. In all the other bicameral legislatures, the members of second chambers have terms of office that are either longer than or equal to those of the first-chamber members.[2]

2. The U.S. House of Representatives is exceptional in that it has a short term of office of only two years. The Australian lower house and the New Zealand unicameral legislature are elected for three years. In Sweden, the term was four years until 1970, when both unicameralism and three-year terms were adopted, but four-year terms were restored from 1994 on. In all other countries, the members of first or only chambers may serve as long as four or five years, but in most parliamentary systems premature dissolutions may shorten these maximum terms.

Third, a common feature of second chambers is their staggered election. One-half of the membership of the Australian and Japanese second chambers is renewed every three years. One-third of the American and Indian second chambers is elected every second year, and one-third of the French second chamber is renewed every three years. Similarly, the members of the Austrian, German, and Swiss federal chambers are selected in a staggered manner but at irregular intervals.

These three differences do affect how the two chambers of the several legislatures operate. In particular, the smaller second chambers can conduct their business in a more informal and relaxed manner than the usually much larger first chambers. But, with one exception to be mentioned shortly, they do not affect the question of whether a country's bicameralism is a truly strong and meaningful institution.

Strong Versus Weak Bicameralism

Three features of bicameral parliaments determine the strength or weakness of bicameralism. The first important aspect is the formal constitutional powers that the two chambers have. The general pattern is that second chambers tend to be subordinate to first chambers. For instance, their negative votes on proposed legislation can frequently be overridden by the first chambers, and in most parliamentary systems the cabinet is responsible exclusively to the first chamber. In two countries, disagreement between the two chambers is settled by a joint session: India and Venezuela. Here the relative sizes of the two chambers, discussed in the previous section, do make a difference with regard to the strength of bicameralism. The Indian second chamber is almost half the size of the first, whereas the Venezuelan senate has less than one-fourth of the members of the lower house. The only examples of bicameral legislatures with formally equal powers in our set of democracies are the legislatures of Colombia, Italy, Switzerland, and the United States;

three countries used to have formally equal chambers—Belgium, Denmark, and Sweden—but the Belgian Senate's power was severely reduced when it was elected in its new federal form in 1995, and Denmark and Sweden abolished their second chambers in 1953 and 1970, respectively.

Second, the actual political importance of second chambers depends not only on their formal powers but also on their method of selection. All first chambers are directly elected by the voters, but the members of most second chambers are elected indirectly (usually by legislatures at levels below that of the national government, as in India, the Netherlands, and, until 1970, in Sweden) or, more frequently, appointed (like the senators in Canada and in the four Commonwealth Caribbean countries, some of the Irish senators, and life peers in the British House of Lords). Second chambers that are not directly elected lack the democratic legitimacy, and hence the real political influence, that popular election confers. Conversely, the direct election of a second chamber may compensate to some extent for its limited power.

On the basis of the above two criteria—the relative formal powers of the two chambers and the democratic legitimacy of the second chambers—bicameral legislatures can be classified as either *symmetrical* or *asymmetrical*. Symmetrical chambers are those with equal or only moderately unequal constitutional powers and democratic legitimacy. Asymmetrical chambers are highly unequal in these respects. The symmetrical category includes the seven legislatures, noted above, that have or had chambers with formally equal powers. Three of these legislatures also have directly elected second chambers—Colombia, Italy, and the United States—and most of the members of the Swiss and Belgian second chambers are popularly elected. In addition, the chambers of four bicameral legislatures are not completely equal but can still be classified as symmetrical according to the above definition: those in Australia, Germany, Japan, and the Netherlands. The entire Australian and Japanese parliaments are elected directly. The Dutch parliament belongs in this category in spite of the second chamber's indirect election by the provincial legislatures, because this chamber has an absolute veto power over all proposed legislation that cannot be overridden by the first chamber. The German second chamber does not owe its strength to either popular election or an absolute legislative veto but to the fact that it is a unique federal chamber, composed of representatives of the *executives* of the member states of the federation—usually ministers in the member state cabinets. It can thus be described as "one of the strongest second chambers in the world" (Edinger 1986, 16). The power relationship between the two houses in the remaining bicameral parliaments is asymmetrical.

The third crucial difference between the two chambers of bicameral legislatures is that second chambers may be elected by different methods or designed so as to overrepresent certain minorities. If this is the case, the two chambers differ in their composition and may be called *incongruent*. The most striking examples are most of the second chambers that serve as federal chambers and that overrepresent the smaller component units of the federation. The greatest degree of overrepresentation occurs when there is equality of state or cantonal representation regardless of the states' or cantons' populations. Such parity can be found in the federal chambers of Switzerland, the United States, and Venezuela (two representatives per state or canton) and Australia (twelve from each state).[3] The German Bundesrat and the Canadian Senate are examples of federal chambers in which the component units are not equally represented but in which the smaller units are overrepresented and the larger ones underrepresented. The Austrian Bundesrat is an exception, as its membership is roughly proportional to the population of the

3. Partial exceptions to parity are the half cantons in Switzerland, which have only one representative each in the federal chamber, and the Australian Capital Territory and Northern Territory, which have two senators each. In Venezuela, former presidents are also members of the Senate.

Table 11.1   Inequality of representation in nine federal
chambers, 1996

	Seats held by given percentages of the most favorably represented voters				Gini Index of Inequality
	10%	*20%*	*30%*	*50%*	
United States	39.7	55.0	67.7	83.8	0.49
Switzerland	38.4	53.2	64.7	80.6	0.46
Venezuela	31.6	47.2	60.0	77.5	0.40
Australia	28.7	47.8	58.7	74.0	0.36
Canada	33.4	46.3	55.6	71.3	0.34
Germany	24.0	41.7	54.3	72.6	0.32
India	15.4	26.9	37.4	56.8	0.10
Austria	11.9	22.5	32.8	52.9	0.05
Belgium	10.8	20.9	31.0	50.9	0.01

Source: Based on data in the Stepan-Swenden Federal Databank, All Souls College, Oxford University

Länder rather than giving special representation to the smaller
Länder. Similarly, the new Belgian Senate gives only slight overrepresentation to the French-speaking and German-speaking
linguistic minorities. India is an intermediate case.

Table 11.1 presents the degree of overrepresentation of the
smaller units in the nine federations in a more precise way—in
terms of the degree of inequality of representation caused by the
favorable treatment of the small units. It shows the percentage of
the membership of the federal chamber that represents the most
favorably represented 10, 20, 30, and 50 percent of the population. The best represented people are those in the smallest component units of the federation. The following example illus-
trates how these percentages are calculated. Assume that the
smallest and best represented state in a federation has 6 percent
of the population and ten of the one hundred seats in the federal
chamber, and that the second smallest and second best represented state has 8 percent of the population and also ten of the
one hundred federal chamber seats. Then the best represented

10 percent of the population are the 6 percent in the smallest state plus half of the people in the second smallest state. Together, these 10 percent of the people have 15 percent of the seats in the federal chamber.

The inequality in the above illustration is minor compared with the actual inequalities that we find in most of the federal chambers. The United States is the most extreme case: the most favorably represented 10 percent of the people, living in the smallest states, have almost 40 percent of the representation in the Senate; 20 percent of the best represented voters have a comfortable majority of 55 percent; and exactly half of them elect an overwhelming majority of almost eighty-four senators. The percentages for Switzerland are close to the American ones, and the Swiss Council of States can therefore be said to be almost as "malapportioned" as the U.S. Senate. In Venezuela, Australia, Canada, and Germany, the inequalities are less extreme but still substantial: 20 percent of the best represented voters do not quite elect majorities in the upper house, but 30 percent do. The Austrian Bundesrat and the Belgian Senate are the only federal chambers in which the degree of overrepresentation is so slight that they can almost be regarded as proportionally apportioned chambers, and they should therefore be classified as congruent with their first chambers. The composition of the Indian federal chambers appears to be closer to the Austrian and Belgian pattern than to that of the other six federal systems; however, because the Indian second chamber is also elected by a different method—the STV form of PR instead of the plurality rule used for lower house elections—it should be classified as incongruent.

The Gini Index of Inequality shown in Table 11.1 is a summary measure of the degree of inequality. It can range from zero when there is complete equality—the Belgian index of 0.01 is close to this point—to a theoretical maximum approximating 1.00 when the most favorably represented unit has all of the seats in the federal chamber and the others get none. The actual Gini

Index of 0.49 for the United States is roughly halfway between these extremes, and the Swiss index of 0.46 follows closely.

Several nonfederal second chambers must also be classified as incongruent. The French Senate is elected by an electoral college in which the small communes, with less than a third of the population, have more than half of the votes; on account of this rural and small-town overrepresentation, Maurice Duverger once characterized the Senate as the "Chamber of Agriculture" (cited in Ambler 1971, 165). The Spanish Senate is incongruent for three reasons: the mainland provinces (but not the islands and the two North African enclaves) are equally represented; most senators are elected by means of the semiproportional limited-vote system (in contrast with the PR method used for the election of the first chamber); and almost one-fifth are elected by the regional autonomous legislatures. The two houses of the Colombian Congress used to be elected by similar methods—PR in relatively low-magnitude districts—but in 1991 the Senate became incongruent because its electoral system was changed to PR in one large nationwide district—making it much easier for minority parties and candidates to get elected.

Many of the other bicameral legislatures are congruent because their two chambers are elected by similar methods: list PR in Italy (until 1992), the Netherlands, and prefederal Belgium; MMP in Italy since 1994; SNTV in Japan until 1996 (although partly list PR for upper house elections since 1983). In the Bahamas, Barbados, and Jamaica, the upper houses are appointed by the governor-general, and in Trinidad by the president, according to various criteria, but always in such a way that the prime minister nominates the majority; thus the majority party in the first chamber also becomes the majority party in the second chamber. Ireland's Senate appears to be incongruent, because a large number of senators have to be elected from candidates nominated by vocational and cultural interest groups, but in the electoral college, composed of national and local legislators, party politics predominates. Hence, the Irish Senate "is composed largely of party politicians not very different from their colleagues in the [first chamber] and, in the case of many of them, with only tenuous connections with the interests they affect to represent" (Chubb 1982, 212).

The Cameral Structures of Thirty-Six Democratic Legislatures

Table 11.2 uses the distinctions between bicameralism and unicameralism, between symmetrical and asymmetrical bicameralism, and between congruent and incongruent bicameralism to construct a classification of the cameral structures of thirty-six democracies as well as an index of bicameralism ranging from 4.0 to 1.0 points. There are four principal categories: strong, medium-strength, and weak bicameralism, and unicameralism. Strong bicameralism is characterized by both symmetry and incongruence. In medium-strength bicameralism, one of these two elements is missing; this category is split into two subclasses according to whether symmetry or incongruence is the missing feature, but both are ranked equally and have the same index of bicameralism (3.0 points). The third category is weak bicameralism in which the chambers are both asymmetrical and congruent. And the fourth category is that of unicameral legislatures. A plausible case can be made for the merger of the last two categories: does a bicameral legislature with two or more identical houses and one house that is much more powerful than the other differ in any significant way from a unicameral legislature? Tsebelis and Money (1997, 211) give an emphatically affirmative answer to this question: "all second chambers exercise influence even if they are considered weak or insignificant."[4] Therefore, for the purpose of measuring the division of

4. This conclusion is also strongly supported by William B. Heller's (1997) findings. In *Democracies*, I used the labels "strong," "weak," and "insignificant" instead of strong, medium-strength, and weak (Lijphart 1984, 99–100); Tsebelis and Money's as well as Heller's arguments have convinced me that "insignificant" bicameralism is a misleading term that should be avoided.

Table 11.2   Cameral structure of legislatures in thirty-six democracies, 1945–96

Strong bicameralism: symmetrical and incongruent chambers [4.0]

Australia	Switzerland	(Colombia after 1991)
Germany	United States	

Medium-strength bicameralism: symmetrical and congruent chambers [3.0]

Belgium	Japan	Colombia [3.1]
Italy	Netherlands	(Colombia before 1991)
		(Denmark before 1953)
		(Sweden before 1970)

Medium-strength bicameralism: asymmetric and incongruent chambers [3.0]

Canada	Spain
France	Venezuela
India	

Between medium-strength and weak bicameralism [2.5]

Botswana	United Kingdom

Weak bicameralism: asymmetrical and congruent chambers [2.0]

Austria	Ireland	Sweden [2.0]
Bahamas	Jamaica	(New Zealand before 1950)
Barbados	Trinidad	

One-and-a-half chambers [1.5]

Norway	Iceland [1.4]
	(Iceland before 1991)

Unicameralism [1.0]

Costa Rica	Malta	Denmark [1.3]
Finland	Mauritius	New Zealand [1.1]
Greece	Papua New Guinea	(Denmark after 1953)
Israel	Portugal	(Iceland after 1991)
Luxembourg		(New Zealand after 1950)
		(Sweden after 1970)

Note: The indexes of bicameralism are in square brackets

legislative power, weak bicameralism still represents a degree of division, whereas unicameralism means complete concentration of power.

As in Table 10.1, which showed the degrees of federalism and decentralization in the previous chapter, Table 11.2 places several countries in intermediate positions between the four principal categories. This is necessary, first, because several countries changed their cameral structure during the period under consideration; for these countries, both their type of cameral structure in each period and their average scores for the entire period are shown.[5] Second, British and Botswanan bicameralism, although technically incongruent, is "demoted" by half a point because the upper houses are relics of a predemocratic era. Third, as discussed earlier, the in-between legislatures of Iceland (until 1991) and Norway should be classified as one-and-a-half cameralism and assigned the commensurate index of 1.5 points. The mean index of bicameralism for all thirty-six countries is 2.2 and the median 2.0 points—both well below the theoretical midpoint of 2.5 points between strong bicameralism on one hand and unicameralism on the other.

Cameral Structure and Degrees of Federalism and Decentralization

As pointed out earlier, there is a strong empirical relationship between the bicameral-unicameral and federal-unitary dichotomies: all formally federal systems have bicameral legislatures, whereas some nonfederal systems have bicameral and others unicameral parliaments. The same strong link appears

5. Somewhat confusingly, Sweden's average score of 2.0 points places it in the asymmetrical and congruent category, although it actually never had this kind of parliament; the explanation is that 2.0 represents the average of two roughly equal periods of symmetrical and congruent chambers (3.0 points) and unicameralism (1.0 point). Belgium's change from medium-strength to weak bicameralism occurred at the end of the period—the new federal senate was not elected until 1995—and is therefore ignored in the table.

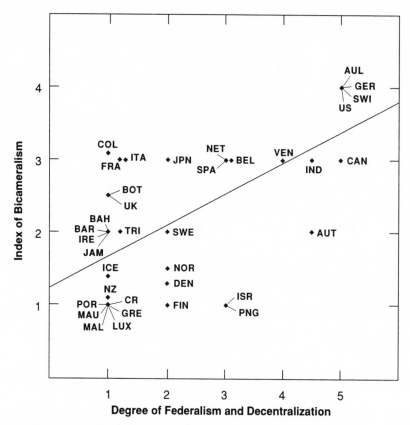

Fig. 11.1 The relationship between federalism-
decentralization and cameral structure in thirty-six
democracies, 1945–96

when the two indexes of federalism and bicameralism are correlated, as Figure 11.1 shows. As the degree of federalism and
decentralization increases, first a shift from unicameralism to
bicameralism takes place and then the strength of bicameralism
increases. The correlation coefficient is 0.64 (significant at the 1
percent level).

Federal Austria is, not unexpectedly, one of the deviant cases as a result of its weakly bicameral legislature. Three Nordic countries that were classified as unitary and decentralized—Finland, Denmark, and Norway—have low bicameralism scores that are more typical of unitary and centralized systems. Similarly, Israel and Papua New Guinea have unicameral parliaments that are at odds with their classification as semifederal systems. On the other side of the regression line, a cluster of three unitary and largely centralized systems—Colombia, France, and Italy—have a much stronger bicameralism than expected. One explanation for these deviant cases appears to be population size. The smaller countries—Austria (which is the second smallest of the nine federal systems), Israel, Papua New Guinea, and the Nordic countries—tend to have unicameral or weakly bicameral legislatures in spite of their federal, semifederal, or decentralized status. By contrast, large countries like Colombia, France, and Italy have a relatively strong bicameralism in spite of their unitary and centralized systems. I noted in the previous chapter that population size was also related to federalism: the federal systems tend to be the larger countries. The three variables are clearly far from perfectly correlated. However, in Chapter 14 I show that population size is closely linked to the entire federal-unitary dimension of which the indexes of federalism and bicameralism are two of the five components.

CHAPTER 12

Constitutions

Amendment Procedures and Judicial Review

In this chapter I discuss two variables, both belonging to the federal-unitary dimension, that have to do with the presence or absence of explicit restraints on the legislative power of parliamentary majorities. Is there a constitution serving as a "higher law" that is binding on parliament and that cannot be changed by a regular parliamentary majority, or is parliament— that is, the majority in parliament—the supreme and sovereign lawmaker? The first variable is the ease or difficulty of amending the constitution: the conventional distinction is between *flexible* constitutions that can be changed by regular majorities and *rigid* constitutions that require supermajorities in order to be amended. The second variable concerns the presence or absence of judicial review; when the constitution and an ordinary law conflict, who interprets the constitution: parliament itself— again meaning the majority in parliament—or a body such as a court or a special constitutional council outside and independent of parliament? In the pure consensus model, the constitution is rigid and protected by judicial review; the pure majoritarian model is characterized by a flexible constitution and the absence of judicial review.

In practice, the two differences are not dichotomies: there are degrees of flexibility or rigidity of constitutions and, when judicial review is present, degrees to which it is actively used. In this chapter I propose four-point scales to measure both constitutional rigidity and judicial review. I also analyze the relationship between the two variables: rigid constitutions tend to have more judicial review protection than more flexible constitutions. In a brief addendum I discuss the role of referendums, which are frequently required in the process of constitutional amendment: should they be seen mainly as majoritarian instruments or rather as incentives for seeking consensus?

Written and Unwritten Constitutions

The distinction between written and unwritten constitutions appears to be relatively unimportant for two reasons. One is that almost all of the constitutions in the world are written; unwritten ones are extremely rare. In our set of thirty-six democracies, only three have unwritten constitutions: the United Kingdom and New Zealand, the two prime examples of majoritarian democracy discussed in Chapter 2, as well as Israel. The absence of a written constitution in Britain and New Zealand is usually explained in terms of their strong consensus on fundamental political norms, which renders a formal constitution superfluous. The opposite explanation applies to the Israeli case. Israel has tried but failed to adopt a written constitution because on a number of key questions, especially the role of religion in the state and in the legal system, agreement could simply not be reached (Gutmann 1988). This dissensus has been solved by an agreement to disagree, while on other fundamental matters the consensus has been strong enough to allow the country to be run without a formal constitution, as in Britain and New Zealand. Second, from the perspective of the fundamental contrast between the majoritarian and consensus models of democracy, it is more relevant to determine whether the constitution, written or unwritten, imposes significant restraints on the majority than to ask whether it is written or not. Written constitutions may be as easily amendable and as free from judicial review as unwritten constitutions.

There are two strong counterarguments, however. First, if the written constitution is a single document, explicitly designated as the country's highest law, the parliamentary majority is likely to feel morally bound to respect it to a greater degree than if it is merely a more or less amorphous collection of basic laws and customs without even a clear agreement on what exactly is and what is not part of the unwritten constitution. Second, even more significant is the fact that unwritten constitutions by their very nature—because they do not have a formal status superior to that of other laws—logically entail both complete flexibility and the absence of judicial review. The use of "entrenched clauses" and "basic laws" in New Zealand and Israel are only apparent exceptions because the entrenchments can be removed or superseded relatively easily.[1] In contrast, written constitutions may be both completely flexible and completely unprotected by judicial review, but in practice this combination is rare; in our set of thirty-three democracies with written constitutions, France between 1958 and about 1974 is the only example.

Flexible and Rigid Constitutions

Democracies use a bewildering array of devices to give their constitutions different degrees of rigidity: special legislative majorities, approval by both houses of bicameral legislatures (even

1. In the important *Bergman* case in 1969, the Israeli Supreme Court for the first time declared an act of the Knesset (parliament) void for violating a basic law; however, this basic law provided for its own amendment by an absolute majority of all members of the Knesset, enabling the Knesset to pass a modified version of the invalidated law with the required absolute majority, but not a supermajority. Presumably the Knesset could also first have amended the absolute-majority requirement of the basic law (by an absolute majority) and then re-passed the invalidated act in its original form (and even without an absolute majority). Three new basic laws adopted in 1992 have the potential of significantly expanding the power of judicial review (Arian 1998, 267–70).

when these are asymmetrical as far as ordinary legislation is concerned), approval by ordinary or special majorities of state or provincial legislatures, approval by referendum, and approval by special majorities in a referendum. Further complications are that some constitutions stipulate different methods of amendment for different provisions in the constitution or alternative methods that may be used for amending any part of the constitution (Maddex 1995). Nevertheless, this great variety of constitutional provisions can be reduced to four basic types, as shown in Table 12.1. These four types are based, first, on the distinction between approval by ordinary majorities—indicating complete flexibility—and by larger than ordinary majorities. Next, three categories of rigidity can be distinguished: (1) approval by two-thirds majorities—a very common rule, based on the idea that supporters of a constitutional change have to outnumber their opponents by a ratio of at least two to one; (2) approval by *less* than a two-thirds majority (but more than an ordinary majority)—for instance, a three-fifths parliamentary majority or an ordinary majority plus a referendum; and (3) approval by *more* than a two-thirds majority, such as a three-fourths majority or a two-thirds majority plus approval by state legislatures.

The only major adjustment that needs to be made concerns the classification of special majorities—also called extraordinary majorities or supermajorities—when these are special parliamentary majorities in parliaments elected by plurality. In such legislatures, large majorities often represent much smaller popular majorities and sometimes merely a popular plurality; moreover, these large majorities are often single-party majorities. For instance, shortly after Indira Gandhi's assassination in 1984, the Indian Congress party won a huge majority of 76.5 percent of the seats—many more than the two-thirds majority needed for amending the constitution—with a mere 48.1 percent of the popular vote. Two-thirds majorities are also required for amending the constitution of Barbados, but in three of the seven elections since 1966 such large one-party majorities were

Table 12.1   Majorities or supermajorities required for
constitutional amendment in thirty-six democracies, 1945–96

Super-majorities greater than two-thirds [4.0]

Australia	Switzerland	Germany [3.5]
Canada	United States	
Japan		

Two-thirds majorities or equivalent [3.0]

Austria	Malta
Bahamas	Mauritius
Belgium	Netherlands
Costa Rica	Norway
Finland	Papua New Guinea
India	Portugal
Jamaica	Spain
Luxembourg	Trinidad

Between two-thirds and ordinary majorities [2.0]

Barbados	Ireland	France [1.6]
Botswana	Italy	(Colombia after 1991)
Denmark	Venezuela	(France after 1974)
Greece		(Sweden after 1980)

Ordinary majorities [1.0]

Iceland	New Zealand	Colombia [1.1]
Israel	United Kingdom	Sweden [1.3]
		(Colombia before 1991)
		(France before 1974)
		(Sweden before 1980)

Note: The indexes of constitutional rigidity are in square brackets

manufactured from between 50 and 60 percent of the popular
votes, and in one from a 48.8 percent plurality.

Supermajorities in plurality systems are clearly much less
constraining than the same supermajorities in PR systems; to
take this difference into account, plurality systems are classified
in Table 12.1 in the category below the one to which they technically belong. The need for this adjustment appears to be recognized by plurality countries themselves: the only countries

that require three-fourths parliamentary majorities for constitutional amendment are the Bahamas, Jamaica, Mauritius, Papua New Guinea, and Trinidad—all plurality countries. These five democracies are classified in the second category of Table 12.1 as the substantive equivalents of countries with two-thirds majority rules. For the same reason, Barbados and Botswana are placed in the third category even though their formal requirements for constitutional amendment are two-thirds majorities.

The problem of different rules for constitutional amendment in the same constitution can be solved relatively easily. First, when alternative methods can be used, the least restraining method should be counted. For instance, the Italian constitution can be amended either by two-thirds majorities in the two chambers or by absolute majorities—that is, majorities of all members of the two chambers, but no supermajorities—followed by a referendum. The latter method is more flexible in terms of the criteria of Table 12.1 and Italy is therefore classified in the third instead of the second category. Second, when different rules apply to different parts of constitutions, the rule pertaining to amendments of the most basic articles of the constitution should be counted. For instance, some provisions of India's lengthy constitution can be changed by regular majorities in both houses, others by absolute majorities of all members of the two houses, and yet others only by two-thirds majorities plus approval by the legislatures of half of the states. The last group contains key provisions like the division of the power between the central and state governments, and it is the rule for amending these that is decisive for the classification of India in the second category of Table 12.1: the two-thirds majorities in a plurality system would only be good for a place in the third category, but the additional requirement of approval by half of the states puts India back in the second.

Rules for constitutional amendments tend to be quite stable, and any changes that do occur tend not to be far-reaching. The changes in Colombia and Sweden merely entailed the addition of a referendum requirement. The last article of the French constitution stipulates that amendments require either majority approval by the two legislative chambers followed by a referendum or a three-fifths majority in a joint session of the legislature; both methods qualify for the third category of Table 12.1. In addition, President Charles de Gaulle's decision in 1962 to circumvent parliament and to submit a proposed amendment directly to a referendum, overwhelmingly approved by the voters, established a purely majoritarian third procedure for constitutional amendment. However, by about 1974 when the first non-Gaullist president was elected, this extra-constitutional method was no longer regarded as a viable option.

Most countries fit the two middle categories of Table 12.1: they require more than ordinary majorities for constitutional amendment but not more than two-thirds majorities or their equivalent. The mean index of constitutional rigidity is 2.6 and the median is 3.0 points. Five countries do have more rigid constitutions. The United States constitution is the least flexible because amendments require two-thirds majorities in both the Senate and the House of Representatives as well as approval by three-fourths of the states. In Canada, several key provisions can only be amended with the approval of every province. In Australia and Switzerland, amendments require the approval in a popular referendum of not just majorities of the voters but also majorities in a majority of the states or cantons; this enables the smallest of the states and cantons with less than 20 percent of the population to block constitutional changes. The Japanese constitution requires two-thirds majorities in both houses of the legislature as well as a referendum. A good case can be made for including the German constitution in the same category because two-thirds majorities are required in two houses and because the Bundesrat's composition differs from that of the Bundestag in several important respects; however, Table 12.1 places it more conservatively between the top two categories. All of these rigid constitutions are also difficult to amend in practice; in fact, the Japanese constitution has never been amended in the more than fifty years of its existence.

Judicial Review

One can argue that a written and rigid constitution is still not a sufficient restraint on parliamentary majorities, unless there is an independent body that decides whether laws are in conformity with the constitution. If parliament itself is the judge of the constitutionality of its own laws, it can easily be tempted to resolve any doubts in its own favor. The remedy that is usually advocated is to give the courts or a special constitutional tribunal the power of judicial review—that is, the power to test the constitutionality of laws passed by the national legislature.

In the famous *Marbury v. Madison* decision (1803), which established judicial review in the United States, Chief Justice John Marshall argued that the presence of a written constitution and an independent judiciary logically implied the Supreme Court's power of judicial review: the court, faced with an incompatibility between the Constitution and an ordinary law, had no choice but to apply the higher law and therefore to invalidate the law with a lower status. The strong appeal of this argument can also be seen in a comment by R. H. S. Crossman, a member of the British Labour cabinet responsible for the controversial 1968 immigration law denying entry into Britain to about a hundred thousand British subjects living in Kenya; he later said that this law "would have been declared unconstitutional in any country with a written constitution and a Supreme Court" (cited in Rose 1974, 138).

The logic of Marshall's and Crossman's reasoning is incontrovertible: even if the constitution does not explicitly prescribe judicial review, it is implied by the higher status of the constitution. Many constitutions, however, do specifically grant this power to the courts. For instance, the Greek constitution states that "the courts shall be bound not to apply laws, the contents of which are contrary to the Constitution" (Brewer-Carías 1989, 169). Article 2 of the Trinidad constitution asserts: "This Constitution is the supreme law of Trinidad and Tobago, and any other law that is inconsistent with this Constitution is void to the extent of the inconsistency." Very similar language is used in the constitutions of the other three Caribbean countries.[2]

Several constitutions explicitly deny the power of judicial review to their courts. Article 120 of the Dutch constitution, for instance, states: "The constitutionality of acts of parliament and treaties shall not be reviewed by the courts." A noteworthy attempt to exclude part of a written constitution from judicial review can be found in the proposed balanced budget amendment to the U.S. Constitution, twice defeated by the Senate in 1995 and 1997: "The judicial power of the United States shall not extend to any case or controversy arising under this [amendment] except as may be specifically authorized by legislation" (*New York Times*, March 1, 1995, A16). Not only in countries without written constitutions but also in those that do have written constitutions but do not have judicial review, parliaments are the ultimate guarantors of the constitution. The logic on which this alternative is based is that of democratic principle: such vital decisions as the conformity of law to the constitution should be made by the elected representatives of the people rather than by an appointed and frequently quite unrepresentative judicial body.

Mainly as a compromise between these two contradictory logics, several countries entrust judicial review to special constitutional courts instead of to the regular court systems. The ordinary courts may submit questions of constitutionality to the special constitutional court, but they may not decide such ques-

2. These constitutions, as well as those of Botswana and Mauritius, also stipulate that the highest court for the purposes of judicial review is the Judicial Committee of the Privy Council in London; however, especially because of dissatisfaction with the liberal rulings of the Judicial Committee in death-penalty cases, the Caribbean countries may replace it with a joint Caribbean Court of Appeal.

tions themselves. This type is called the centralized system of judicial review. It was proposed by the famous Austrian jurist Hans Kelsen and first adopted by Austria in 1920. It is now also used in Germany, Italy, Spain, Portugal, and Belgium. The alternative, decentralized judicial review, in which all courts may consider the constitutionality of laws, is still the more common system (Favoreu 1986, Cappelletti 1989, 132–66).

France was long considered the prime example of a country in which the principle of popular sovereignty was said to prevent any application of judicial review. The constitution of the Fifth Republic did set up a constitutional council, but at first this body served mainly to protect executive power against legislative encroachments; only the president, the prime minister, and the presidents of the two chambers were permitted to submit questions of constitutionality to the council. However, a constitutional amendment passed in 1974 also gave relatively small minorities in the legislature—sixty members of either chamber—the right to appeal to the constitutional council, and the council itself has strongly asserted its power of judicial review (Stone 1992). Although the courts still cannot turn to the constitutional council, parliament is no longer the ultimate interpreter of the constitutionality of its own laws, and therefore France must now also be counted among the countries with judicial review of the centralized kind.

Judicial Review and Judicial Activism

The impact of judicial review depends only partly on its formal existence and much more vitally on the vigor and frequency of its use by the courts, especially supreme and constitutional courts. Table 12.2 presents a fourfold classification of the strength of judicial review based, first, on the distinction between the presence and absence of judicial review and, second, on three degrees of activism in the assertion of this power by the courts. There are only a few countries where judicial review is

Table 12.2   The strength of judicial review in thirty-six democracies, 1945–96

Strong judicial review [4.0]		
Germany*	United States	(Canada after 1982)
India		
Medium-strength judicial review [3.0]		
Australia	Papua New Guinea	Canada [3.3]
Austria*	Spain*	Italy [2.8]
Mauritius		(Belgium after 1984*)
		(Canada before 1982)
		(Colombia after 1981)
		(France after 1974*)
		(Italy after 1956*)
Weak judicial review [2.0]		
Bahamas	Jamaica	Belgium [1.5]
Barbados	Japan	Colombia [2.4]
Botswana	Malta	France [2.2]
Costa Rica	Norway	(Colombia before 1981)
Denmark	Portugal*	(Italy before 1956)
Greece	Sweden	
Iceland	Trinidad	
Ireland	Venezuela	
No judicial review [1.0]		
Finland	New Zealand	(Belgium before 1984)
Israel	Switzerland	(France before 1974)
Luxembourg	United Kingdom	
Netherlands		

*Centralized judicial review by special constitutional courts

Note: The indexes of judicial review are in square brackets

very strong: the United States, Germany, India, and, since 1982, Canada. The activist American courts and the Supreme Court in particular have been accused of forming an "imperial judiciary" (Franck 1996), but the German Constitutional Court has been even more activist: from 1951 to 1990, it invalidated almost 5 percent of all federal laws (Landfried 1995, 308). India's courts were not very assertive in their early days, but Carl Baar (1992) argues that from 1977 on they have become "the world's most active judiciary." The Supreme Court of India has been described as "the closest analogue—not just non-Western analogue—to the American Supreme Court as both a policy-making and politically important institution. It has declared over 100 laws and ordinances unconstitutional and shows no hesitation in standing up to the Prime Minister and Parliament" (Gadbois 1987, 137–38). In Canada, the adoption of the Charter of Rights and Freedoms in 1982 began "an era of judicial activism" (Baar 1991, 53).

Medium-strength judicial review characterizes five countries during their entire periods under consideration—Australia, Austria, Mauritius, Papua New Guinea, and Spain—and five countries during shorter periods: Canada until 1982, Belgium after the establishment of the Court of Arbitration in 1984 (see Chapter 3), France after the Constitutional Council became a true organ of judicial review in 1974, Italy after the constitutional court provided for in the postwar constitution finally began functioning in 1956, and Colombia as a result of several increasingly assertive supreme court decisions in the early 1980s. Almost half of the democracies are in the category of weak judicial review. Mauro Cappelletti (1989, 141) writes that judges in Denmark, Norway, and Sweden exercise their decentralized power of judicial review "with extreme caution and moderation." These Scandinavian countries are probably among the weakest systems in this respect, and a few of the others—like Portugal and, after 1982, Malta (Agius and Grosselfinger 1995)—can be rated as slightly stronger, but the differences are not great.

The general pattern shown in Table 12.2 is one of relatively weak judicial review. The mean score is 2.2 and the median 2.0 points, well below the midpoint of 2.5 on the four-point scale. However, there appears to be a trend toward more and stronger judicial review: the five countries that are classified in different categories of Table 12.2 during different periods all moved from lower to higher degrees of strength of judicial review. Moreover, the four countries with written constitutions but still no judicial review are older European democracies; the newer democracies, without exception, do have judicial review. Finally, like the United Kingdom (see Chapter 2), these four older European democracies have accepted the supranational judicial review of the European Court of Justice and/or the European Court of Human Rights (Cappelletti 1989, 202). These trends confirm, to cite the title of a recent book, "the global expansion of judicial power" (Tate and Vallinder 1995).

Table 12.2 also shows that countries with centralized judicial review tend to have stronger judicial review than countries with decentralized systems: six of the seven centralized systems are in the top two categories. This is a rather surprising conclusion because centralized review was originally developed as a compromise between not having judicial review at all and the decentralized type of it. The explanation must be that, if a special body is created for the express and exclusive purpose of reviewing the constitutionality of legislation, it is very likely to carry out this task with some vigor.

Constitutional Rigidity and Judicial Review

There are two reasons to expect that the variables of constitutional rigidity versus flexibility and the strength of judicial review will be correlated. One is that both rigidity and judicial review are antimajoritarian devices and that completely flexible constitutions and the absence of judicial review permit unrestricted majority rule. Second, they are also logically linked in that judicial review can work effectively only if it is backed up by constitutional rigidity and vice versa. If there is strong judicial review but the constitution is flexible, the majority in the legislature can easily respond to a declaration of unconstitutionality by amending the constitution. Similarly, if the constitution is rigid but not protected by judicial review, the parliamentary

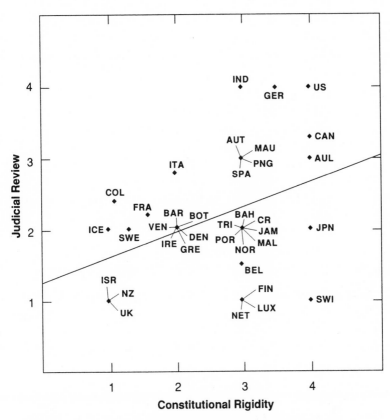

Fig. 12.1 The relationship between constitutional rigidity and judicial review in thirty-six democracies, 1945–96

majority can interpret any constitutionally questionable law it wants to pass as simply not being in violation of the constitution.

Figure 12.1 shows the empirical relationship between the two variables for the thirty-six democracies. The correlation coefficient is 0.39—not exceptionally strong but still statistically significant at the 1 percent level. One prominent outlier is Switzerland, where, as emphasized in Chapter 3, the absence of judicial review is the only majoritarian characteristic in an otherwise solidly consensual democracy. The other main deviant cases are Finland, the Netherlands, and Luxembourg—countries with two-thirds majority rules for constitutional amendment but no judicial review—and India and Germany—where very strong judicial review is combined with rigid but not maximally rigid constitutions. Analysts of judicial review also often note its frequent use in federal systems (Becker 1970, 222). In fact, both judicial review and rigid constitutions are linked with federalism as well as with the other two variables of the federal-unitary dimension: bicameralism and independent central banks. Central banks are subject of the next chapter, and the links among all five federal-unitary variables are discussed in Chapter 14.

Addendum: Referendums and Consensus Democracy

A striking feature of the amendment procedures specified by written constitutions is their frequent use of the referendum either as an absolute requirement or as an optional alternative: in twelve of the thirty-three written constitutions (as of 1996). If majority approval in a referendum is the only procedure required for constitutional amendment, the referendum serves as a majoritarian device; however, the only example of this kind of referendum in our set of democracies was President de Gaulle's extraconstitutional use of it in France. In all of the other cases, the referendum is prescribed in addition to legislative approval by ordinary or extraordinary majorities, making amendments harder to adopt and constitutions more rigid—and hence serving as an antimajoritarian device (Gallagher 1995).

This function of the referendum conflicts with the conventional view that the referendum is the most extreme majoritarian method of decision-making—that is, even more majoritarian than representative majoritarian democracy, since elected legislatures offer at least some opportunities for minorities to present their case in unhurried discussion and to engage in bargaining and logrolling. David Butler and Austin Ranney (1978, 36) state: "Because they cannot measure intensities of beliefs or work things out through discussion and discovery, referendums are bound to be more dangerous than representative assemblies to minority rights." Although Butler and Ranney's argument has considerable force in most situations, it clearly requires modification. Its use in the process of constitutional amendment, as a requirement in addition to legislative approval, is more anti-majoritarian than majoritarian: in particular, it offers dissatisfied minorities the opportunity to launch a campaign against the proposed amendment.

There is an additional important way in which referendums differ from the blunt majoritarian character that the conventional wisdom attributes to them. In fact, this happens when they assume their strongest form: in combination with the popular initiative. Switzerland is the prime example. Here the referendum and initiative give even very small minorities a chance to challenge any laws passed by the majority of the elected representatives. Even if this effort does not succeed, it forces the majority to pay the cost of a referendum campaign. Hence the potential calling of a referendum by a minority is a strong stimulus for the majority to be heedful of minority views. Franz Lehner (1984, 30) convincingly argues that in Switzerland "any coalition with a predictable and safe chance of winning has to include all parties and organizations that may be capable of calling for a successful referendum." The referendum-plus-initiative has thus reinforced two Swiss traditions: the broad four-party coalitions in the executive Federal Council and the search for legislative majorities on particular bills that are as close to unanimity as possible. Both the logic of the referendum-plus-initiative and the example of how it has worked in Switzerland support the conclusion that it can be seen as a strong consensus-inducing mechanism and the very opposite of a blunt majoritarian instrument (Jung 1996).

CHAPTER 13

Central Banks
Independence Versus Dependence

The fifth and last variable in the federal-unitary dimension concerns central banks and how much independence and power they enjoy. Central banks are key governmental institutions that, compared with the other main organs of government, tend to be neglected in political science. In single-country and comparative descriptions of democratic political systems, political scientists invariably cover the executive, the legislature, political parties, and elections, and often also interest groups, the court system, the constitutional amendment process, and central-noncentral government relations—but hardly ever the operation and power of the central bank.[1]

When central banks are strong and independent, they play a critical role in the policy process. For instance, Robert B. Reich (1997, 80), secretary of labor in the first Clinton administration, describes not President Clinton but Alan Greenspan, chairman of the Federal Reserve Board, as "the most powerful man in the world." Conversely, when central banks are dependent branches of the executive and hence relatively weak, this weakness is also

1. For instance, in the authoritative and widely used comparative politics textbook edited by Gabriel A. Almond and G. Bingham Powell (1996), central banks are not mentioned in the comparative section, and the twelve country studies contain only cursory references to the Bank of England and the Bank of Brazil—but not to the mighty German Bundesbank or the Federal Reserve System in the United States. Of course, *Democracies* did not cover central banks either!

a highly relevant attribute of the democratic system—just as the weakness of a legislature or the reluctance of a supreme court to use judicial review is a significant indicator of the kind of democracy to which these institutions belong. Giving central banks independent power is yet another way of dividing power and fits the cluster of divided-power characteristics (the second dimension) of the consensus model of democracy; central banks that are subservient to the executive fit the concentrated-power logic of majoritarian democracy.

Fortunately, economists have paid a great deal of attention to central banks and have developed precise measures of central bank autonomy that can be used for the purpose of this study: in particular, the index of legal central bank independence that Alex Cukierman, Steven B. Webb, and Bilin Neyapti (1994) have constructed for seventy-two industrialized and developing countries, including thirty-two of our thirty-six democracies, for the long period from 1950 to 1989. In addition, Cukierman, Webb, and Neyapti have proposed an alternative indicator, based on the turnover rate of the central bank governor, which is an especially good indicator of central bank independence in developing countries; and Vittorio Grilli, Donato Masciandaro, and Guido Tabellini (1991) have independently developed an index of the political and economic autonomy of central banks in eighteen developed countries. These three measures are combined into a comprehensive measure of central bank independence for our thirty-six democracies—a much more precise measure of this fifth variable than the four-point and five-point scales used for the measurement of the other federal-unitary variables.

The Duties and Powers of Central Banks

The most important task of central banks is the making of monetary policy—that is, the regulation of interest rates and the supply of money. Monetary policy has a direct effect on price stability and the control of inflation, and it indirectly, but also very strongly, affects levels of unemployment, economic growth, and fluctuations in the business cycle. Other duties that central banks frequently perform are managing the government's financial transactions; financing the government's budget deficits by buying government securities, making loans from their reserves, or printing money; financing development projects; regulating and supervising commercial banks; and, if necessary, bailing out insolvent banks and publicly owned enterprises. These other tasks may conflict with the task of controlling inflation, and the power of central banks over monetary policy can therefore be enhanced by not giving them these additional duties: "Although most governments recognize the long-term benefit of price stability, other goals often loom larger in the short run . . . Assuring price stability, therefore, usually requires ensuring that the central bank is not forced to perform these [other] functions, at least not when they would cause inflation" (Cukierman, Webb, and Neyapti 1994, 2).

Central banks and their role in monetary policy have become especially important since 1971 when President Nixon devalued the U.S. dollar—breaking the fixed link of the dollar to gold and of nondollar currencies to the dollar, fashioned in the Bretton Woods agreement of 1944. In the much more uncertain situation of floating exchange rates, central bank independence became an even more important tool to limit price instability. Central bank autonomy in most countries, however, was not greatly enhanced until after 1990. As Sylvia Maxfield (1997, 7–11) points out, the dramatic increases in independence that many countries, especially in Europe and Latin America, gave to their central banks in the 1990s were largely due to the Maastricht Treaty in 1992, which requires central bank independence as a condition for participating in the common European currency, and to the globalization of finance, which makes it important for developing countries to "signal their creditworthiness" to international investors.

Measuring the Independence of Central Banks

The powers and functions of central banks are usually defined by bank charters that are statute laws and not by means of constitutional provisions; nevertheless, these charters have tended to harden into "conventions with quasi-constitutional force" (Elster 1994, 68). Cukierman, Webb, and Neyapti (1994, 5–12) analyze sixteen variables concerning the legal independence of central banks, each coded from zero to one—the lowest to the highest level of independence. Their overall index of legal independence is a weighted average of these sixteen ratings. There are four clusters of variables: the appointment and tenure of the bank's governor (chief executive officer), policy formulation, central bank objectives, and limitations on lending.

To give a few examples, the highest (most independent) ratings are given to a governor whose term of office is eight years or longer, who cannot be dismissed, and who may not simultaneously hold other offices in government. The lowest (least independent) ratings are given to governors who are appointed for less than four years, who can be dismissed at the discretion of the executive, and who is not barred from holding another government appointment. As far as policy formulation is concerned, the highest ratings go to banks that have exclusive responsibility to formulate monetary policy and play an active role in the government's budgetary process; central banks that have no influence on monetary and budgetary policy are given the lowest ratings.

With regard to objectives, the highest rating is accorded when "price stability is the major or only objective in the charter, and the central bank has the final word in case of conflict with other government objectives." Medium ratings are given when "price stability is one goal [together] with other compatible objectives, such as a stable banking system," and, slightly lower, "when price stability is one goal, with potentially conflicting

Table 13.1   Central bank independence in thirty-six democracies,
1945–96

	Cukierman-Webb-Neyapti index	Grilli-Masciandaro-Tabellini index	Governors' turnover rate index	Mean
Germany	0.69	0.69	—	0.69
Switzerland	0.56	0.64	—	0.60
United States	0.48	0.64	—	0.56
Austria	0.63	0.48	—	0.55
Canada	0.45	0.58	—	0.52
Netherlands	0.42	0.53	—	0.48
Denmark	0.50	0.42	—	0.46
Mauritius	—	—	0.43	0.43
Australia	0.36	0.48	—	0.42
Papua New Guinea	0.36	—	0.47	0.42
Ireland	0.44	0.37	—	0.41
Malta	0.44	—	0.39	0.41
Bahamas	0.41	—	0.39	0.40
Barbados	0.38	—	0.43	0.40
Costa Rica	0.47	—	0.31	0.39
Israel	0.39	—	0.39	0.39
Trinidad	—	—	0.39	0.39
Greece	0.55	0.21	—	0.38
India	0.34	—	0.35	0.35

objectives, such as full employment." The lowest rating is given
when the goals stated in the charter do not include price stability. Finally, central banks are rated as independent when they
are allowed to lend only to the central government and when
they fully control the terms of lending; conversely, they are the
least independent when they can lend to all levels of government, to public enterprises, and to the private sector and when
the terms of lending are decided by the executive branch of
government.

Cukierman, Webb, and Neyapti rate central banks in each of
the four decades from the 1950s to the 1980s. The first column of
Table 13.1 contains either the averages of these four ratings or

Table 13.1 *Continued*

	Cukierman-Webb-Neyapti index	Grilli-Masciandaro-Tabellini index	Governors' turnover rate index	Mean
Jamaica	—	—	0.35	0.35
Iceland	0.34	—	—	0.34
Colombia	0.27	—	0.39	0.33
Luxembourg	0.33	—	—	0.33
Botswana	0.33	—	0.31	0.32
France	0.27	0.37	—	0.32
Venezuela	0.38	—	0.27	0.32
United Kingdom	0.30	0.32	—	0.31
Sweden	0.29	—	—	0.29
Finland	0.28	—	—	0.28
Portugal	0.41	0.16	—	0.28
Belgium	0.16	0.37	—	0.27
Italy	0.25	0.27	—	0.26
Japan	0.18	0.32	—	0.25
Spain	0.23	0.27	—	0.25
New Zealand	0.22	0.16	—	0.19
Norway	0.17	—	—	0.17

Source: Based on data in Cukierman, Webb, and Neyapti 1994, 40–57; Grilli, Masciandaro, and Tabellini 1991, 368–69; and data provided by Neville Francis, Hansraj Mathur, Ron May, and Ralph R. Premdas

the averages of the ratings for the relevant later decades in the case of countries that were not yet independent and democratic by the early 1950s. We can assume that these ratings are representative for the entire period of analysis of each of our democracies, although they do not include the 1990–96 period in which, as noted above, central bank independence was increased in several countries. However, these changes affect only a few short years: the new central bank charters of Colombia and Venezuela were not adopted until the very end of 1992, and legislation providing greater central bank autonomy was passed in Italy and Portugal in 1992, in Belgium, France, and Greece in 1993, and in Spain in 1994 (Maxfield 1997, 51–56, 62–63). The one similar change that took place several years earlier occurred in New Zealand in 1989, as noted in Chapter 2. In the decades before 1990, legal central bank independence was remarkably stable in most countries.

Four countries were not included in the Cukierman-Webb-Neyapti study: Jamaica, Mauritius, Papua New Guinea, and Trinidad. However, because Papua New Guinea's central bank charter was modeled after the Australian one, it can be assigned the same index as Australia's. Two other indexes can be used to make up for the missing data and also to take advantage of additional expert judgments in order to arrive at an overall index of central bank independence that is as accurate and valid as possible. One is the index of political and economic independence of central banks designed by Grilli, Masciandaro, and Tabellini (1991, 366–71) and applied by them to the central banks of eighteen industrialized countries. Although these three economists use the term "political and economic independence," they emphasize formal rules, and hence their index is, in principle, quite similar to the Cukierman-Webb-Neyapti index. They differ, however, with regard to several of the specific variables on which they focus and the weighting of these variables.

The third index is based on a simple variable—the rate of turnover in the governorship of the central bank during the 1980s—which Cukierman, Webb, and Neyapti (1994, 13–19, 37–42) found to be a better indicator of central bank independence and a better predictor of inflation rates for the less developed countries than their more complex legal measure: the greater the turnover rate of the central bank governor, the less the independence of the central bank. The two additional indexes were transformed to the same zero to one scale used for the Cukierman-Webb-Neyapti index.[2] They are shown in the

2. The empirical range of the Grilli-Masciandaro-Tabellini index for eighteen countries is from three to thirteen points, compared with the range of 0.16 to 0.69 of the Cukierman-Webb-Neyapti index for the same countries; in order to convert the former into the latter, three points were taken to be the equivalent of

second and third columns of Table 13.1. The two separate indexes that are available for 28 countries are strongly correlated—the coefficient is 0.54, significant at the 1 percent level—but they are far from identical. The differences in the indexes for Belgium, Greece, and Portugal especially are quite sizable. Both the overall similarity and the differences for particular cases justify the use of more than one index.

The fourth column of Table 13.1 shows the mean of the two separate indexes of independence for twenty-eight of the thirty-six central banks and the one index that is available for the remaining eight central banks; the values in the fourth column constitute the comprehensive index of central bank independence that will be used henceforth in this study. The thirty-six countries are listed in descending order of central bank independence. The index can theoretically range from one to zero, but the empirical range is only about half as large. Only five countries have indexes that are greater than 0.50—the point that in the Cukierman-Webb-Neyapti coding scheme represents semi-independence. The midpoint of the empirical range is 0.43, but the mean and median are lower—0.38 and 0.36, respectively—indicating that more countries are concentrated in the lower half of the empirical range. The German, Swiss, and American central banks head the list and are also generally regarded as the world's strongest, but even these banks do not always earn the highest scores. For instance, only the German Bundesbank governor has an eight-year term of office; in Switzerland, the term is six and in the United States four years (Capie, Goodhart, and Schnadt 1994, 58). The Bundesbank's mandated goal is to safeguard price stability, but it also has to support the general economic policy of the federal government

---

0.16; thirteen points as the equivalent of 0.69; and four to twelve points at commensurate places in between. The empirical range of governors' turnover was from five to zero turnovers, compared with a range of 0.27 to 0.47 for the same countries on the Cukierman-Webb-Neyapti index; the same procedure was used to convert the former into the latter.

(Lohmann 1998); in the United States, both price stability and full employment are central bank objectives; and price stability is not explicitly mentioned in the Swiss charter.

Federalism and Central Bank Independence

Central bank independence has been linked to several other institutional characteristics of democracies. Peter A. Hall (1994) argues that corporatist institutions facilitate central bank independence: they allow central banks to control inflation without having to pay the full price of higher unemployment, because coordinated wage bargaining can counteract the tendency for unemployment to increase. In our set of thirty-six democracies, however, there is little or no systematic relationship between the two. The correlation between the independence of the central bank and interest group pluralism is a weak and insignificant −0.07.

John B. Goodman (1991, 346) argues that central bank independence is mainly a function of the time horizons of the politicians who are in power: "Politicians generally wish to maintain a high degree of freedom in their actions. However, they will be willing to change the status of the central bank to bind the hands of their successors, a decision they will make when they expect a short tenure in office." Goodman's argument suggests that central banks should have less autonomy in majoritarian democracies where executives are stronger and more durable than in consensus democracies. However, the correlation between executive dominance and central bank independence is an insignificant −0.06.

A third suggestion of an institutional connection—between central bank independence and federalism—is much more fruitful (Banaian, Laney, and Willett 1986). The correlation between our indexes of federalism and decentralization on one hand and central bank independence on the other is a strong 0.57 (significant at the 1 percent level). The shape of the relationship is

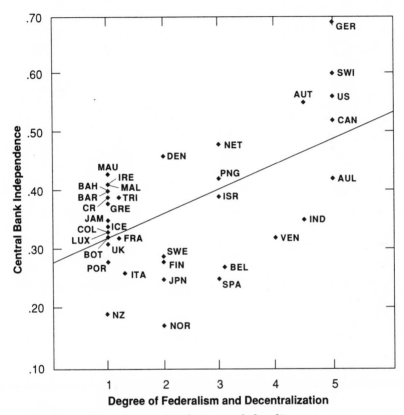

Fig. 13.1 The relationship between federalism-decentralization and central bank independence in thirty-six democracies, 1945–96

shown in Figure 13.1. The five central banks with the greatest independence all operate in federal systems: Germany, Switzerland, the United States, Austria, and Canada. In the rank order of Table 13.1, Australia is in ninth place, and India is approximately in the middle. Only the Venezuelan central bank clearly belongs to the bottom half according to its degree of independence; Venezuela was also the only federal system described as centralized in Chapter 10. The ninth federal system, Belgium, has one of the lowest indexes of bank independence, but Belgium did not become federal until 1993, and as discussed in Chapter 3, it made its central bank much more independent at about the same time. As is shown in the next chapter, central bank independence is also strongly correlated with the other three variables of the federal-unitary dimension.

CHAPTER 14

The Two-Dimensional Conceptual Map of Democracy

In this brief chapter I summarize the main findings of Chapters 5 through 13, which have dealt with each of the ten basic majoritarian versus consensus variables. I focus on two aspects of the "grand picture": the two-dimensional pattern formed by the relationships among the ten variables and the positions of each of the thirty-six democracies in this two-dimensional pattern. In addition, I explore the changes in these positions from the pre-1970 to the post-1971 period of twenty-six of the thirty-six democracies for which a sufficiently long time span is available in the first period.

The Two Dimensions

In Chapter 1, I previewed one of the most important general findings of this book: the clustering of the ten institutional variables along two clearly separate dimensions, which I have called the executives-parties and federal-unitary dimensions—although, as I explained in Chapter 1, it might be more accurate and theoretically more meaningful to call the two dimensions the joint-power and divided-power dimensions. In Chapters 5 through 13, too, I have repeatedly called attention to the close links among some of the variables within each cluster. Table 14.1 now presents the overall pattern by means of the correlation

Table 14.1 Correlation matrix of the ten variables distinguishing majoritarian from consensus democracy in thirty-six democracies, 1945–96

Variable 1: Effective number of parliamentary parties
Variable 2: Minimal winning one-party cabinets
Variable 3: Executive dominance
Variable 4: Electoral disproportionality
Variable 5: Interest group pluralism
Variable 6: Federalism-decentralization
Variable 7: Bicameralism
Variable 8: Constitutional rigidity
Variable 9: Judicial review
Variable 10: Central bank independence

	[1]	[2]	[3]	[4]	[5]	[6]	[7]	[8]	[9]	[10]
[1]	1.00									
[2]	−0.87**	1.00								
[3]	−0.71**	0.68**	1.00							
[4]	−0.50**	0.57**	0.33*	1.00						
[5]	−0.55**	0.68**	0.38*	0.56**	1.00					
[6]	0.26	−0.25	−0.23	−0.16	−0.28	1.00				
[7]	0.02	0.00	0.01	0.10	0.05	0.64**	1.00			
[8]	0.02	−0.06	−0.09	−0.02	−0.06	0.54**	0.35*	1.00		
[9]	−0.13	0.06	−0.05	0.26	0.20	0.48**	0.41**	0.39**	1.00	
[10]	−0.01	−0.14	−0.06	−0.06	−0.07	0.57**	0.34*	0.42**	0.39**	1.00

*Statistically significant at the 5 percent level (one-tailed test)
**Statistically significant at the 1 percent level (one-tailed test)

matrix for all ten variables. It shows strong relationships within each cluster and only weak connections between variables belonging to different clusters. All of the correlations within the two clusters are statistically significant: sixteen of the twenty at the 1 percent level and the remaining four at the 5 percent level; the correlation coefficients are shown in the two highlighted triangles in Table 14.1. In sharp contrast, none of the twenty-five correlations between variables in the different clusters, shown in the bottom left of the table, are statistically significant at either level.

The first cluster of variables has somewhat stronger interconnections than the second cluster: the averages of the absolute values of the correlation coefficients are 0.58 and 0.45, respectively. Within the first cluster, the percentage of minimal winning one-party cabinets is a particularly strong element: it has the highest correlations with the other variables. This finding is of great theoretical interest because, as argued earlier (in the beginning of Chapter 5), this variable can also be seen as conceptually close to the essence of the distinction between concentration of power and the joint exercise of power. The effective number of parliamentary parties is a second key component in this cluster. In the second cluster, the federalism and decentralization variable emerges as the strongest element. This finding is theoretically significant, too, because this variable can be seen as conceptually at the heart of the federal-unitary dimension.

An even better and more succinct summary of the relationships among the ten variables can be achieved by means of factor analysis. The general purpose of factor analysis is to detect whether there are one or more common underlying dimensions among several variables. The factors that are found can then be seen as "averages" of the closely related variables. Table 14.2 presents the results of the factor analysis of our ten basic variables. The values that are shown for each variable are the factor loadings, which may be interpreted as the correlation coefficients between the variable and the first and second factors detected by

Table 14.2   Varimax orthogonal rotated factor matrix of the ten variables distinguishing majoritarian from consensus democracy in thirty-six democracies, 1945–96

Variable	Factor I	Factor II
Effective number of parliamentary parties	−0.90	0.02
Minimal winning one-party cabinets	0.93	−0.07
Executive dominance	0.74	−0.10
Electoral disproportionality	0.72	0.09
Interest group pluralism	0.78	−0.01
Federalism-decentralization	−0.28	0.86
Bicameralism	0.06	0.74
Constitutional rigidity	−0.05	0.71
Judicial review	0.20	0.73
Central bank independence	−0.07	0.71

Note: The factor analysis is a principal components analysis with eigenvalues over 1.0 extracted

the factor analysis. The same two clusters emerge prominently from this analysis; they are also clearly separate clusters, because the factor analysis used an orthogonal rotation, which guarantees that the two factors are completely uncorrelated.

The factor loadings are very high within each of the two clusters and much lower—in fact, close to zero in most cases—outside of the clusters. The percentage of minimal winning one-party cabinets again turns out to be the strongest variable in the first dimension: its factor loading of 0.93 means that it almost coincides with the factor. The effective number of parties is an almost equally strong element with a factor loading of −0.90. And the federalism variable emerges once more as the strongest element in the second dimension with a factor loading of 0.86. The remaining factor loadings within the two clusters are lower but still impressively strong: all between 0.70 and 0.80.

The Conceptual Map of Democracy

The two-dimensional pattern formed by the ten basic variables allows us to summarize where the thirty-six individual countries are situated between majoritarian and consensus democracy. Their characteristics on each of the two sets of five variables can be averaged so as to form just two summary characteristics, and these can be used to place each of the democracies on the two-dimensional conceptual map of democracy shown in Figure 14.1.[1] The horizontal axis represents the executives-parties and the vertical axis the federal-unitary dimension. Each unit on these axes represents one standard deviation; high values indicate majoritarianism and low values consensus. On the executives-parties dimension, all countries are within two standard deviations from the middle; on the federal-unitary dimension, two countries—Germany and the United States—are at the greater distance of almost two and a half standard deviations below the middle. The exact scores of each of the thirty-six countries on the two dimensions can be found in Appendix A.[2]

Most of the prototypical cases of majoritarian and consensus democracy discussed in Chapters 2 and 3 are in the expected positions on the map. The United Kingdom and New Zealand are in the top right corner. The United Kingdom is slightly more majoritarian on the executives-parties dimension, but New Zealand is a great deal more so on the federal-unitary dimension and its overall position is therefore more extreme—in line with the proposition that, until 1996, New Zealand was the purer

1. In order for the five variables in each of the two clusters to be averaged, they first had to be standardized (so as to have a mean of 0 and a standard deviation of 1), because they were originally measured on quite different scales. Moreover, their signs had to be adjusted so that high values on each variable represented either majoritarianism or consensus and low values the opposite characteristic; for the purpose of constructing the conceptual map, I arbitrarily gave the high values to majoritarianism (which entailed reversing the signs of the effective number of parties and of all five variables in the federal-unitary dimension). After averaging these standardized variables, the final step was to standardize the averages so that each unit on the two axes represents one standard deviation.

2. Note, however, that in Appendix A all values on the two dimensions are expressed in terms of degrees of consensus democracy; these can be converted easily into degrees of majoritarian democracy by reversing the signs.

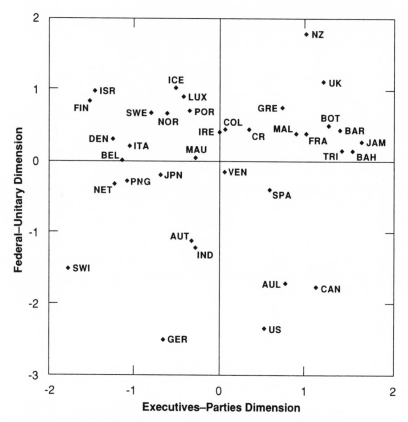

Fig. 14.1 The two-dimensional conceptual map of democracy

example of the Westminster model. Chapter 2 used Barbados as an exemplar of majoritarian democracy on the executives-parties dimension only and not as typically majoritarian on the federal-unitary dimension; its location below the United Kingdom and New Zealand but also somewhat farther to the right fits this description well. Switzerland is, as expected, in the bottom left corner but not quite as far down as several other countries, mainly due to its one nonconsensual characteristic—the absence of judicial review. It is still the clearest consensual prototype, however, because it is more than one and a half standard deviations away from the center on both dimensions, whereas Germany—which the map suggests could also have served as the prototype—is located far down but less than one standard deviation left of the center.[3] Belgium is the one exemplar case not to be in an extreme position, but this is not unexpected either because it only became fully federal in 1993; it does, however, have a strong consensual position on the executives-parties dimension.

The two-dimensional map also reveals prototypes of the two combinations of consensus and majoritarian characteristics. In the top left corner, Israel represents the combination of consensus democracy on the executives-parties dimension (in particular, frequent oversized coalition cabinets, multipartism, highly proportional PR elections, and interest group corporatism) but, albeit somewhat less strongly, majoritarianism on the federal-unitary dimension (an unwritten constitution and a unicameral parliament, moderated, however, by intermediate characteristics with regard to federalism and central bank independence). In the bottom right-hand corner, Canada is the strongest candidate for the opposite prototype of majoritarianism on the executives-parties and consensus on the federal-unitary dimension: on one hand, dominant one-party cabinets, a roughly two-and-a-third party system, plurality elections, and interest group pluralism, but on the other hand, strong federalism and judicial review, a rigid constitution, an independent central bank, and a bicameral parliament (albeit of only medium strength). The United States is located in the same corner and is stronger on

3. However, Germany's location on the clearly consensual side of both dimensions does confirm Manfred G. Schmidt's (1996, 95) characterization of Germany as "the grand coalition state"; he writes that "it is almost impossible in the Federal Republic not to be governed by a formal or informal Grand Coalition of the major established parties and a formal or hidden Grand Coalition of federal government and state governments."

the federal-unitary dimension—but not exceptionally majoritarian on the executives-parties dimension, especially due to the
executive-legislative balance in its presidential system.

Explanations

Are any general patterns revealed by the distribution of the
thirty-six democracies on the map? Is there, for instance, any correspondence between the conceptual and geographical maps?
There does appear to be such a relationship as far as the consensus side of the executives-parties dimension is concerned: most
continental European countries are located on the left side of
the map, including the five Nordic countries, which have been
called "the consensual democracies" with a "distinctively Scandinavian culture of consensus and . . . structures for conciliation
and arbitration" (Elder, Thomas, and Arter 1988, 221). On the
right-hand side, the three Latin American democracies are close
together and only slightly to the right of the center. Considerably
farther to the right, the four Caribbean countries are located near
one another. But most of the countries on the right-hand side of
the conceptual map are geographically distant from one another.
Instead, the striking feature that many of these countries, including those in the Caribbean, have in common is that they are
former British colonies. In fact, it is the presence or absence of a
British political heritage that appears to explain the distribution
on the left and right side of the executives-parties dimension
better than any geographical factor.

There are several obvious exceptions to this twofold division
based on the influence of a British heritage. The three Latin
American countries constitute one exception but not a major
exception, because they are located more in the center than
on the right. Farther to the right, however, are Spain, Greece,
and especially France. In view of French president de Gaulle's
deeply felt and frequently expressed antagonism toward *les*

anglo-saxons, it is ironic that the republic he created is the most Anglo-Saxon of any of the continental European democracies. There are exceptions on the left side of this dimension, too: India, Israel, and Mauritius emerged from British colonial rule, and Papua New Guinea was ruled by Australia (itself a former British colony). However, what also unites these four countries is that they are plural societies—suggesting that it is the degree of pluralism that explains why countries are consensual rather than majoritarian on the executives-parties dimension. Of the eighteen plural and semiplural societies listed in Table 4.3, twelve are located on the left side of the map.

Regression analysis confirms that both explanations are important but also that British political heritage is the stronger influence. The correlation between British heritage—a dummy variable with a value of one for Britain itself and for the fifteen countries it formerly ruled, and zero for the other twenty countries—and majoritarian democracy on the executives-parties dimension has a coefficient of 0.54 (significant at the 1 percent level); the correlation with degree of plural society—plural versus semiplural versus nonplural—is -0.32 (significant at the 5 percent level). When both of the independent variables are entered into the regression equation, the multiple correlation coefficient is 0.65, and both variables are now significant explanatory variables at the 1 percent level. Finally, in a stepwise regression analysis, British heritage explains 28 percent of the variance in majoritarian democracy, and the degree of pluralism adds another 11 percent for a total of 39 percent of the variance explained (measured in terms of the adjusted R-squared).[4]

4. It can be argued that three additional countries—Austria, Germany, and Japan—should also be coded as having had a strong degree of British, or rather Anglo-American, influence on their political systems. The postwar Japanese constitution was drafted by General Douglas MacArthur's staff and was largely inspired by the British model. American and British occupation authorities also oversaw the reestablishment of democracy in Germany and Austria, and they had an especially strong and direct hand in the shaping of the postwar German

The degree to which countries are plural societies also appears to explain the location of the thirty-six democracies on the federal-unitary dimension. Of the thirteen countries situated below the middle (including Belgium, which, with a score of -0.01, is barely below the middle), ten are plural or semiplural societies. An additional explanation suggested by the map is population size. The three largest countries—India, the United States, and Japan—are all located in the bottom part of the map, and of the fifteen countries with populations greater than ten million, ten are in the bottom part. This potential explanation is bolstered by Robert A. Dahl and Edward R. Tufte's (1973, 37) finding that size is related to federalism and decentralization, the key variable in the federal-unitary dimension: "the larger the country, the more decentralized its government, whether federal or not."

Regression analysis again confirms both of these impressions. The correlation coefficients are -0.50 for population size (logged) and -0.40 for degree of pluralism (both significant at the 1 percent level). In the multiple regression, both remain significant explanatory variables (although pluralism only at the 5 percent level), and the multiple correlation coefficient is 0.57. Population size by itself explains 23 percent of the variance, and pluralism adds another 6 percent for a total of 29 percent explained variance. The degree of pluralism is again the weaker variable, but it can be regarded as the strongest overall explanation because it can explain a significant portion of the variation in the locations of the thirty-six democracies on both dimensions.[5] Although the joint-power and divided-power as-

---

democratic system (Muravchik 1991, 91–114). However, assigning these three countries a code of 1 on the British heritage variable weakens all of the correlations; for instance, the total variance explained goes down from 39 to 28 percent.

5. British political heritage is not related to the second dimension. Neither is population size related to the first dimension—contradicting Dahl and Tufte's (1973, 91) argument that "the small system, being more homogeneous, is . . .

pects of consensus democracy are conceptually and empirically distinct dimensions, they represent complementary institutional mechanisms for the accommodation of deep societal divisions. This finding strengthens Sir Arthur Lewis's recommendation, stated in Chapter 3, that both dimensions of consensus democracy—in particular, Lewis advocates power-sharing cabinets and federalism—are needed in plural societies.

Shifts on the Conceptual Map

The locations of the thirty-six democracies on the conceptual map are *average* locations over a long period: close to fifty years for the twenty older democracies and a minimum of nineteen years for the three newest democracies (see Table 4.1). These averages conceal any large or small changes that may have taken place. Obviously, political systems can and do change; for instance, in previous chapters I called attention to changes in the party, electoral, and interest group systems of the thirty-six democracies as well as in their degrees of decentralization, the cameral structure of their legislatures, and the activism of their judicial review. To what extent have these changes added up to shifts in the direction of greater majoritarianism or greater consensus on either or both of the dimensions?

To explore this question, I divided the period 1945–96 in two roughly equal parts: the period until the end of 1970 and the period from 1971 to the middle of 1996. For countries with a sufficiently long time span in the first period, scores on both of the dimensions were calculated for each period. This could be done for the twenty countries covered since the middle or late

likely to be more consensual [and that] the larger system, being more heterogeneous, is . . . likely to be more conflictual." Our thirty-six democracies also differ a great deal with regard to level of development, but this variable (measured in terms of the human development index) is not related to either of the two dimensions.

1940s and for six additional countries: Costa Rica, France, Colombia, Venezuela, Trinidad, and Jamaica.[6] Figure 14.2 shows the shifts that took place in these twenty-six democracies from the pre-1970 period to the post-1971 period. The arrows point to the positions in the later period.

The general picture is one of many relatively small shifts, but no radical transformations: not a single country changed from a clearly majoritarian democracy to a clearly consensual democracy or vice versa. There are more shifts from left to right or vice versa than from higher to lower locations or vice versa—a pattern that reflects the greater stability of the institutional characteristics of the federal-unitary dimension because these are more often anchored in constitutional provisions. The arrows appear to point in different directions almost randomly, suggesting that there was no general trend toward more majoritarianism or consensus. This suggestion is largely correct, although there were actually tiny shifts toward greater consensus on both dimensions: an average of 0.03 of a standard deviation on the first and an average of 0.06 on the second dimension—such small shifts that they deserve to be disregarded.[7]

Although the overall pattern is one of great stability, some countries shifted considerably more than others. The least change took place in the United States and the most in Belgium. In addition to Belgium, sizable shifts also occurred in Germany, Jamaica, Sweden, Norway, France, and Venezuela. The shift toward greater majoritarianism in Germany reflects the change from frequent oversized cabinets in the first period to mainly minimal winning cabinets in the second period, from short-

6. Costa Rica is covered from 1953 on; France, Colombia, and Venezuela from 1958; Trinidad from 1961; and Jamaica from 1962. Botswana, Barbados, and Malta were not included in this analysis because the time span from the beginning of their coverage in 1965 and 1966 until 1970 was much too short; the remaining seven countries became independent and democratic, or were re-democratized, after 1971.

7. Because the scores for the second period (1971–96) may be of special interest to other researchers, they are included in Appendix A.

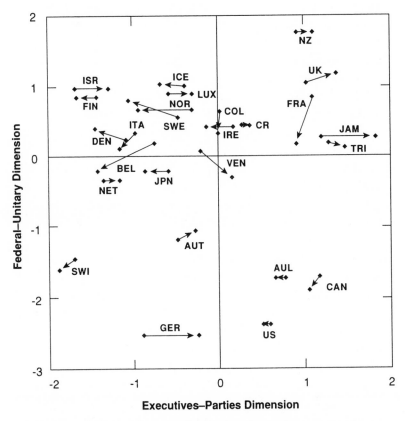

Fig. 14.2   Shifts on the two-dimensional map by twenty-six democracies from the period before 1971 to the period 1971–96

lived to longer-lived cabinets, and to a slight reduction in the effective number of parties—only slightly counterbalanced by more proportional election results in the second period. Jamaica moved in the same direction and about the same distance, but from an already strongly majoritarian early period; its party system changed from roughly a two-party system to a one-and-a-half party system, and the disproportionality of its elections escalated from about 9 percent to more than 21 percent. Norway and Sweden moved in the other direction: more minority and coalition cabinets, shorter cabinet duration, increases in the effective number of parties, and lower disproportionality; Sweden's slight shift on the federal-unitary dimension mainly reflects its adoption of unicameralism in 1970.

Belgium, France, and Venezuela experienced significant changes on both dimensions. Belgium moved down, mainly due to the adoption of judicial review, and to the left, largely caused by an increase in oversized cabinets and a sharp increase in multipartism from a roughly three-party to a five-and-a-half party system. Most of France's move was toward greater consensus on the federal-unitary dimension, reflecting its more rigid constitution and active judicial review from 1974 on and its decentralization after 1981—counterbalanced, however, by a decrease in the independence of the Bank of France; the small shift to the left was primarily caused by small increases in multipartism and proportionality. Finally, Venezuela became more majoritarian on the executives-parties dimension mainly as a result of having fewer coalition and oversized cabinets and the change from an approximately four-party to a three-party system; the shift away from majoritarianism on the federal-unitary dimension reflects the substantial increase in the legal independence of the central bank.

All of the other countries experienced less change, although these changes may loom larger when compared with changes in the other direction in neighboring countries. For instance, Peter Mair (1994, 99) has argued that, while the trend toward less consensus democracy in the Netherlands on the executives-parties dimension since the early 1970s may not have been all that impressive by itself, "many of the other European democracies seem to have adopted a more consensual style of politics"—rendering the Dutch shift away from consensus a more notable development in relative terms. Figure 14.2 bears out Mair's point: especially compared with the shifts toward consensus by all of the smaller democracies in northwestern Europe (except

Luxembourg), the change in the other direction by the Nether-lands presents a sizable contrast.

The second-period (1971–96) scores of the twenty-six de-mocracies on the two dimensions, introduced in this chapter, are used again in the next two chapters (together with the scores for the other ten democracies that are covered from only a few years before or after 1970 on). These chapters analyze the conse-quences that type of democracy may have for the effectiveness, democratic character, and general policy orientation of govern-ments. Reliable data on these variables are generally available only for recent decades; moreover, focusing on the more recent period enables us to include as many of the thirty-six democ-racies as possible in the analysis. It therefore also makes sense to measure the degrees of consensus or majoritarianism of the twenty-six longer-term democracies in terms of their charac-teristics in the second period.

CHAPTER 15

Macro-Economic Management and the Control of Violence

Does Consensus Democracy Make a Difference?

In this chapter and the next I deal with the "so what?" question: does the difference between majoritarian and consensus democracy make a difference for the operation of democracy, especially for how well democracy works? The conventional wisdom—which is often stated in terms of the relative advantages of PR versus plurality and majority elections but which can be extended to the broader contrast between consensus and majoritarian democracy along the executives-parties dimension—is that there is a trade-off between the quality and the effectiveness of democratic government. On one hand, the conventional wisdom concedes that PR and consensus democracy may provide more accurate representation and, in particular, better minority representation and protection of minority interests, as well as broader participation in decision-making. On the other hand, the conventional wisdom maintains that the one-party majority governments typically produced by plurality elections are more decisive and hence more effective policymakers. This view is reflected in the adage, recently restated by Samuel Beer (1998, 25), that "representative government must not only represent, it must also govern"—with its clear implication that representativeness comes at the expense of effective government.

Conventional wisdom has long been widely accepted without adequate empirical examination, perhaps because its logic appears to be so strong that no test was thought to be needed. For instance, I have already called attention (in Chapter 5) to Lowell's (1896) assertion that it was a self-evident "axiom" that one-party majority cabinets were needed for effective policy-making. The first part of the conventional wisdom, which concerns democratic quality, is discussed in the next chapter. In this chapter I critically examine the second part, which posits a link between majoritarian democracy and effective decision-making.

Hypotheses and Preliminary Evidence

The theoretical basis for Lowell's axiom is certainly not implausible: concentrating political power in the hands of a narrow majority can promote unified, decisive leadership and hence coherent policies and fast decision-making. But there are several counterarguments. Majoritarian governments may be able to make decisions faster than consensus governments, but fast decisions are not necessarily wise decisions. In fact, the opposite may be more valid, as many political theorists—notably the venerable authors of the *Federalist Papers* (Hamilton, Jay, and Madison 1788)—have long argued. The introduction of the so-called poll tax, a new local government tax in Britain in the 1980s, is a clear example of a policy, now universally acknowledged to have been a disastrous policy, that was the product of fast decision-making; in all probability, the poll tax would never have been introduced had it been more carefully, and more slowly, debated (Butler, Adonis, and Travers 1994).

Moreover, the supposedly coherent policies produced by majoritarian governments may be negated by the alternation of these governments; this alternation from left to right and vice versa may entail sharp changes in economic policy that are too frequent and too abrupt. In particular, S. E. Finer (1975) has forcefully argued that successful macroeconomic management requires not so much a *strong* hand as a *steady* one and that PR and coalition governments are better able to provide steady, centrist policy-making.[1] Policies supported by a broad consensus, furthermore, are more likely to be carried out successfully and to remain on course than policies imposed by a "decisive" government against the wishes of important sectors of society. Finally, for maintaining civil peace in divided societies, conciliation and compromise—goals that require the greatest possible inclusion of contending groups in the decision-making process—are probably much more important than making snap decisions. These counterarguments appear to be at least slightly stronger than the argument in favor of majoritarian government that is based narrowly on the speed and coherence of decision-making.

The empirical evidence is mixed. Peter Katzenstein (1985) and Ronald Rogowski (1987) have shown that small countries adopted PR and corporatist practices to compensate for the disadvantages of their small size in international trade; that is, these consensus elements served as sources of strength instead of weakness. Richard Rose (1992) and Francis G. Castles (1994) find no significant differences in economic growth, inflation, and unemployment between PR and non-PR systems among the industrialized democracies. Nouriel Roubini and Jeffrey D. Sachs (1989) do find a clear connection between multiparty coalition government and governments with a short average tenure—both characteristics of consensus democracy—on one hand and large budget deficits on the other; their methods and conclusions, however, have been challenged by Stephen A. Borrelli and Terry J. Royed (1995) and by Sung Deuk Hahm, Mark S. Kamlet, and David C. Mowery (1996). Markus M. L. Crepaz (1996) finds that, in the OECD countries, consensual institutions are not related to economic growth but do have significantly favorable effects on inflation, unemployment, and the number of working days lost as a result of industrial unrest. Finally, G. Bingham Powell (1982) finds that "representational"

1. That PR also provides greater electoral justice is an added bonus but, in Finer's eyes, not the main advantage.

democracies—similar to what I call consensus democracies—
have a better record than majoritarian democracies with regard
to controlling violence.[2]

The above tests all had to do with macroeconomic management and the control of violence. These are excellent performance indicators both because they involve crucial functions of
government and because precise quantitative data are available.
I therefore also focus on these two sets of variables. Because the
theoretical arguments and the empirical evidence are mixed but
give a slight edge to consensus democracy, my working hypothesis is that consensus democracy produces better results—but
without the expectation that the differences will be very strong
and significant. Another reason not to expect major differences
is that economic success and the maintenance of civil peace are
not solely determined by government policy. As far as British
macroeconomic policy is concerned, for instance, Rose (1992,
11) points out that "many influences upon the economy are
outside the control of the government. . . . Decisions taken independently of government by British investors, industrialists,
consumers and workers can frustrate the intentions of the government of the day. In an open international economy, Britain is
increasingly influenced too by decisions taken in Japan, Washington, New York, Brussels, or Frankfurt."

Rose's point should obviously not be exaggerated: the fact
that governments are not in full control does not mean that they
have no control at all. When the economy performs well—when
economic growth is high, and inflation, unemployment, and

2. Powell (1982) also examines the performance of democracies with regard
to voter turnout and government stability. He finds that voter participation in
elections is better in the representational systems—a topic to which I return in
Chapter 16—but that majoritarian democracies have a better record on government stability. Note, however, that Powell's measure of government stability is
executive durability. As discussed in Chapter 7, this kind of durability is indeed
a good indicator of political power, but executive strength does not necessarily
spell effective policy-making. A strong executive mainly means relatively weak
legislative power, and an imbalance in executive-legislative power favoring the
executive is simply part of the syndrome of majoritarian characteristics.

budget deficits are low—governments routinely claim credit for this happy state of affairs. And voters are known to reward government parties in good economic times and to punish them when the economy is in poor shape. The Maastricht Treaty, concluded in 1992 among the members of the European Union, was also based on the assumption that governments do have the capacity to control macroeconomic forces because it obligated the signatories inter alia to keep inflation low—defined as not exceeding the average of the three countries with the lowest inflation rates by more than 1.5 percent—and to keep their national budget deficits below 3 percent of gross domestic product.

Rose's argument, however, does point up the need to take these other influences into account. To the extent that they are identifiable and measurable variables, they should be controlled for in the statistical analyses. For economic performance, the level of economic development is such a potentially important explanatory variable. For the control of violence, the degree of societal division should be controlled for, because deep divisions make the maintenance of public order and peace more difficult. A third variable whose influence must be checked is population, if only because our democracies differ widely in this respect. It may also be hypothesized that large countries face greater problems of public order than smaller ones. In other respects, it is not clear whether size is a favorable or an unfavorable factor. Large countries obviously have greater power in international relations, which they can use, for instance, to gain economic benefits for their citizens. And yet, greater international influence also means more responsibility and hence higher expenses, especially for military purposes.

Fortuitous events may also affect economic success, such as the good luck experienced by Britain and Norway when they discovered oil in the North Sea. The effects of such fortuitous events as well as external influences that cannot be clearly identified and controlled for can be minimized when economic performance is examined over a long period and for many coun-

tries. These two desiderata are frequently in conflict: extending
the period of analysis often means that some countries have to be
excluded. And they may both conflict with a third desidera-
tum—that the most accurate and reliable data be used. Therefore, in the analysis below, I usually report the results for different periods, different sets of countries, and different types of
data in order to provide as complete and robust a test of the hy-
potheses as possible. Finally, in testing the influence of the type
of democracy on the economic performance variables, I limit the
potential disturbing impact of external forces by excluding the
five smallest democracies with populations of less than half
a million—the Bahamas, Barbados, Iceland, Luxembourg and
Malta—from the analysis because these small countries are obviously extremely vulnerable to international influences.

Consensus Democracy and Successful
Macro-Economic Management

Table 15.1 shows the results of the bivariate regression analyses of the effect of consensus democracy on six groups of macroeconomic variables (as well as on four indicators of violence,
discussed in the next section). The independent variable is the
degree of consensus democracy on the executives-parties dimension; because all of the economic variables are for the 1970s
or later years, the consensus variable used is the degree of consensus democracy in the period 1971–96. The estimated regression coefficient is the increase or decrease in the dependent
variable for each unit increase in the independent variable—in
our case, each increase by one standard deviation of consensus
democracy. Because the range in the degrees of consensus democracy is close to four standard deviations (see Figure 14.1),
the distance between the "average" consensus democracy and
the "average" majoritarian democracy is about two standard deviations. Therefore, in answer to the question "How much difference does consensus democracy make?" the reply can be—

roughly—twice the value of the estimated regression coefficient. For instance, based on the first row of Table 15.1, the effect of consensus democracy on economic growth is approximately twice the estimated regression coefficient of −0.07 percent, or about one-seventh (0.14) of a percent less annual growth than majoritarian democracy.

Because the table reports bivariate regression results, the standardized regression coefficient in the second column equals the correlation coefficient. The statistical significance of the correlations depends on the absolute t-value, shown in the third column, and the number of cases, shown in the fourth column. Whether the correlations are significant is indicated by asterisks; three levels of significance are reported, including the least demanding 10 percent level. If the number of countries is twenty-one or lower, the countries are usually the OECD countries and the data are usually the most reliable OECD data; when the number is above twenty-one, the developing countries are also included to the extent that the necessary data on them are available.

The first set of three dependent variables are average annual economic growth figures in three periods and for three sets of countries. The first is for thirty-one countries, that is, all of our democracies except the five with the smallest populations. The majoritarian democracies appear to have a slightly better record with 0.14 percent greater annual growth than the consensus democracies (twice the estimated regression coefficient, as explained above)—obviously a very small and completely insignificant difference. This small difference is reduced to zero when the level of development, measured in terms of the human development index, is introduced into the equation; the level of development is itself highly correlated with economic growth (at the 1 percent level), with the less developed countries having higher growth rates. Introducing population size (logged) as an additional control does not affect the results. Among the thirty-one countries, Botswana is an unusual outlier with an astounding 9.5 percent average annual growth rate in the fourteen years from 1980 to 1993—and it is this case that is responsible for the overall higher economic growth of the majoritarian democracies. When Botswana is removed from the analysis, the consensus democracies actually show better growth—by approximately half of a percent (the estimated regression coefficient is 0.24 percent)—which is not affected when the level of development is controlled for, but the relationship is not statistically significant.

The second economic growth figure is for eighteen OECD countries from 1970 to 1995, and the third for the shorter period 1980–95 but for three additional countries: Spain, Portugal, and Greece, which became democratic during the 1970s. The majoritarian democracies again appear to have a slightly better record with 0.28 percent and 0.14 percent higher growth, respectively, in the two periods. The first percentage is reduced to 0.17 percent when the level of development and population size, which are not significant themselves, are controlled for, but the second percentage is not affected. The positive relationships between majoritarianism and growth remain, but they are obviously very small and not statistically significant.

Average annual inflation levels are again reported for different sets of countries and periods, and also in terms of two measures: the GDP deflator and the consumer price index. The consumer price index is the more widely used measure, but the GDP deflator is the more comprehensive index because it measures inflation in the entire economy instead of merely consumer items; the two measures, however, are usually not far apart. The consensus democracies have the better record regardless of the differences in periods, countries, and measures used, and two of the bivariate relationships are statistically significant at the 10 percent level. The greatest difference in inflation levels occurs in the period 1980–93 period for thirty-one countries: the typical consensus democracy has about 3.7 percentage points less inflation than the typical majoritarian democracy. Higher

Table 15.1 Bivariate regression analyses of the effect of consensus democracy (executives-parties dimension) on nineteen macroeconomic performance variables and on four indicators of violence

	Estimated regression coefficient	Standardized regression coefficient	Absolute t-value	Countries (N)
Economic growth (1980–93)	−0.07	−0.04	0.22	31
Economic growth (1970–95)	−0.14	−0.20	0.81	18
Economic growth (1980–95)	−0.07	−0.13	0.57	21
GDP deflator (1980–93)	−1.87*	−0.28	1.58	31
GDP deflator (1970–95)	−0.51	−0.25	1.04	18
GDP deflator (1980–95)	−1.01	−0.28	1.26	21
Consumer price index (1970–95)	−0.56	−0.30	1.25	18
Consumer price index (1980–95)	−1.13*	−0.31	1.44	21
Unemployment, standardized (1971–95)	−0.70	−0.35	1.22	13
Unemployment, unstandardized (1971–95)	−0.69	−0.27	1.13	18
Unemployment, standardized (1980–95)	−1.38*	−0.38	1.42	14
Unemployment, unstandardized (1980–95)	−1.19*	−0.32	1.45	21

Strike activity (1970–94)	−39.02	−0.23	0.95	18
Strike activity (1980–94)	−71.99	−0.26	1.28	25
Budget deficits (1970–95)	−0.07	−0.02	0.09	16
Budget deficits (1980–95)	−0.41	−0.12	0.48	19
GLB freedom index (1993–95)	−0.14	−0.16	0.89	32
HJK freedom index (1996)	0.04	0.09	0.52	35
Freedom House index (1996)	0.04	0.01	0.07	26
Riots (1948–82)	−0.40	−0.12	0.51	19
Riots (1963–82)	−1.26***	−0.55	3.14	25
Political deaths (1948–82)	−2.62*	−0.33	1.42	19
Political deaths (1963–82)	−35.37**	−0.39	2.03	25

*Statistically significant at the 10 percent level (one-tailed test)
**Statistically significant at the 5 percent level (one-tailed test)
***Statistically significant at the 1 percent level (one-tailed test)

Source: Based on data in United Nations Development Programme 1996, 186–87, 208; United Nations Development Programme 1997, 202–3, 223; OECD 1990, 194; OECD 1991, 208–9; OECD 1995, 22–23; OECD 1996a, A4, A17, A19, A24–A25, A33; OECD 1996b, 22–23; International Labour Organization 1996 (and earlier volumes); Gwartney, Lawson, and Block 1996, xxi; Holmes, Johnson, and Kirkpatrick 1997, xxix–xxxii; Messick 1996, 12–14; Taylor and Jodice 1983, 1:91–93, 2:33–36, 48–51; Taylor 1986

levels of development and, more weakly, population size are associated with lower inflation, but when these variables are controlled for, the negative relationship between consensus democracy and inflation remains significant.

For the OECD countries, there is a statistically significant negative bivariate correlation between consensus democracy and inflation in the period 1980–95 when the consumer price index is used to measure inflation. When the level of development and population size are controlled for, all of the correlations become statistically significant: at the 5 percent level in the period 1970–95 and at the 1 percent level in the period 1980–95. Two countries are outliers with unusually high average inflation rates: Italy in the period 1970–95 with a GDP deflator of 11.4 percent and consumer price inflation of 10.5 percent, and Greece in the period 1980–95 with inflation percentages of 16.9 and 17.8 percent according to the two measures. When these countries are removed from the analysis, however, and with the controls still in place, all four correlations remain significant, three at the 1 percent level.

Unemployment statistics are available for the OECD countries, and Table 15.1 reports the results for the usual two periods and for two measures: the standardized unemployment percentages, which are fully comparable across the different countries but are available for fewer countries, and the unstandardized and hence somewhat less reliable percentages. Here again, the consensus democracies have the better record and the two bivariate correlations for the period 1980–95 are significant at the 10 percent level. However, Spain had exceptionally high unemployment in the period 1980–95—annual averages of 18.4 and 18.8 percent according to the standardized and unstandardized measures, respectively—and when it is removed from the analysis, the relationships are no longer significant. Controlling for the level of development and population size strengthens all of the correlations slightly but not enough to give them statistical significance. However, all of the relationships remain negative, indicating that the consensus democracies performed at least slightly better.

Strike activity is measured in terms of working days lost per thousand workers per year. The differences between countries on this variable are huge; in the period 1970–94, for instance, the numbers for Italy and Canada were 570 and 497 compared with 1 and 5 for Switzerland and Austria. The countries included in the years 1970–94 are mainly OECD countries but also Israel. For the period 1980–94, not only Spain, Portugal, and Greece but also India, Costa Rica, Mauritius, and Trinidad were added. The estimated regression coefficients give the impression of a considerably better record for the consensus democracies compared with the majoritarian countries: they lost about 78 and 144 fewer working days per thousand workers in the two periods. The differences are not statistically significant, however, mainly because there are several big exceptions to the tendency of consensus countries to be less strike-prone than majoritarian democracies: especially majoritarian France with relatively few strikes and mainly consensual Finland and Italy with high strike levels (see also Cornwall 1990, 120–21). Controlling for the level of development and population size barely affects these relationships.[3]

There are also large differences between countries with regard to budget deficits. Italy had the highest annual deficits in both periods—9.7 and 10.4 percent of gross domestic product—whereas Norway and Finland had, on average, slight budget surpluses. Overall, the consensus democracies show a somewhat

3. I should point out that the type of democracy and strike levels are not defined completely independently of each other. I relied on Siaroff's (1998) measure of the degree of interest group pluralism and corporatism, which is based in part on differential strike levels in different countries; and the degree of corporatism is a component of the degree of consensus democracy. However, only one-eighth of Siaroff's measure is based on strikes, and only one-fifth of the degree of corporatism goes into the overall measure of consensus democracy. Hence, only 2.5 percent of the degree of consensus democracy is defined in terms of low strike levels.

better performance, but the differences are not great and not statistically significant. Controlling for the level of development and population size strengthens the correlations considerably, but not enough to make them statistically significant.

Table 15.1 also reports the correlations between consensus democracy and three economic freedom indexes—not because economic freedom itself is an appropriate indicator of macro-economic performance but because many economists believe that long-term economic growth depends on it. The three indexes were independently developed by James Gwartney, Robert Lawson, and Walter Block (1996) and by Kim R. Holmes, Bryan T. Johnson, and Melanie Kirkpatrick (1997) for most of the countries of the world, including most of our thirty-six democracies, and by Freedom House for the larger countries (Messick 1996). The results are mixed: consensus democracy is negatively correlated with the first index and positively with the other two, but the negative correlation is the strongest. However, even this correlation is far from statistically significant.[4]

The results of these tests of macroeconomic management can be summarized as follows: the evidence with regard to economic growth and economic freedom is mixed, but with regard to all of the other indicators of economic performance, the consensus democracies have a slightly better record and a significantly better record as far as inflation is concerned.

Consensus Democracy and the Control of Violence

The last four performance variables shown in Table 15.1 are measures of violence: numbers of riots and numbers of deaths

4. The HJK index ranges from one (the highest economic freedom) to five (the least economic freedom). I reversed the signs so that high values would indicate high degrees of economic freedom. The GLB index is measured on a ten-point and the Freedom House index on a seventeen-point scale. The three indexes are highly correlated: r=0.81 between the GLB and HJK indices, r=0.85 between HJK and Freedom House, and r=0.58 between GLB and Freedom House.

from political violence per million people. These data are only available for the period from 1948 to 1982. A separate shorter period, from 1963 to 1982, was constructed to be able to include countries that were not yet independent and democratic before 1963. Both the longer and shorter periods overlap the two separate periods (1945–70 and 1971–96) for which degrees of consensus democracy were calculated; therefore, the independent variable for this part of the analysis is the degree of consensus democracy in the entire period.[5]

The simple bivariate relationships all show that consensus democracy is associated with less violence, and three of the four correlations are statistically significant. This evidence is weakened, however, when controls are introduced and two extreme outliers are removed. Violence tends to occur more in plural, populous, and less developed societies. The strongest negative relationship, significant at the 1 percent level, is between consensus democracy and riots in the period 1963–82. When level of development, degree of societal pluralism, and population are controlled for, the significance decreases to 5 percent. In the analyses of the relationship between consensus democracy and deaths from political violence, the United Kingdom is an extreme outlier in the period 1948–82 as a result of the Northern Ireland problem, and Jamaica is an extreme outlier in the period 1963–82 mainly as a result of large-scale violence surrounding the 1980 election. When the same three controls are introduced and the outliers removed, the statistical significance disappears completely, although both correlations remain negative— showing at least a slightly better performance of the consensus democracies.

5. Because in Israel international and domestic violence cannot be clearly separated, I excluded this country from the analysis. Because the degree of societal pluralism is an important control variable, and because most of the violence in the United Kingdom was concentrated in Northern Ireland, the United Kingdom is regarded as a plural society for the purpose of this analysis.

The Effects of the Federalist Dimension
of Consensus Democracy

In this chapter I have concentrated so far on the consequences of the executives-parties dimension of consensus democracy. These are the effects that the conventional wisdom
addresses and posits to be unfavorable. The conventional wisdom does not concern itself explicitly with the federal-unitary
dimension, but its logic applies to this second dimension as
well. Federalism, second chambers, rigid constitutions, strong
judicial review, and independent central banks can all be assumed to inhibit the decisiveness, speed, and coherence of the
central government's policy-making compared with unitary systems, unicameralism, flexible constitutions, weak judicial review, and weak central banks. For this reason, I repeated the
twenty-three regression analyses reported in Table 15.1 but now
with consensus democracy on the federal-unitary dimension as
the independent variable. With one big exception, discussed
shortly, all of the relationships are extremely weak. Consensus
democracy again has a slight edge over majoritarianism: it is
positively related to the economic growth variables and negatively to strike activity and to deaths from political violence; the
results for budget deficits, unemployment, and riots are mixed.
To repeat, however, the correlations are so weak that they do not
allow any substantive conclusions in favor of one or the other
type of democracy.

The big exception is inflation. For all five indicators of inflation, the correlations with consensus democracy are very strong
and significant (at the 1 and 5 percent levels). The results of
the regression analyses are shown in Table 15.2. Consensus democracy is uniformly associated with lower levels of inflation.
Among the thirty-one countries in the period 1980–93, the typical consensus democracy had almost 4.8 percentage points less
inflation (twice the estimated regression coefficient) than the
typical majoritarian democracy. As mentioned earlier in this

Table 15.2 Bivariate regression analyses of the effect of consensus democracy (federal-unitary dimension) on five measures of inflation

	Estimated regression coefficient	Standardized regression coefficient	Absolute t-value	Countries (N)
GDP deflator (1980–93)	−2.38**	−0.36	2.07	31
GDP deflator (1970–95)	−1.06***	−0.62	3.14	18
GDP deflator (1980–95)	−1.41**	−0.45	2.21	21
Consumer price index (1970–95)	−1.04***	−0.65	3.42	18
Consumer price index (1980–95)	−1.41**	−0.46	2.26	21

*Statistically significant at the 10 percent level (one-tailed test)
**Statistically significant at the 5 percent level (one-tailed test)
***Statistically significant at the 1 percent level (one-tailed test)

Source: Based on data in United Nations Development Programme 1996, 186–87, 208; OECD 1996a, A17, A19

chapter, the level of development and, to some extent, population size are inversely related to inflation, but when these two variables are controlled for, all five correlations remain as strong and significant as the bivariate correlations. When, in addition, outlier Italy is removed from the two 1970–95 regression analyses and outlier Greece is removed from the 1980–95 analyses, the four relationships survive intact at the same levels of significance.

This important finding is obviously not surprising. One of the five ingredients of consensus democracy on the federal-unitary dimension is central bank independence, and the most important reason why central banks are made strong and independent is to give them the tools to control inflation. It should be noted that the underlying logic of central bank independence is diametrically at odds with the logic of the conventional wisdom: strong and coherent policy-making here is posited to flow from the division of power instead of the concentration of power.

The findings of this chapter warrant three conclusions. First, on balance, consensus democracies have a better performance record than majoritarian democracies, especially with regard to the control of inflation but also, albeit much more weakly, with regard to most of the other macroeconomic performance variables and the control of violence; majoritarian democracies do not have an even slightly better record on any of the six groups of performance variables. Second, however, the overall results are relatively weak and mixed; when controls were introduced and outliers were removed, few statistically significant correlations were found. Hence, the empirical results do not permit the definitive conclusion that consensus democracies are better decision-makers and better policy-makers than majoritarian systems. Therefore, third, the most important conclusion of this chapter is negative: majoritarian democracies are clearly *not* superior to consensus democracies in managing the economy and in maintaining civil peace. This means that the second part of conventional wisdom does not—or not yet—need to be completely *reversed:* it is not proven that consensus democracies are actually better at governing. What is proven beyond any doubt, however, is that the second part of the conventional wisdom is clearly wrong in claiming that majoritarian democracies are the better governors. The first part of the conventional wisdom, which concedes that consensus democracies are better at representing, is the subject of the next chapter.

The Quality of Democracy and a "Kinder, Gentler" Democracy

Consensus Democracy Makes a Difference

The conventional wisdom, cited in the previous chapter, argues—erroneously, as I have shown—that majoritarian democracy is better at governing, but admits that consensus democracy is better at representing—in particular, representing minority groups and minority interests, representing everyone more accurately, and representing people and their interests more inclusively. In the first part of this chapter I examine several measures of the quality of democracy and democratic representation and the extent to which consensus democracies perform better than majoritarian democracies according to these measures. In the second part of the chapter I discuss differences between the two types of democracy in broad policy orientations. Here I show that consensus democracy tends to be the "kinder, gentler" form of democracy. I borrow these terms from President George Bush's acceptance speech at the Republican presidential nominating convention in August 1988, in which he asserted: "I want a kinder, and gentler nation" (*New York Times*, August 19, 1988, A14). Consensus democracies demonstrate these kinder and gentler qualities in the following ways: they are more likely to be welfare states; they have a better record with regard to the protection of the environment; they put fewer people in prison and are less likely to use the death penalty; and the

consensus democracies in the developed world are more generous with their economic assistance to the developing nations.

Consensus Democracy and Democratic Quality

Table 16.1 presents the results of bivariate regression analyses of the effect of consensus democracy on eight sets of indicators of the quality of democracy. The organization of the table is
similar to that of Tables 15.1 and 15.2 in the previous chapter.
The independent variable is the degree of consensus democracy
on the executives-parties dimension, generally in the period
1971–96 (unless indicated otherwise). The first two indicators
are general indicators of democratic quality. Many studies have
attempted to distinguish between democracy and nondemocratic forms of government not in terms of a dichotomy but in terms
of a scale with degrees of democracy from perfect democracy to
the complete absence of democracy. These degrees of democracy can also be interpreted as degrees of the quality of democracy: how democratic a country is reflects the degree to which it
approximates perfect democracy. Unfortunately, most of these
indexes cannot be used to measure different degrees of democratic quality among our thirty-six democracies because there is
insufficient variation: all or most of our democracies are given
the highest ratings. For instance, both the ratings of the Freedom
House Survey Team (1996) and those by Keith Jaggers and Ted
Robert Gurr (1995), which I used in Chapter 4 to defend the selection of the thirty-six democracies for the analysis in this book,
place almost all of these countries in their highest category.

There are two exceptions. One is Robert A. Dahl's (1971,
231–45) *Polyarchy,* in which 114 countries are placed in thirty-
one scale types from the highest type of democracy to the lowest
type of nondemocracy as of approximately 1969. All of our democracies that were independent and democratic at that time,
except Barbados, Botswana, and Malta, were rated by Dahl—a
total of twenty-six of our thirty-six democracies—and their rat-

ings span nine scale types. To give a few examples, the highest summary ranking goes to Belgium, Denmark, and Finland; Austria and Germany are in the middle; and Colombia and Venezuela at the bottom. Table 16.1 shows that consensus democracy is strongly and significantly correlated (at the 1 percent level) with the Dahl rating of democratic quality.[1] The difference between consensus and majoritarian democracy is more than three points (twice the estimated regression coefficient) on the nine-point scale. Dahl's rating contains a slight bias in favor of consensus democracy because it is partly based on a higher ranking of multiparty compared with two-party systems. However, this difference represents only a third of the variation on one of ten components on which the rating is based; if it could somehow be discounted, the very strong correlation between consensus democracy and the rating of democratic quality would only be reduced marginally. A more serious potential source of bias is that the Third World democracies are all placed in the lowest three categories. However, when the level of development is used as a control variable, the estimated regression coefficient goes down only slightly (to 1.28 points) and the correlation remains statistically significant at the 1 percent level.

The second rating of democratic quality is the average of Tatu Vanhanen's (1990, 17–31) indexes of democratization for each year from 1980 to 1988 for almost all of the countries in the world, including all thirty-six of our democracies. Vanhanen bases his index on two elements: the degree of competition, defined as the share of the vote received by all parties except the largest party, and participation, defined as the percentage of the total population that voted in the most recent election; these two numbers are multiplied to arrive at the overall index. The values of the index range from a high of 43.2, for Belgium, to a low of zero; for our thirty-six countries the lowest value is 5.7 for

1. The independent variable is consensus democracy in the 1945–70 period. On Dahl's scale, 1 is the highest and 9 the lowest point; I reversed the sign in order to make the higher values represent higher degrees of democratic quality.

Table 16.1 Bivariate regression analyses of the effect of consensus democracy (executives-parties dimension) on seventeen indicators of the quality of democracy

	Estimated regression coefficient	Standardized regression coefficient	Absolute t-value	Countries (N)
Dahl rating (1969)	1.57****	0.58	3.44	26
Vanhanen rating (1980–88)	4.89****	0.54	3.75	36
Women's parliamentary representation (1971–95)	3.33***	0.46	3.06	36
Women's cabinet representation (1993–95)	3.36**	0.33	2.06	36
Family policy (1976–82)	1.10*	0.33	1.41	18
Rich-poor ratio (1981–93)	−1.41**	−0.47	2.50	24
Decile ratio (c. 1986)	−0.38**	−0.49	2.20	17
Index of power resources (c. 1990)	3.78*	0.26	1.57	36
Voter turnout (1971–96)	3.07*	0.24	1.46	36
Voter turnout (1960–78)	3.31*	0.30	1.49	24

Satisfaction with democracy (1995–96)	8.42*	0.36	1.55	18
Differential satisfaction (1990)	−8.11***	−0.83	4.51	11
Government distance (1978–85)	−0.34**	−0.62	2.51	12
Voter distance (1978–85)	−5.25**	−0.64	2.63	12
Corruption index (1997)	−0.32	−0.14	0.71	27
Popular cabinet support (1945–96)	1.90*	0.22	1.32	35
J. S. Mill criterion (1945–96)	2.51	0.07	0.42	35

*Statistically significant at the 10 percent level (one-tailed test)
**Statistically significant at the 5 percent level (one-tailed test)
***Statistically significant at the 1 percent level (one-tailed test)

Source: Based on data in Dahl 1971, 232; Vanhanen 1990, 27–28; Inter-Parliamentary Union 1995; Banks 1993; Banks, Day, and Muller 1996; Wilensky 1990, 2, and additional data provided by Harold L. Wilensky; United Nations Development Programme 1996, 170–71, 198; Atkinson, Rainwater, and Smeeding 1995, 40; Vanhanen 1997, 86–89; International IDEA 1997, 51–95; Powell 1980, 6; Klingemann 1999; Anderson and Guillory 1997, and additional data provided by Christopher J. Anderson; Huber and Powell 1994, and additional data provided by John D. Huber; Transparency International 1997

Botswana. The first element effectively distinguishes one-party rule from democratic electoral contestation, but it also necessarily suffers from the bias that two-party systems tend to get lower scores than multiparty systems. Moreover, this bias affects one of the two components of Vanhanen's index and therefore has a much greater impact than the slight bias in Dahl's index. Because the Vanhanen index is widely used and because it is available for all of our democracies, I report the result of its regression on consensus democracy in Table 16.1 anyway. The correlation is impressively strong and remains strong at the same level of significance when the level of development is controlled for and when Botswana, which is somewhat of an outlier, is removed from the analysis. However, its sizable bias in favor of multiparty systems makes the Vanhanen index a less credible index of democratic quality than the Dahl index.

Women's Representation

The next three indicators in Table 16.1 measure women's political representation and the protection of women's interests. These are important measures of the quality of democratic representation in their own right, and they can also serve as indirect proxies of how well minorities are represented generally. That there are so many kinds of ethnic and religious minorities in different countries makes comparisons extremely difficult, and it therefore makes sense to focus on the "minority" of women—a political rather than a numerical minority—that is found everywhere and that can be compared systematically across countries. As Rein Taagepera (1994, 244) states, "What we know about women's representation should [also] be applicable to ethnoracial minorities."

The average percentage of women elected to the lower or only houses of parliament in all elections from 1971 to 1995 in our thirty-six democracies ranges from a high of 30.4 percent in Sweden to a low of 0.9 percent in Papua New Guinea. These differences are strongly and significantly related to the degree of consensus democracy. The percentage of women's parliamentary representation is 6.7 percentage points higher (again, twice the estimated regression coefficient) in consensus democracies than in majoritarian systems. Women tend to be better represented in developed than in developing countries, but when the level of development is controlled for, the relationship between consensus democracy and women's legislative representation weakens only slightly and is still significant at the 1 percent level. It can be argued that in presidential systems the percentage of women's representation should not be based only on women's election to the legislature but also, perhaps equally, on their election to the presidency. If this were done, the relationship between consensus democracy and women's political representation would be reinforced because not a single woman president was elected in Colombia, Costa Rica, France, the United States, and Venezuela in the entire period under consideration and because all five presidential democracies are on the majoritarian side of the spectrum (see Figures 14.1 and 14.2).

The pattern is similar for the representation of women in cabinets in two recent years—1993 and 1995—although the correlation is significant only at the 5 percent level.[2] The percentages range from 42.1 percent in Norway to 0 percent in Papua New Guinea. Here again, the level of development is also a strong explanatory variable, but controlling for it does not affect the correlation between consensus democracy and women's cabinet representation.

As a measure of the protection and promotion of women's interests, I examined Harold L. Wilensky's (1990) rating of the industrialized democracies with regard to the innovativeness and expansiveness of their family policies—a matter of special concern to women. On Wilensky's thirteen-point scale, from a

2. The percentages are based on data in the *Political Handbook of the World* (Banks 1993; Banks, Day, and Muller 1996); 1993 is the first year for which the *Political Handbook* reports the gender of cabinet members.

maximum of twelve to a minimum of zero, France and Sweden have the highest score of eleven points and Australia and Ireland the lowest score of one point.[3] Consensus democracies score more than two points higher on the scale, and the correlation is significant at the 10 percent level and unaffected by level of development. France is an unusual deviant case: it is a mainly majoritarian system but receives one of the highest family-policy scores. When it is removed from the analysis, the correlation becomes stronger and is statistically significant at the 5 percent level.

Political Equality

Political equality is a basic goal of democracy, and the degree of political equality is therefore an important indicator of democratic quality. Political equality is difficult to measure directly, but economic equality can serve as a valid proxy, since political equality is more likely to prevail in the absence of great economic inequalities: "Many resources that flow directly or indirectly from one's position in the economic order can be converted into political resources" (Dahl 1996, 645). The rich-poor ratio is the ratio of the income share of the highest 20 percent to that of the lowest 20 percent of households. The United Nations Development Programme (1996) has collected the relevant statistics for twenty-four of our democracies, including six of the developing countries: Botswana, Colombia, Costa Rica, India, Jamaica, and Venezuela. The ratio varies between 16.4 in highly inegalitarian Botswana and 4.3 in egalitarian Japan. Consensus democracy and inequality as measured by the rich-poor ratio are

3. Wilensky's (1990, 2) ratings are based on a five-point scale, from four to zero, "for each of three policy clusters: existence and length of maternity and parental leave, paid and unpaid; availability and accessibility of public daycare programs and government effort to expand daycare; and flexibility of retirement systems. They measure government action to assure care of children and maximize choices in balancing work and family demands for everyone."

negatively and very strongly related (statistically significant at the 5 percent level and almost at the 1 percent level). The difference between the average consensus democracy and the average majoritarian democracy is about 2.8. The more developed countries have less inequality than the developing countries; when the level of development is controlled for, the correlation between consensus democracy and equality weakens only slightly and is still significant at the 5 percent level. When, in addition, the most extreme case of Botswana is removed from the analysis, the relationship remains significant at the same level.

The decile ratio is a similar ratio of income differences: the income ratio of the top to the bottom decile. It is available for most of the OECD countries, based on the most painstaking comparative study of income differences that has been done so far (Atkinson, Rainwater, and Smeeding 1995). Consensus democracies are again the more egalitarian; the correlation is significant at the 5 percent level and is not affected when level of development is controlled for. Finland has the lowest decile ratio, 2.59, and the United States has the highest, 5.94. The United States is an extreme case: the midpoint between its ratio and that of Finland is 4.26, and the sixteen other democracies are all below this midpoint; the country with the next highest decile ratio after the United States is Ireland with a ratio of 4.23. When the United States is removed from the analysis, the correlation between consensus democracy and income equality becomes even stronger although not enough to become significant at the higher level.

Vanhanen's (1997, 43, 46) Index of Power Resources is an indicator of equality based on several indirect measures such as the degree of literacy ("the higher the percentage of literate population, the more widely basic intellectual resources are distributed") and the percentage of urban population ("the higher [this] percentage . . . , the more diversified economic activities and economic interest groups there are and, consequently, the more economic power resources are distributed among various groups"). Although Vanhanen's index is an indirect and obviously rough measure, it has the great advantage that it can be calculated for many countries, including all of our thirty-six democracies. The highest value, 53.5 points, is found in the Netherlands, and the lowest, 3.3 points, in Papua New Guinea. Consensus democracy is positively correlated with the Index of Power Resources but only at the 10 percent level of significance. However, when level of development, which is also strongly correlated with Vanhanen's index, is controlled for, the relationship becomes stronger and is significant at the 5 percent level.

Electoral Participation

Voter turnout is an excellent indicator of democratic quality for two reasons. First, it shows the extent to which citizens are actually interested in being represented. Second, turnout is strongly correlated with socioeconomic status and can therefore also serve as an indirect indicator of political equality: high turnout means more equal participation and hence greater political equality; low turnout spells unequal participation and hence more inequality (Lijphart 1997b). Table 16.1 uses the turnout percentages in national elections that attract the largest numbers of voters: legislative elections in parliamentary systems and, in presidential systems, whichever elections had the highest turnout—generally the presidential rather than the legislative elections and, where presidents are chosen by majority-runoff, generally the runoff instead of the first-ballot elections. The basic measure is the number of voters as a percentage of voting-age population.[4]

4. This is a more accurate measure of turnout than actual voters as a percent of registered voters, because voter registration procedures and reliability differ greatly from country to country. The only problem with the voting-age measure is that it includes noncitizens and hence tends to depress the turnout percentages of countries with large noncitizen populations. Because this prob-

In the period 1971–96, Italy had the highest average turnout, 92.4 percent, and Switzerland the lowest, 40.9 percent. Consensus democracy and voter turnout are positively correlated, but the correlation is significant only at the 10 percent level. However, several controls need to be introduced. First of all, compulsory voting, which is somewhat more common in consensus than in majoritarian democracies, strongly stimulates turnout.[5] Second, turnout is severely depressed by the high frequency and the multitude of electoral choices to be made both in consensual Switzerland and the majoritarian United States. Third, turnout tends to be higher in more developed countries. When compulsory voting and the frequency of elections (both in the form of dummy variables) as well as the level of development are controlled for, the effect of consensus democracy on voter turnout becomes much stronger and is now significant at the 1 percent level. With these controls in place, consensus democracies have approximately 7.5 percentage points higher turnout than majoritarian democracies.

The regression analysis was repeated with the average turnout figures collected by G. Bingham Powell (1980) for an earlier period, 1960–78.[6] Both the bivariate and multivariate relationships are very similar to the pattern reported in the previous paragraph. The bivariate correlation is significant at the 10 percent level, but when the three control variables are added, the correlation between consensus democracy and turnout becomes

---

lem assumes extreme proportions in Luxembourg with its small citizen and relatively very large noncitizen population, I made an exception in this case and used the turnout percentage based on registered voters.

5. The democracies with compulsory voting in the 1971–96 period are Australia, Belgium, Costa Rica, Greece, Italy, Luxembourg, and Venezuela. Compulsory voting was abolished in the Netherlands in 1970. For the regression analysis with the 1960–78 Powell data, reported below, the Netherlands is counted as having compulsory voting, and the average Dutch turnout percentage is only for the elections in which voting was still compulsory.

6. The independent variable here is the degree of consensus democracy for the entire 1945–96 period.

strong and significant at the 1 percent level. The difference in turnout between consensus and majoritarian democracies is about 7.3 percentage points—very close to the 7.5 percent difference in the period 1971–96.[7]

Satisfaction with Democracy

Does the type of democracy affect citizens' satisfaction with democracy? Hans-Dieter Klingemann (1999) reports the responses to the following survey question asked in many countries, including eighteen of our democracies, in 1995 and 1996: "On the whole, are you very satisfied, fairly satisfied, not very satisfied, or not at all satisfied with the way democracy works in (your country)?" The Danes and Norwegians expressed the highest percentage of satisfaction with democracy: 83 and 82 percent, respectively, said that they were "very" or "fairly" satisfied. The Italians and Colombians were the least satisfied: only 19 and 16 percent, respectively, expressed satisfaction. Generally, as Table 16.1 shows, citizens in consensus democracies are significantly more satisfied with democratic performance in their countries than citizens of majoritarian democracies; the difference is approximately 17 percentage points.

In an earlier study of eleven European democracies, Christopher J. Anderson and Christine A. Guillory (1997) found that, in each of these countries, respondents who had voted for the winning party or parties were more likely to be satisfied with how well democracy worked in their country than respondents who had voted for the losing party or parties. Because it is easy to be satisfied when one is on the winning side, the degree to which winners and losers have similar responses can be regarded as a

7. PR is probably the most important institutional element responsible for the strong relationships between consensus democracy on one hand and voter turnout and women's representation on the other; PR is the usual electoral system in consensus democracies, and it has been found to be a strong stimulant to both voter participation and women's representation (Blais and Carty 1990, Rule and Zimmerman 1994).

more sensitive measure of the *breadth* of satisfaction than simply the number of people who say they are very or fairly satisfied. The largest difference, 37.5 percentage points, was in Greece, where 70.3 percent of the respondents on the winning side expressed satisfaction compared with only 32.8 percent of the losers; the smallest difference occurred in Belgium, where 61.5 percent of the winners were satisfied compared with 56.8 percent of the losers—a difference of only 4.7 percentage points. The general pattern discovered by Anderson and Guillory was that in consensus democracies the differences between winners and losers were significantly smaller than in majoritarian democracies. My replication of Anderson and Guillory's analysis, using the degree of consensus democracy on the executives-parties dimension in the period 1971–96, strongly confirms their conclusion. As Table 16.1 shows, the difference in satisfaction is more than 16 percentage points smaller in the typical consensus than in the typical majoritarian democracy. The correlation is highly significant (at the 1 percent level).[8]

Government-Voter Proximity

The next two variables can be used to test the following key claim that is often made on behalf of majoritarian democracy: because in the typical two-party system the two major parties are both likely to be moderate, the government's policy position is likely to be close to that of the bulk of the voters. John D. Huber and G. Bingham Powell (1994) compared the government's position on a ten-point left-right scale with the voters' positions on the same scale in twelve Western democracies in

8. In Anderson and Guillory's eleven countries, there was also a positive, but not statistically significant, relationship between consensus democracy and the percentage of respondents expressing satisfaction with democracy. However, Italy is an extreme outlier, with only 21.7 percent of the respondents expressing satisfaction; the percentages in the other countries range from 83.8 percent in Germany to 44.7 percent in Greece. When the Italian case is removed from the analysis, the correlation becomes significant at the 5 percent level.

the period 1978–85. One measure of the distance between government and voters is simply the distance between the government's position on the left-right scale and the position of the median voter; this measure is called "government distance" in Table 16.1. The other measure is the percentage of voters between the government and the median citizen, called "voter distance" in the table. The smaller these two distances are, the more representative the government is of the citizens' policy preferences.

Government distance ranges from a high of 2.39 points on the ten-point scale in the United Kingdom to a low of 0.47 in Ireland. Voter distance is the greatest in Australia, 37 percent, and the smallest in Ireland, 11 percent. Contrary to the majoritarian claim, both distances are actually smaller in consensus than in majoritarian democracies: the differences in the respective distances are about two-thirds of a point on the ten-point scale and more than 10 percent of the citizens. Both correlations are significant at the 5 percent level.

Accountability and Corruption

Another important claim in favor of majoritarian democracy is that its typically one-party majority governments offer clearer responsibility for policy-making and hence better accountability of the government to the citizens—who can use elections either to "renew the term of the incumbent government" or to "throw the rascals out" (Powell 1989, 119). The claim is undoubtedly valid for majoritarian systems with pure two-party competition. However, in two-party systems with significant third parties, "rascals" may be repeatedly returned to office in spite of clear majorities of the voters voting for other parties and hence against the incumbent government; all reelected British cabinets since 1945 fit this description. Moreover, it is actually easier to change governments in consensus democracies than in majoritarian democracies, as shown by the shorter duration of cabinets in consensus systems (see the first two columns of Table 7.1). Admittedly, of course, changes in consensus democracies tend to be partial changes in the composition of cabinets, in contrast with the more frequent complete turnovers in majoritarian democracies.

A related measure is the incidence of corruption. It may be hypothesized that the greater clarity of responsibility in majoritarian democracies inhibits corruption and that the consensus systems' tendency to compromise and "deal-making" fosters corrupt practices. The indexes of perceived corruption in a large number of countries, including twenty-seven of our democracies, by Transparency International (1997) can be used to test this hypothesis. An index of 10 means "totally corrupt" and 0 means "totally clean."[9] Among our democracies, India and Colombia are the most corrupt, with scores between 7 and 8; at the other end of the scale, six countries are close to "totally clean" with scores between 0 and 1: Denmark, Finland, Sweden, New Zealand, Canada, and the Netherlands. Contrary to the hypothesis, there is no significant relationship between consensus democracy and corruption. Moreover, the weak relationship that does appear is actually negative: consensus democracies are slightly *less* likely to be corrupt than majoritarian systems (by about two-thirds of a point on the index). This relationship becomes a bit stronger, but is still not statistically significant, when the level of development, which is strongly and negatively correlated with the level of corruption, is controlled for.

John Stuart Mill's Hypotheses

The final two variables that measure the quality of democracy are inspired by John Stuart Mill's (1861, 134) argument that majority rule is the most fundamental requirement of democ-

9. Transparency International's highest scores are for the "cleanest" and the lowest scores for the most "corrupt" countries. I changed this 10–0 scale to a 0–10 scale so that higher values would indicate more corruption.

racy and that the combination of plurality or majority elections and parliamentary government may lead to minority rule. He proves his point by examining the most extreme case: "Suppose . . . that, in a country governed by equal and universal suffrage, there is a contested election in every constituency, and every election is carried by a small majority. The Parliament thus brought together represents little more than a bare majority of the people. This Parliament proceeds to legislate, and adopts important measures by a bare majority of itself." Although Mill does not state so explicitly, the most important of these "important measures" is the formation of a cabinet supported by a majority of the legislators. Mill continues: "It is possible, therefore, and even probable" that this two-stage majoritarian system delivers power "not to a majority but to a minority." Mill's point is well illustrated by the fact that, as I showed in Chapter 2, the United Kingdom and New Zealand have tended to be *pluralitarian* instead of majoritarian democracies since 1945 because their parliamentary majorities and the one-party cabinets based on them have usually been supported by only a plurality—the largest minority—of the voters.

Mill argues that the best solution is to use PR for the election of the legislature, and he is obviously right that under a perfectly proportional system the problem of minority control cannot occur. His argument further means that consensus democracies, which frequently use PR and which in addition tend to have more inclusive coalition cabinets, are more likely to practice true majority rule than majoritarian democracies. Two measures can be used to test this hypothesis derived from Mill. One is popular cabinet support: the average percentage of the voters who gave their votes to the party or parties that formed the cabinet, or, in presidential systems, the percentage of the voters who voted for the winning presidential candidate, weighted by the time that each cabinet or president was in office. The second measure may be called the John Stuart Mill Criterion: the percentage of time that the majority-rule requirement—the requirement that the cabinet or president be supported by popular majorities—is fulfilled. Both measures can be calculated for the entire period 1945–96 for all democracies except Papua New Guinea due to the large number of independents elected to its legislature and frequently participating in its cabinets.[10] The highest average popular cabinet support occurred in Switzerland (76.6 percent), Botswana (71.2 percent), and Austria (70.7 percent), and the lowest in Denmark (40.3 percent) and Spain (40.7 percent). The John Stuart Mill Criterion was always satisfied—100 percent of the time—in the Bahamas, Botswana, Jamaica, Luxembourg, and Switzerland, and never—0 percent of the time—in Norway, Spain, and the United Kingdom. These examples already make clear that the best and the poorest performers on these measures include both consensus and majoritarian democracies. We should therefore not expect strong statistical correlations between consensus democracy and either measure. Table 16.1 shows that, though both correlations are positive, they are fairly weak and only one is statistically significant. Popular cabinet support is only about 3.8 percent greater in consensus than in majoritarian democracies.

The evidence does not lend stronger support to Mill's line of thinking for three reasons. One is that the smallest majoritarian democracies—Botswana, the Bahamas, Jamaica, Trinidad, and Barbados—have high popular cabinet support as a result of their almost pure two-party systems in which the winning party usually also wins a popular majority or at least a strong popular plurality. This finding is in line with Robert A. Dahl and Edward R. Tufte's (1973, 98–108) conclusion that smaller units have fewer political parties even when they use PR. Dag Anckar (1993) argues that, in addition to size, insularity plays a role in

10. In a few other countries, relatively short periods had to be excluded: for instance, the period 1958–65 in France because the president was not popularly elected, and the periods 1979–80 and 1984–86 in India and Mauritius, respectively, because the cabinets contained fragments of parties that had split after the most recent elections. Moreover, nonpartisan cabinets and cabinets formed after boycotted elections were excluded.

reducing the number of parties. The case of the small island state of Malta, with PR elections but virtually pure two-party competition, bears out both arguments. When population size is controlled for, the correlation between consensus democracy and popular cabinet support becomes statistically significant at the 5 percent level. Controlling for population has an even more dramatic effect on the correlation between consensus democracy and the John Stuart Mill Criterion: it is now both strong and highly significant (at the 1 percent level).

The second explanation is that the presidential systems are on the majoritarian half of the spectrum but that they tend to do well in securing popular support for the executive: competition tends to be between two strong presidential candidates, and majority support is guaranteed—or, perhaps more realistically speaking, contrived—when the majority-runoff method is used.

Third, consensus democracies with frequent minority cabinets, especially the Scandinavian countries, have relatively low popular cabinet support. There is still a big difference, of course, between cabinets with only minority popular support but also minority status in the legislature, as in Scandinavia, and cabinets with minority popular support but with majority support in parliament, as in Britain and New Zealand; the lack of popular support is clearly more serious in the latter case. Moreover, popular cabinet support is based on actual votes cast and does not take into account strategic voting, that is, the tendency—which is especially strong in plurality elections—to vote for a party not because it is the voters' real preference but because it appears to have a chance to win. Hence, if popular cabinet support could be calculated on the basis of the voters' sincere preferences instead of their actual votes, the consensus democracies would do much better on this indicator of democratic quality.

The general conclusion is that consensus democracies have a better record than majoritarian democracy on all of the measures of democratic quality in Table 16.1, that all except two correlations are statistically significant, and that most of the correlations are significant at the 1 or 5 percent level. For reasons of space, I am not presenting a table, similar to Table 16.1, with the bivariate correlations between consensus democracy on the federal-unitary dimension and the seventeen indicators of democratic quality. The reason is that there are no interesting results to report: the only strongly significant bivariate relationship (at the 5 percent level) is a negative correlation between consensus democracy and voter turnout in the period 1971–96. However, when compulsory voting, the frequency of elections, and level of development are controlled for, the correlation becomes very weak and is no longer significant.

Consensus Democracy and Its Kinder, Gentler Qualities

The democratic qualities discussed so far in this chapter should appeal to all democrats: it is hard to find fault with better women's representation, greater political equality, higher participation in elections, closer proximity between government policy and voters' preferences, and more faithful adherence to John Stuart Mill's majority principle. In addition, consensus democracy (on the executives-parties dimension) is associated with some other attributes that I believe most, though not necessarily all, democrats will also find attractive: a strong community orientation and social consciousness—the kinder, gentler qualities mentioned in the beginning of this chapter. These characteristics are also consonant with feminist conceptions of democracy that emphasize, in Jane Mansbridge's (1996, 123) words, "connectedness" and "mutual persuasion" instead of self-interest and power politics: "The processes of persuasion may be related to a more consultative, participatory style that seems to characterize women more than men." Mansbridge further relates these differences to her distinction between "adversary" and "unitary" democracy, which is similar to the majoritarian-consensus contrast. Accordingly, consensus democracy may also be thought of as the more feminine model and majoritarian democracy as the more masculine model of democracy.

There are four areas of government activity in which the kinder and gentler qualities of consensus democracy are likely to manifest themselves: social welfare, the protection of the environment, criminal justice, and foreign aid. My hypothesis is that consensus democracy will be associated with kinder, gentler, and more generous policies. Table 16.2 presents the results of the bivariate regression analyses of the effect of consensus democracy on ten indicators of the policy orientations in these four areas. The independent variable in all cases is the degree of consensus democracy on the executives-parties dimension in the period 1971–96.

The first indicator of the degree to which democracies are welfare states is Gøsta Esping-Andersen's (1990) comprehensive measure of "decommodification"—that is, the degree to which welfare policies with regard to unemployment, disability, illness, and old age permit people to maintain decent living standards independent of pure market forces. Among the eighteen OECD countries surveyed by Esping-Andersen in 1980, Sweden has the highest score of 39.1 points and Australia and the United States the lowest—13.0 and 13.8 points, respectively. Consensus democracy has a strong positive correlation with these welfare scores. The difference between the average consensus democracy and the average majoritarian democracy is almost ten points. Wealthy countries can afford to be more generous with welfare than less wealthy countries, but when the level of development is controlled for, the correlation between consensus democracy and welfare becomes even a bit stronger.

Esping-Andersen's measure has been severely criticized for understating the degree to which Australia, New Zealand, and the United Kingdom are welfare states (Castles and Mitchell 1993). Because these three countries are, or were, also mainly majoritarian systems, this criticism throws doubt on the link between consensus democracy and welfare statism. In order to test whether the original finding was entirely driven by Esping-Andersen's classification of Australia, New Zealand, and the United Kingdom, I re-ran the regression without these three disputed cases. The result is reported in the second row of Table 16.2. The relationship between consensus democracy and the welfare state is weakened only slightly, and it is still statistically significant at the 5 percent level.

Another indicator of welfare statism is social expenditure as a percentage of gross domestic product in the same eighteen OECD countries in 1992, analyzed by Manfred G. Schmidt (1997). Sweden is again the most welfare-oriented democracy with 37.1 percent social expenditure, but Japan now has the lowest percentage, 12.4 percent, followed by the United States with 15.6 percent. The correlation with consensus democracy is again strong and significant, and it is not affected when level of development is controlled for. Consensus democracies differ from majoritarian democracies in that they spend an additional 5.3 percent of their gross domestic product on welfare.

Environmental performance can be measured by means of two indicators that are available for all or almost all of our thirty-six democracies. The first is Monte Palmer's (1997) composite index of concern for the environment, based mainly on carbon dioxide emissions, fertilizer consumption, and deforestation. This index ranges from a theoretical high of one hundred points, indicating the best environmental performance to a low of zero points for the worst performance. The highest score among our democracies is for the Netherlands, seventy-seven points, and the lowest score is Botswana's, zero points.[11] Consensus democracies score almost ten points higher than majoritarian

11. Palmer (1997, 16) gives the highest scores to "the most environmentally troubled nations." I changed his 0–100 scale to a 100–0 scale so that higher scores would indicate better environmental performance.

Table 16.2 Bivariate regression analyses of the effect of consensus democracy (executives-parties dimension) on ten indicators of welfare statism, environmental performance, criminal justice, and foreign aid

	Estimated regression coefficient	Standardized regression coefficient	Absolute t-value	Countries (N)
Welfare state index (1980)	4.90***	0.68	3.70	18
Adjusted welfare index (1980)	4.29**	0.58	2.60	15
Social expenditure (1992)	2.66**	0.44	1.94	18
Palmer index (c. 1990)	4.99*	0.30	1.67	31
Energy efficiency (1990–94)	0.93***	0.51	3.50	36
Incarceration rate (1992–95)	−32.12*	−0.30	1.39	22
Death penalty (1996)	−0.35***	−0.44	2.86	36
Foreign aid (1982–85)	0.09*	0.30	1.38	21
Foreign aid (1992–95)	0.10**	0.39	1.86	21
Aid versus defense (1992–95)	5.94***	0.51	2.58	21

*Statistically significant at the 10 percent level (one-tailed test)
**Statistically significant at the 5 percent level (one-tailed test)
***Statistically significant at the 1 percent level (one-tailed test)

Source: Based on data in Esping-Andersen 1990, 52; Schmidt 1997, 155; Palmer 1997, 16–20; World Bank 1992, 26–27; World Bank 1993, 26–27; World Bank 1994, 26–27; World Bank 1995, 26–27; World Bank 1997, 26–27; Mauer 1994, 3; Mauer 1997, 4; Bedau 1997, 78–82; United Nations Development Programme 1994, 197; United Nations Development Programme 1995, 204, 206; United Nations Development Programme 1996, 199, 201; United Nations Development Programme 1997, 214–15

democracies; the correlation is statistically significant at the 10 percent level and is not affected when level of development is controlled for.

An even better overall measure of environmental responsibility is energy efficiency. Table 16.2 uses the World Bank's figures for the gross domestic product divided by total energy consumption for the years from 1990 to 1994. The most environmentally responsible countries produce goods and services with the lowest relative consumption of energy; the least responsible countries waste a great deal of energy. Among our thirty-six democracies, Switzerland has the highest value, an annual average of $8.70, and Trinidad the lowest, $0.80. The correlation between consensus democracy and energy efficiency is extremely strong (significant at the 1 percent level) and unaffected by the introduction of level of development as a control variable.

One would also expect the qualities of kindness and gentleness in consensus democracies to show up in criminal justice systems that are less punitive than those of majoritarian democracies, with fewer people in prison and with less or no use of capital punishment. To test the hypothesis with regard to incarceration rates, I used the average rates in 1992–93 and 1995 collected by the Sentencing Project (Mauer 1994, 1997). These rates represent the number of inmates per hundred thousand population. The highest and lowest rates are those for the United States and India: 560 and 24 inmates per hundred thousand population, respectively. Consensus democracy is negatively correlated with incarceration, but only at the modest 10 percent level of significance. However, this result is strongly affected by the extreme case of the United States: its 560 prisoners per hundred thousand people is more than four times as many as the 131 inmates in the next most punitive country, New Zealand. When the United States is removed from the analysis, the negative correlation between consensus democracy and the incarceration rate is significant at the 5 percent level; when in addition the level of development is controlled for, the correlation becomes significant at the 1 percent level. The remaining twenty-one countries range from 24 to 131 inmates per hundred thousand population; with level of development controlled, the consensus democracies put about 26 fewer people per hundred thousand population in prison than the majoritarian democracies.

As of 1996, eight of our thirty-six democracies retained and used the death penalty for ordinary crimes: the Bahamas, Barbados, Botswana, India, Jamaica, Japan, Trinidad, and the United States. The laws of twenty-two countries did not provide for the death penalty for any crime. The remaining six countries were in intermediate positions: four still had the death penalty but only for exceptional crimes such as wartime crimes—Canada, Israel, Malta, and the United Kingdom—and two retained the death penalty but had not used it for at least ten years—Belgium and Papua New Guinea (Bedau 1997, 78–82). On the basis of these differences, I constructed a three-point scale with a score of two for the active use of the death penalty, zero for the absence of the death penalty, and one for the intermediate cases. The negative correlation between consensus democracy and the death penalty is strong and highly significant (at the 1 percent level), and is not affected by controlling for level of development.

In the field of foreign policy, one might plausibly expect the kind and gentle characteristics of consensus democracy to be manifested by generosity with foreign aid and a reluctance to rely on military power.[12] Table 16.2 uses three indicators for twenty-one OECD countries: average annual foreign aid—that is, economic development assistance, not military aid—as a percentage of gross national product in the period 1982–85 before the end of the Cold War; average foreign aid levels in the post—

12. This hypothesis can also be derived from the "democratic peace" literature (Ray 1997). The fact that democracies are more peaceful, especially in their relationships with each other, than nondemocracies is often attributed to their stronger compromise-oriented political cultures and their institutional checks and balances. If this explanation is correct, one should expect consensus democracies to be even more peace-loving than majoritarian democracies.

Cold War years from 1992 to 1995; and foreign aid in the latter period as a percent of defense expenditures. In the period 1982–85, foreign aid ranged from a high of 1.04 percent of gross national product (Norway) to a low of 0.04 percent (Portugal); in the period 1992–95, the highest percentage was 1.01 percent (Denmark and Norway) and the lowest 0.14 percent (the United States). The highest foreign aid as a percent of defense expenditure was Denmark's 51 percent, and the lowest that of the United States, 4 percent.

In the bivariate regression analysis, consensus democracy is significantly correlated with all three indicators, albeit at different levels. However, two important controls need to be introduced. First, because wealthier countries can better afford to give foreign aid than less wealthy countries, the level of development should be controlled for. Second, because large countries tend to assume greater military responsibilities and hence tend to have larger defense expenditures, which can be expected to limit their ability and willingness to provide foreign aid, population size should be used as a control variable; Dahl and Tufte (1973, 122–23) found a strong link between population and defense spending. When these two controls are introduced, the correlations between consensus democracy and the three measures of foreign aid remain significant, all at the 5 percent level. With the controls in place, the typical consensus democracy gave about 0.20 percent more of its gross national product in foreign aid than the typical majoritarian democracy in both the Cold War and post–Cold War periods, and its aid as a percent of defense spending was about 9.5 percentage points higher.

Similar regression analyses can be performed to test the effect of the other (federal-unitary) dimension of consensus democracy on the above ten indicators, but few interesting results appear. The only two significant bivariate correlations are between consensus democracy on one hand and the incarceration rate and social expenditure on the other, both at the 5 percent level. The negative correlation with social expenditure is not affected when the level of development is controlled for; the explanation is that three federal systems—Australia, Canada, and the United States—are among the only four countries with social spending below 20 percent of gross domestic product. The positive correlation with the rate of incarceration is entirely driven by the extreme case of the United States; when the United States is removed from the analysis, the relationship disappears.

As the subtitle of this chapter states: consensus democracy makes a difference. Indeed, consensus democracy—on the executives-parties dimension—makes a big difference with regard to almost all of the indicators of democratic quality and with regard to all of the kinder and gentler qualities. Furthermore, when the appropriate controls are introduced, the positive difference that consensus democracy makes generally tends to become even more impressive.

CHAPTER 17

Conclusions and Recommendations

Two conclusions of this book stand out as most important. The first is that the enormous variety of formal and informal rules and institutions that we find in democracies can be reduced to a clear two-dimensional pattern on the basis of the contrasts between majoritarian and consensus government. The second important conclusion has to do with the policy performance of democratic governments: especially as far as the executives-parties dimension is concerned, majoritarian democracies do not outperform the consensus democracies on macroeconomic management and the control of violence—in fact, the consensus democracies have the slightly better record— but the consensus democracies do clearly outperform the majoritarian democracies with regard to the quality of democracy and democratic representation as well as with regard to what I have called the kindness and gentleness of their public policy orientations. On the second dimension, the federal institutions of consensus democracy have obvious advantages for large countries, and the independent central banks that are part of this same set of consensus characteristics effectively serve the purpose of controlling inflation.

These conclusions have an extremely important practical implication: because the overall performance record of the consensus democracies is clearly superior to that of the majoritarian democracies, the consensus option is the more attractive option for countries designing their first democratic constitutions or contemplating democratic reform. This recommendation is particularly pertinent, and even urgent, for societies that have deep cultural and ethnic cleavages, but it is also relevant for more homogeneous countries.

The Good News

Two pieces of good news and two pieces of bad news are attached to this practical constitutional recommendation. The first bit of good news is that, contrary to the conventional wisdom, there is no trade-off at all between governing effectiveness and high-quality democracy—and hence no difficult decisions to be made on giving priority to one or the other objective. Both dimensions of consensus democracy have advantages that are not offset by countervailing disadvantages—almost too good to be true, but the empirical results presented in Chapters 15 and 16 demonstrate that it *is* true.

Additional good news is that it is not difficult to write constitutions and other basic laws in such a way as to introduce consensus democracy. Divided-power institutions—strong federalism, strong bicameralism, rigid amendment rules, judicial review, and independent central banks—can be prescribed by means of constitutional stipulations and provisions in central bank charters. How these constitutional provisions work also depends on how they are interpreted and shaped in practice, of course, but the independent influence of explicit written rules should not be underestimated. It may also be possible to strengthen these institutions by choosing a particular form of them; for instance, if one wants to stimulate active and assertive judicial review, the best way to do so is to set up a special constitutional court (see Chapter 12). A central bank can be made particularly strong if its independence is enshrined not just in a central bank charter but in the constitution.

The institutions of consensus democracy on the executives-parties dimension do not depend as directly on constitutional provisions as the divided-power institutions. But two formal elements are of crucial indirect importance: proportional representation and a parliamentary system of government. Especially when they are used in combination, and if the PR system is proportional not just in name but reasonably proportional in practice, they provide a potent impetus toward consensus democracy. On the conceptual map of democracy (see Figure 14.1), almost all of the democracies that have both PR and parliamentary systems are on the left, consensual side of the map, and almost all of the democracies that have plurality or majority elections or presidential systems of government or both are on the right, majoritarian side.[1]

Because the hybrid Swiss system can be regarded as more parliamentary than presidential (see Chapter 7) and because the Japanese SNTV electoral system can be regarded as closer to PR than to plurality (see Chapter 8), there are, among our thirty-six democracies, only three major and three minor exceptions to the proposition that PR and parliamentarism produce consensus democracy. Four PR-parliamentary systems are not clearly on the consensus side of the map: Ireland, Greece, Spain, and Malta. Ireland is almost exactly in the middle and hence not a significant exception. Greece and Spain are the two PR countries with notoriously impure PR systems (see Chapter 8) and are therefore not major exceptions either. The only major exception is Malta, where the proportional STV system has not

1. Because our set of thirty-six democracies includes only five presidential systems, and because France is a rather unusual presidential system, the conclusion concerning the effects of presidentialism cannot be regarded as definitive. Remember, however, that several majoritarian features are inherent in the nature of presidentialism, especially the majoritarian character of presidential cabinets and the disproportionality of presidential elections, and that presidentialism strongly promotes a system with relatively few parties. It is clearly not a coincidence that Costa Rica, Colombia, and Venezuela end up on the majoritarian side of the executives-parties dimension even though presidentialism in these three countries is combined with PR in legislative elections.

prevented the development and persistence of an almost pure two-party system. The two exceptions on the other side—clear and significant exceptions—are India and Mauritius: their ethnic and religious pluralism and the multiplicity of their ethnic and religious groups have produced multiparty systems and coalition or minority cabinets in spite of plurality elections.

Both parliamentarism and PR can be fine-tuned to fit the conditions of particular countries and also to allay any fears that the combination of PR and parliamentary government will lead to weak and unstable cabinets—however exaggerated such fears may be, given the analysis in Chapter 15 of this book. One reinforcement of parliamentary government that has been introduced in several countries is the German-style constructive vote of no confidence, which requires that parliament can dismiss a cabinet only by simultaneously electing a new cabinet.[2] One problem with this rule is that a parliament that has lost confidence in the cabinet but is too divided internally to elect a replacement may render the cabinet impotent by rejecting all or most of its legislative proposals; this scenario is similar to the divided-government situation that often afflicts presidential democracies. This problem can be solved, however, by adding the French rule that gives the cabinet the right to make its legislative proposals matters of confidence—which means that parliament can reject such proposals only by voting its lack of confidence in the cabinet by an absolute majority (see Chapter 6). The combination of these German and French rules can prevent both cabinet instability and executive-legislative deadlock without taking away parliament's ultimate power to install a cabinet in which it does have confidence.

Similarly, PR systems can be designed so as to control the degree of multipartism. The evidence does not support fears that PR, if it is too proportional, will inevitably lead to extreme

2. In the German model, it is the prime minister (chancellor) rather than the cabinet as a whole who is elected by parliament and who can be constructively replaced by parliament, but in practice this distinction is not significant.

party proliferation. Nor is there a strong connection between the degree of proportionality of PR and the effective number of parliamentary parties (see Figure 8.2). Nevertheless, if, for instance, one wants to exclude small parties with less than 5 percent of the vote from legislative representation, it is easy to do so by writing a threshold clause into the electoral law and (unlike the German electoral law) not allowing any exceptions to this rule.[3]

And the (Seemingly) Bad News

Unfortunately, there are also two pieces of bad news: both institutional and cultural traditions may present strong resistance to consensus democracy. As far as the four institutional patterns defined by the PR-plurality and parliamentary-presidential contrasts are concerned, there is a remarkable congruence with four geographical regions of the world, defined roughly in terms of the Eastern, Western, Northern, and Southern hemispheres (Powell 1982, 66–68). In the Eastern hemisphere, the "North" (western and central Europe) is mainly PR-parliamentary, whereas the "South" (especially the former British dependencies in Africa, Asia, and Australasia) is characterized by the plurality-parliamentary form of government. In the Western hemisphere, the "South" (Latin America) is largely PR-presidential in character, whereas the "North" (the United States) is the world's principal example of plurality-presidential government.[4]

Most of the older democracies, but only a few of the newer

3. The only danger of electoral thresholds, especially if they are as high as 5 percent or even higher, is that in unconsolidated party systems there may be many small parties that will be denied representation—leading to an extremely high degree of disproportionality.

4. The congruence is far from perfect, of course. France is a major exception in the PR-parliamentary "North-East"; the plurality-presidential—or majority-presidential—"North-West" has extensions into East Asia (especially the Philippines), Central Asia (the former Soviet republics), and eastern Europe (Ukraine, Belarus, and Moldova); and the plurality-parliamentary "South-East" has important representatives in other regions (Canada and former British colonies in the Caribbean as well as the United Kingdom itself in western Europe).

ones (like the Czech Republic, Hungary, Slovenia, Estonia, and Latvia), are in the PR-parliamentary "North-East." Most of the newer democracies—both those analyzed in this book and the somewhat younger ones—as well as most of the democratizing countries are in the "South-East" and "South-West." These two regions are characterized by either plurality elections or presidentialism. The majoritarian propensities of these institutions and the strength of institutional conservatism are obstacles to consensus democracy that may not be easy to overcome.

The second piece of bad news appears to be that consensus democracy may not be able to take root and thrive unless it is supported by a consensual political culture. Although the focus of this book has been on institutions rather than culture, it is clear that a consensus-oriented culture often provides the basis for and connections between the institutions of consensus democracy. For instance, four of the five elements of the executives-parties dimension are structurally connected—PR leading to multipartism, multipartism to coalition cabinets, and so on—but there is no such structural connection between these four and the fifth element of interest group corporatism. The most plausible explanation is cultural. Consensus democracy and majoritarian democracy are alternative sets of political institutions, but more than that: they also represent what John D. Huber and G. Bingham Powell (1994) call the "two visions" of democracy.

Similarly, four of the five elements of the second dimension of consensus democracy are structurally and functionally linked to the requirements of operating a federal system, as theorists of federalism have long insisted (see Chapter 1). But there is no such link with central bank independence. Instead, the most likely connection is a political-cultural predisposition to think in terms of dividing power among separate institutions. My final example concerns the connection found in Chapter 16 between consensus democracy and several kinder and gentler public policies. It appears more plausible to assume that both consensus democracy and these kinder, gentler policies stem from an underlying consensual and communitarian culture than that these policies are the direct result of consensus institutions.

Grounds for Optimism

These two items of bad news do not necessarily mean that consensus democracy has no chance in newly democratic and democratizing countries, because there are two important counter-arguments. One is that we tend to think of culture and structure in terms of cause and effect, respectively, but that there is actually a great deal of interaction between them; this is especially true of political culture and political structure. As Gabriel A. Almond and Sidney Verba (1963, 35) argued in *The Civic Culture,* structural and cultural phenomena are variables in "a complex, multidirectional system of causality." This means that, although a consensual culture may lead to the adoption of consensus institutions, these institutions also have the potential of making an initially adversarial culture less adversarial and more consensual. Consensus democracies like Switzerland and Austria may have consensual cultures today, but they have not always been so consensual: the Swiss fought five civil wars from the sixteenth to the middle of the nineteenth century, and the Austrians fought a brief but bloody civil war as recently as 1934. In the late 1990s, Belgium, India, and Israel have—and clearly need—consensus institutions, but they do not have consensual cultures. Observers of the Belgian political scene often wonder whether the country can stay together or will fall apart. Israel and India, too, can only be described as having highly contentious and conflictual political cultures.

Moreover, although the institutional traditions in the "South-East" and "South-West," where most of the newly democratic and democratizing countries are located, are not favorable to consensus democracy, the prevalent political cultures in these areas of the world are much more consensual than majoritarian.

In his classic work *From Empire to Nation,* Rupert Emerson (1960, 284) argued that the assumption that the majority has the "right to overrule a dissident minority after a period of debate does violence to conceptions basic to non-Western peoples." While he conceded that there were important differences among the traditions of Asian and African peoples, "their native inclination is generally toward extensive and unhurried deliberation aimed at ultimate consensus. The gradual discovery of areas of agreement is the significant feature and not the ability to come to a speedy resolution of issues by counting heads." Sir Arthur Lewis (1965, 86), a native of St. Lucia in the Caribbean and of African descent, not only strongly advocated consensus democracy for the West African countries (see Chapter 3) but also emphasized their strong consensually oriented traditions: "The tribe has made its decisions by discussion, in much the way that coalitions function; this kind of democratic procedure is at the heart of the original institutions of the people."

More recently, the same point has been made forcefully and repeatedly in the book *Will of the People: Original Democracy in Non-Western Societies* by Philippine statesman and scholar Raul S. Manglapus (1987, 69, 78, 82, 103, 107, 123, 129). He argues not only that the non-West has strong democratic traditions but that these traditions are much more consensual than majoritarian: "the common characteristic [is] the element of consensus as opposed to adversarial decisions." And time and again he describes the non-Western democratic process as a "consensual process" based on a strong "concern for harmony." My final example is a statement by Nigerian scholar and former United Nations official Adebayo Adedeji (1994, 126): "Africans are past masters in consultation, consensus, and consent. Our traditions abhor exclusion. Consequently, there is no sanctioned and institutionalized opposition in our traditional system of governance. Traditionally, politics for us has never been a zero-sum game."

Such statements are often regarded as suspect because they

have been abused by some non-Western political leaders to justify deviations from democracy (Bienen and Herbst 1991, 214). But the fact that they have been used for illegitimate purposes does not make them less valid. All of the authors I have cited are both sincere democrats and sensitive observers without ulterior nondemocratic motives. Hence the consensus-oriented political cultures of the non-Western world can be regarded as a strong counterforce to its majoritarian institutional conservatism, and they may well be able to provide fertile soil for consensus democracy.

Two Dimensions and Ten Basic Variables, 1945–96 and 1971–96

The following list contains the values of the executives-parties and federal-unitary dimensions and of the ten basic variables during the 1945–96 and 1971–96 periods. Please note that the exact years that mark the beginning of the first and longest period differ from country to country and, in fact, range from 1945 to 1977 (see Table 4.1). For the ten democracies whose period of analysis started in 1965 or later, the first year of the period 1971–96 ranges from 1965 to 1977. The thirty-six democracies are identified by the first three characters of their English names, except that AUL means Australia, AUT Austria, CR Costa Rica, JPN Japan, NZ New Zealand, PNG Papua New Guinea, UK United Kingdom, and US United States.

The values of all of the "so what?" variables analyzed in Chapters 15 and 16 are not included in this appendix for reasons of space, but may be obtained from the author. Please write to Arend Lijphart, Department of Political Science (0521), University of California, San Diego, 9500 Gilman Drive, La Jolla, CA 92093–0521; or email to alijphar@ucsd.edu.

	First (executives-parties) dimension		Second (federal-unitary) dimension		Effective number of parliamentary parties		Minimal winning one-party cabinets (%)	
	45–96	71–96	45–96	71–96	45–96	71–96	45–96	71–96
AUL	−0.78	−0.67	1.71	1.72	2.22	2.19	81.9	85.3
AUT	0.33	0.26	1.12	1.08	2.48	2.72	41.4	65.1
BAH	−1.53	−1.54	−0.16	−0.15	1.68	1.68	100.0	100.0
BAR	−1.39	−1.40	−0.44	−0.44	1.76	1.76	100.0	100.0
BEL	1.08	1.42	0.01	0.21	4.32	5.49	37.5	28.8
BOT	−1.26	−1.27	−0.50	−0.50	1.35	1.35	100.0	100.0
CAN	−1.12	−1.07	1.78	1.88	2.37	2.35	91.0	95.2
COL	−0.06	0.01	−0.46	−0.34	3.32	3.64	55.7	58.5
CR	−0.34	−0.38	−0.44	−0.44	2.41	2.42	89.4	90.0
DEN	1.25	1.45	−0.31	−0.38	4.51	5.11	30.2	23.9
FIN	1.53	1.66	−0.84	−0.83	5.03	5.17	12.8	6.0
FRA	−1.00	−0.93	−0.39	−0.17	3.43	3.54	62.5	63.5
GER	0.67	0.23	2.52	2.53	2.93	2.84	36.2	46.2
GRE	−0.73	−0.74	−0.75	−0.75	2.20	2.20	96.9	96.9
ICE	0.52	0.66	−1.03	−1.03	3.72	4.00	45.6	48.0
IND	0.29	0.29	1.22	1.23	4.11	4.11	52.5	52.5
IRE	0.01	0.12	−0.42	−0.42	2.84	2.76	58.9	57.3
ISR	1.47	1.27	−0.98	−0.97	4.55	4.16	10.8	7.9
ITA	1.07	1.16	−0.21	−0.11	4.91	5.22	10.9	9.2
JAM	−1.64	−1.83	−0.28	−0.27	1.62	1.50	100.0	100.0
JPN	0.70	0.85	0.21	0.22	3.71	4.07	48.1	31.4
LUX	0.43	0.29	−0.90	−0.89	3.36	3.68	44.1	50.0
MAL	−0.89	−0.90	−0.40	−0.39	1.99	1.99	100.0	100.0
MAU	0.29	0.29	−0.04	−0.04	2.71	2.71	14.0	14.0
NET	1.23	1.16	0.33	0.35	4.65	4.68	25.3	37.3
NZ	−1.00	−1.12	−1.78	−1.77	1.96	1.96	99.5	99.1
NOR	0.63	0.92	−0.66	−0.65	3.35	3.61	63.1	45.1
PNG	1.09	1.10	0.29	0.29	5.98	5.98	23.0	23.0
POR	0.36	0.36	−0.70	−0.70	3.33	3.33	40.2	40.2
SPA	−0.59	−0.59	0.41	0.42	2.76	2.76	73.0	73.0
SWE	0.82	1.04	−0.67	−0.79	3.33	3.52	47.5	41.4
SWI	1.77	1.87	1.52	1.61	5.24	5.57	4.1	0.0
TRI	−1.41	−1.47	−0.15	−0.12	1.82	1.83	99.1	98.7
UK	−1.21	−1.39	−1.12	−1.19	2.11	2.20	96.7	93.3
US	−0.54	−0.52	2.36	2.36	2.40	2.41	81.2	80.1
VEN	−0.05	−0.18	0.16	0.28	3.38	3.07	73.4	82.4

	Index of executive dominance		Index of dispropor-tionality (%)		Index of interest group pluralism		Index of federalism	
	45–96	71–96	45–96	71–96	45–96	71–96	45–96	71–96
AUL	5.06	4.02	9.26	10.15	2.66	2.56	5.0	5.0
AUT	5.47	5.52	2.47	1.34	0.62	0.62	4.5	4.5
BAH	5.52	5.52	15.47	15.47	3.30	3.30	1.0	1.0
BAR	5.48	5.48	15.75	15.75	2.80	2.80	1.0	1.0
BEL	1.98	1.95	3.24	3.09	1.25	1.25	3.1	3.2
BOT	5.52	5.52	11.74	11.74	2.60	2.60	1.0	1.0
CAN	4.90	4.17	11.72	12.16	3.56	3.50	5.0	5.0
COL	3.00	3.25	10.62	9.35	2.50	2.50	1.0	1.0
CR	1.00	1.00	13.65	14.31	2.50	2.50	1.0	1.0
DEN	2.28	2.09	1.83	1.78	1.00	1.12	2.0	2.0
FIN	1.24	1.49	2.93	3.17	1.31	1.00	2.0	2.0
FRA	5.52	5.52	21.08	18.65	2.84	3.00	1.2	1.3
GER	2.82	5.52	2.52	1.48	1.38	1.38	5.0	5.0
GRE	2.88	2.88	8.08	8.08	3.50	3.50	1.0	1.0
ICE	2.48	2.27	4.25	2.80	2.25	2.25	1.0	1.0
IND	2.08	2.08	11.38	11.38	2.30	2.30	4.5	4.5
IRE	3.07	2.49	3.45	3.20	2.94	2.88	1.0	1.0
ISR	1.58	1.40	2.27	3.48	1.12	1.62	3.0	3.0
ITA	1.14	1.10	3.25	3.82	3.12	3.00	1.3	1.5
JAM	5.52	5.52	17.75	21.14	3.30	3.30	1.0	1.0
JPN	2.57	2.98	5.03	5.28	1.25	1.25	2.0	2.0
LUX	4.39	5.42	3.26	3.93	1.38	1.38	1.0	1.0
MAL	5.52	5.52	2.36	2.36	3.30	3.30	1.0	1.0
MAU	1.79	1.79	16.43	16.43	1.60	1.60	1.0	1.0
NET	2.72	2.66	1.30	1.29	1.19	1.25	3.0	3.0
NZ	4.17	3.68	11.11	14.63	3.00	3.12	1.0	1.0
NOR	3.17	2.56	4.93	4.70	0.44	0.50	2.0	2.0
PNG	1.57	1.57	10.06	10.06	2.10	2.10	3.0	3.0
POR	2.09	2.09	4.04	4.04	3.00	3.00	1.0	1.0
SPA	4.36	4.36	8.15	8.15	3.25	3.25	3.0	3.0
SWE	3.42	2.73	2.09	1.77	0.50	0.50	2.0	2.0
SWI	1.00	1.00	2.53	2.98	1.00	1.00	5.0	5.0
TRI	5.52	5.52	13.66	14.89	3.30	3.30	1.2	1.3
UK	5.52	5.52	10.33	14.66	3.38	3.50	1.0	1.0
US	1.00	1.00	14.91	15.60	3.31	3.12	5.0	5.0
VEN	2.00	2.00	14.41	14.19	1.90	1.90	4.0	4.0

	Index of bicameralism		Index of constitutional rigidity		Index of judicial review		Index of central bank independence	
	45–96	71–96	45–96	71–96	45–96	71–96	45–96	71–96
AUL	4.0	4.0	4.0	4.0	3.0	3.0	0.42	0.42
AUT	2.0	2.0	3.0	3.0	3.0	3.0	0.55	0.53
BAH	2.0	2.0	3.0	3.0	2.0	2.0	0.40	0.40
BAR	2.0	2.0	2.0	2.0	2.0	2.0	0.40	0.40
BEL	3.0	3.0	3.0	3.0	1.5	2.0	0.27	0.28
BOT	2.5	2.5	2.0	2.0	2.0	2.0	0.32	0.32
CAN	3.0	3.0	4.0	4.0	3.3	3.6	0.52	0.52
COL	3.1	3.2	1.1	1.2	2.4	2.6	0.33	0.33
CR	1.0	1.0	3.0	3.0	2.0	2.0	0.39	0.39
DEN	1.3	1.0	2.0	2.0	2.0	2.0	0.46	0.46
FIN	1.0	1.0	3.0	3.0	1.0	1.0	0.28	0.28
FRA	3.0	3.0	1.6	1.9	2.2	2.8	0.32	0.29
GER	4.0	4.0	3.5	3.5	4.0	4.0	0.69	0.69
GRE	1.0	1.0	2.0	2.0	2.0	2.0	0.38	0.38
ICE	1.4	1.4	1.0	1.0	2.0	2.0	0.34	0.34
IND	3.0	3.0	3.0	3.0	4.0	4.0	0.35	0.35
IRE	2.0	2.0	2.0	2.0	2.0	2.0	0.41	0.41
ISR	1.0	1.0	1.0	1.0	1.0	1.0	0.39	0.39
ITA	3.0	3.0	2.0	2.0	2.8	3.0	0.26	0.26
JAM	2.0	2.0	3.0	3.0	2.0	2.0	0.35	0.35
JPN	3.0	3.0	4.0	4.0	2.0	2.0	0.25	0.25
LUX	1.0	1.0	3.0	3.0	1.0	1.0	0.33	0.33
MAL	1.0	1.0	3.0	3.0	2.0	2.0	0.41	0.41
MAU	1.0	1.0	3.0	3.0	3.0	3.0	0.43	0.43
NET	3.0	3.0	3.0	3.0	1.0	1.0	0.48	0.48
NZ	1.1	1.0	1.0	1.0	1.0	1.0	0.19	0.20
NOR	1.5	1.5	3.0	3.0	2.0	2.0	0.17	0.17
PNG	1.0	1.0	3.0	3.0	3.0	3.0	0.42	0.42
POR	1.0	1.0	3.0	3.0	2.0	2.0	0.28	0.28
SPA	3.0	3.0	3.0	3.0	3.0	3.0	0.25	0.25
SWE	2.0	1.0	1.3	1.6	2.0	2.0	0.29	0.29
SWI	4.0	4.0	4.0	4.0	1.0	1.0	0.60	0.63
TRI	2.0	2.0	3.0	3.0	2.0	2.0	0.39	0.39
UK	2.5	2.5	1.0	1.0	1.0	1.0	0.31	0.28
US	4.0	4.0	4.0	4.0	4.0	4.0	0.56	0.56
VEN	3.0	3.0	2.0	2.0	2.0	2.0	0.32	0.37

Alternative Measures of Multipartism, Cabinet Composition, and Disproportionality, 1945–96 and 1971–96

As explained in Chapter 5, closely allied parties in three democracies (Australia, Belgium, and Germany) and factionalized parties in five democracies (Colombia, India, Italy, Japan, and the United States) are both counted as one-and-a-half parties in this book. However, for readers who prefer to accept the parties' own definition of "parties"—which entails that closely allied parties are counted as two parties and factionalized parties as one party—the corresponding values of the eight countries on the three variables that are affected (in the periods 1945–96 and 1971–96) are listed below:

	Effective number of parliamentary parties		Minimal winning one-party cabinets (%)		Index of disproportionality (%)	
	45–96	71–96	45–96	71–96	45–96	71–96
AUL	2.50	2.44	63.8	70.8	8.94	10.05
BEL	5.05	6.83	33.7	23.9	3.24	2.99
GER	3.23	3.12	31.3	42.5	2.46	1.46
COL	2.22	2.45	57.1	60.6	11.34	9.71
IND	3.34	3.34	71.7	71.7	12.37	12.37
ITA	4.16	4.60	16.0	13.1	3.49	4.00
JPN	3.08	3.04	64.3	51.0	5.30	5.68
US	1.93	1.91	86.6	83.8	15.55	16.32

References

Adedeji, Adebayo. 1994. "An Alternative for Africa." *Journal of Democracy* 5, no. 4 (October): 119–32.

Agius, Carmel A., and Nancy A. Grosselfinger. 1995. "The Judiciary and Politics in Malta." In C. Neal Tate and Torbjörn Vallinder, eds., *The Global Expansion of Judicial Power,* 381–402. New York: New York University Press.

Alen, André, and Rusen Ergec. 1994. *Federal Belgium After the Fourth State Reform of 1993.* Brussels: Ministry of Foreign Affairs.

Almond, Gabriel A. 1983. "Corporatism, Pluralism, and Professional Memory." *World Politics* 35, no. 2 (January): 245–60.

Almond, Gabriel A., and G. Bingham Powell, Jr., eds. 1996. *Comparative Politics: A World View,* 6th ed. New York: HarperCollins.

Almond, Gabriel A., and Sidney Verba. 1963. *The Civic Culture: Political Attitudes and Democracy in Five Nations.* Princeton: Princeton University Press.

Ambler, John S. 1971. *The Government and Politics of France.* Boston: Houghton Mifflin.

Amorim Neto, Octavio, and Gary W. Cox. 1997. "Electoral Institutions, Cleavage Structures, and the Number of Parties." *American Journal of Political Science* 41, no. 1 (January): 149–74.

Anckar, Dag. 1993. "Notes on the Party Systems of Small Island States." In Tom Bryder, ed., *Party Systems, Party Behaviour and Democracy,* 153–68. Copenhagen: Copenhagen Political Studies Press.

Anderson, Christopher J., and Christine A. Guillory. 1997. "Political Institutions and Satisfaction with Democracy: A Cross-National Analysis of Consensus and Majoritarian Systems." *American Political Science Review* 91, no. 1 (March): 66–81.

Andeweg, Rudy B. 1997. "Institutional Reform in Dutch Politics: Elected Prime Minister, Personalized PR, and Popular Veto in Comparative Perspective." *Acta Politica* 32, no. 3 (Autumn): 227–57.

Arian, Asher. 1998. *The Second Republic: Politics in Israel.* Chatham, N.J.: Chatham House.

Armingeon, Klaus. 1997. "Swiss Corporatism in Comparative Perspective." *West European Politics* 20, no. 4 (October): 164–79.

Aron, Raymond. 1982. "Alternation in Government in the Industrialized Countries." *Government and Opposition* 17, no. 1 (Winter): 3–21.

Ashford, Douglas E. 1979. "Territorial Politics and Equality: Decentralization in the Modern State." *Political Studies* 27, no. 1 (March): 71–83.

Atkinson, Anthony B., Lee Rainwater, and Timothy M. Smeeding. 1995. *Income Distribution in OECD Countries: Evidence from the Luxembourg Income Study.* Paris: Organisation for Economic Co-operation and Development.

Axelrod, Robert. 1970. *Conflict of Interest: A Theory of Divergent Goals with Applications to Politics.* Chicago: Markham.

Baar, Carl. 1991. "Judicial Activism in Canada." In Kenneth M. Holland, ed., *Judicial Activism in Comparative Perspective,* 53–69. New York: St. Martin's.

——. 1992. "Social Action Litigation in India: The Operation and Limits of the World's Most Active Judiciary." In Donald W. Jackson and C. Neal Tate, eds., *Comparative Judicial Review and Public Policy,* 77–87. Westport, Conn.: Greenwood.

Baerwald, Hans H. 1986. *Party Politics in Japan.* Boston: Allen and Unwin.

Banaian, King, Leroy O. Laney, and Thomas D. Willett. 1986. "Central Bank Independence: An International Comparison." In Eugenia Froedge Toma and Mark Toma, eds., *Central Bankers, Bureaucratic Incentives, and Monetary Policy,* 199–217. Dordrecht: Kluwer Academic.

Banks, Arthur S. 1993. *Political Handbook of the World: 1993.* Binghamton, N.Y: CSA.

Banks, Arthur S., Alan J. Day, and Thomas C. Muller. 1996. *Political Handbook of the World: 1995–1996.* Binghamton, N.Y.: CSA.

———. 1997. *Political Handbook of the World: 1997.* Binghamton, N.Y.: CSA.

Becker, Theodore. 1970. *Comparative Judicial Politics.* New York: Rand McNally.

Bedau, Hugh Adam, ed. 1997. *The Death Penalty in America: Current Controversies.* New York: Oxford University Press.

Beer, Samuel. 1998. "The Roots of New Labour: Liberalism Rediscovered." *Economist* (February 7): 23–25.

Beetham, David, ed. 1994. *Defining and Measuring Democracy.* London: Sage.

Bergman, Torbjörn. 1995. *Constitutional Rules and Party Goals in Coalition Formation: An Analysis of Winning Minority Governments in Sweden.* Umeå: Department of Political Science, Umeå University.

Bienen, Henry, and Jeffrey Herbst. 1991. "Authoritarianism and Democracy in Africa." In Dankwart A. Rustow and Kenneth Paul Erickson, eds., *Comparative Political Dynamics: Global Research Perspectives,* 211–32. New York: HarperCollins.

Bienen, Henry, and Nicolas van de Walle. 1991. *Of Time and Power: Leadership Duration in the Modern World.* Stanford: Stanford University Press.

Blais, André, and R. K. Carty. 1990. "Does Proportional Representation Foster Voter Turnout?" *European Journal of Political Research* 18, no. 2 (March): 167–81.

Blais, André, Louis Massicotte, and Agnieszka Dobrzynska. 1997. "Direct Presidential Elections: A World Summary." *Electoral Studies* 16, no. 4 (December): 441–55.

Blondel, Jean. 1968. "Party Systems and Patterns of Government in Western Democracies." *Canadian Journal of Political Science* 1, no. 2 (June): 180–203.

Borrelli, Stephen A., and Terry A. Royed. 1995. "Government 'Strength' and Budget Deficits in Advanced Democracies." *European Journal of Political Research* 28, no. 2 (September): 225–260.

Boston, Jonathan, Stephen Levine, Elizabeth McLeay, and Nigel S. Roberts, eds. 1996. *New Zealand Under MMP: A New Politics?* Auckland: Auckland University Press.

Bowman, Larry W. 1991. *Mauritius: Democracy and Development in the Indian Ocean.* Boulder, Colo.: Westview.

Brass, Paul R. 1990. *The Politics of India Since Independence.* Cambridge: Cambridge University Press.

Bräutigam, Deborah. 1997. "Institutions, Economic Reform, and Democratic Consolidation in Mauritius." *Comparative Politics* 30, no. 1 (October): 45–62.

Brewer-Carías, Allan R. 1989. *Judicial Review in Comparative Law.* Cambridge: Cambridge University Press.

Browne, Eric C., and John P. Frendreis. 1980. "Allocating Coalition Payoffs by Conventional Norm: An Assessment of the Evidence from Cabinet Coalition Situations." *American Journal of Political Science* 24, no. 4 (November): 753–68.

Budge, Ian, and Valentine Herman. 1978. "Coalitions and Government Formation: An Empirically Relevant Theory." *British Journal of Political Science* 8, no. 4 (October): 459–77.

Budge, Ian, David Robertson, and Derek Hearl, eds. 1987. *Ideology, Strategy and Party Change: Spatial Analyses of Post-War Election Programmes in 19 Democracies.* Cambridge: Cambridge University Press.

Busch, Andreas. 1994. "Central Bank Independence and the Westminster Model." *West European Politics* 17, no. 1 (January): 53–72.

Butler, David. 1978. "Conclusion." In David Butler, ed., *Coalitions in British Politics,* 112–18. New York: St. Martin's.

Butler, David, Andrew Adonis, and Tony Travers. 1994. *Failure in British Government: The Politics of the Poll Tax.* Oxford: Oxford University Press.

Butler, David, and Austin Ranney. 1978. "Theory." In David Butler and Austin Ranney, eds., *Referendums: A Comparative Study of Practice and Theory,* 23–37. Washington, D.C.: American Enterprise Institute.

Buxton, James, John Kampfner, and Brian Groom. 1997. "Blair Says Scots' Home Rule Vote Will Affect Rest of UK." *Financial Times* (September 13–14): 1.

Capie, Forrest, Charles Goodhart, and Norbert Schnadt. 1994. "The

Development of Central Banking." In Forrest Capie, Charles Goodhart, Stanley Fischer, and Norbert Schnadt, eds., *The Future of Central Banking: The Tercentenary Symposium of the Bank of England*, 1–231. Cambridge: Cambridge University Press.

Cappelletti, Mauro. 1989. *The Judicial Process in Comparative Perspective*. Oxford: Clarendon.

Castles, Francis G. 1994. "The Policy Consequences of Proportional Representation: A Sceptical Commentary." *Political Science* 46, no. 2 (December): 161–71.

Castles, Francis G., and Deborah Mitchell. 1993. "Worlds of Welfare and Families of Nations." In Francis G. Castles, ed., *Families of Nations: Patterns of Public Policy in Western Democracies*, 93–128. Aldershot: Dartmouth.

Chubb, Basil. 1982. *The Government and Politics of Ireland*, 2d ed. Stanford: Stanford University Press.

Codding, George Arthur, Jr. 1961. *The Federal Government of Switzerland*. Boston: Houghton Mifflin.

Committee on the Constitutional System. 1987. *A Bicentennial Analysis of the American Political Structure: Report and Recommendations*. Washington, D.C.: Committee on the Constitutional System.

Coombs, David. 1977. "British Government and the European Community." In Dennis Kavanagh and Richard Rose, eds., *New Trends in British Politics: Issues for Research*, 83–103. London: Sage.

Coppedge, Michael. 1993. "Parties and Society in Mexico and Venezuela: Why Competition Matters." *Comparative Politics* 25, no. 3 (April): 253–74.

———. 1994. *Strong Parties and Lame Ducks: Presidential Partyarchy and Factionalism in Venezuela*. Stanford: Stanford University Press.

Cornwall, John. 1990. *The Theory of Economic Breakdown: An Institutional-Analytical Approach*. Cambridge: Basil Blackwell.

Cox, Gary W. 1997. *Making Votes Count: Strategic Coordination in the World's Electoral Systems*. Cambridge: Cambridge University Press.

Crepaz, Markus M. L. 1996. "Consensus Versus Majoritarian Democracy: Political Institutions and Their Impact on Macroeconomic Performance and Industrial Disputes." *Comparative Political Studies* 29, no. 1 (February): 4–26.

Crisp, Brian. 1994. "Limitations to Democracy in Developing Capitalist Societies: The Case of Venezuela." *World Development* 22, no. 10 (October): 1491–1509.

Crowe, Edward W. 1980. "Cross-Voting in the British House of Commons: 1945–74." *Journal of Politics* 42, no. 2 (May): 487–510.

Cukierman, Alex, Steven B. Webb, and Bilin Neyapti. 1994. *Measuring Central Bank Independence and Its Effect on Policy Outcomes.* San Francisco: ICS.

Dahl, Robert A. 1956. *A Preface to Democratic Theory.* Chicago: University of Chicago Press.

———. 1971. *Polyarchy: Participation and Opposition.* New Haven: Yale University Press.

———. 1996. "Equality versus Inequality." *PS: Political Science and Politics* 29, no. 4 (December): 639–48.

Dahl, Robert A., and Edward R. Tufte. 1973. *Size and Democracy.* Stanford: Stanford University Press.

de Swaan, Abram. 1973. *Coalition Theories and Cabinet Formations: A Study of Formal Theories of Coalition Formation Applied to Nine European Parliaments After 1918.* Amsterdam: Elsevier.

Diamond, Larry. 1989. "Introduction: Persistence, Erosion, Breakdown, and Renewal." In Larry Diamond, Juan J. Linz, and Seymour Martin Lipset, eds., *Democracy in Developing Countries: Asia,* 1–52. Boulder, Colo.: Lynne Rienner.

———. 1992. "Economic Development and Democracy Reconsidered." In Gary Marks and Larry Diamond, eds., *Reexamining Democracy: Essays in Honor of Seymour Martin Lipset,* 93–139. Newbury Park, Calif.: Sage.

Dicey, A. V. 1915. *Introduction to the Study of the Law of the Constitution,* 8th ed. London: Macmillan.

Dixon, Robert G., Jr. 1968. *Democratic Representation: Reapportionment in Law and Politics.* New York: Oxford University Press, 1968.

Dodd, Lawrence C. 1976. *Coalitions in Parliamentary Government.* Princeton: Princeton University Press.

Dogan, Mattei. 1989. "Irremovable Leaders and Ministerial Instability in European Democracies." In Mattei Dogan, ed., *Pathways to*

Power: Selecting Rulers in Pluralist Democracies, 239–75. Boulder, Colo.: Westview.

———. 1994. "Use and Misuse of Statistics in Comparative Research: Limits to Quantification in Comparative Politics." In Mattei Dogan and Ali Kazancigil, eds., *Comparing Nations: Concepts, Strategies, Substance,* 35–71. Oxford: Blackwell.

Druckman, James N. 1996. "Party Factionalism and Cabinet Durability." *Party Politics* 2, no. 3 (July): 397–407.

Duchacek, Ivo D. 1970. *Comparative Federalism: The Territorial Dimension of Politics.* New York: Holt, Rinehart and Winston.

Duncan, Neville. 1994. "Barbados: Democracy at the Crossroads." In Carlene J. Edie, ed., *Democracy in the Caribbean: Myths and Realities,* 75–91. Westport, Conn.: Praeger.

Duverger, Maurice. 1964. *Political Parties: Their Organization and Activity in the Modern State,* 3d ed. London: Methuen.

———. 1980. "A New Political System Model: Semi-Presidential Government." *European Journal of Political Research* 8, no. 2 (June): 165–87.

———. 1986. "Duverger's Law: Forty Years Later." In Bernard Grofman and Arend Lijphart, eds. *Electoral Laws and Their Political Consequences,* 69–84. New York: Agathon.

Edinger, Lewis J. 1986. *West German Politics.* New York: Columbia University Press.

Elazar, Daniel J. 1968. "Federalism." In David L. Sills, ed., *International Encyclopedia of the Social Sciences,* 5, 353–67. New York: Macmillan and Free Press.

———. 1987. *Exploring Federalism.* Tuscaloosa: University of Alabama Press.

———. 1997. "Contrasting Unitary and Federal Systems." *International Political Science Review* 18, no. 3 (July): 237–51.

Elder, Neil, Alastair H. Thomas, and David Arter. 1988. *The Consensual Democracies? The Government and Politics of the Scandinavian States,* rev. ed. Oxford: Basil Blackwell.

Elster, Jon. 1994. "Constitutional Courts and Central Banks: Suicide Prevention or Suicide Pact?" *East European Constitutional Review,* 3, nos. 3–4 (Summer–Fall): 66–71.

Emerson, Rupert. 1960. *From Empire to Nation: The Rise to Self-Assertion of Asian and African Peoples.* Cambridge, Mass.: Harvard University Press.

Emmanuel, Patrick A. M. 1992. *Elections and Party Systems in the Commonwealth Caribbean, 1944–1991.* St. Michael, Barbados: Caribbean Development Research Services.

Esping-Andersen, Gøsta. 1990. *The Three Worlds of Welfare Capitalism.* Princeton: Princeton University Press.

Favoreu, Louis. 1986. *Les cours constitutionnelles.* Paris: Presses Universitaires de France.

Feldstein, Martin. 1997. "EMU and International Conflict." *Foreign Affairs* 76, no. 6 (November–December): 60–73.

Fenno, Richard F., Jr. 1959. *The President's Cabinet: An Analysis in the Period from Wilson to Eisenhower.* Cambridge, Mass.: Harvard University Press.

Finer, S. E., ed. 1975. *Adversary Politics and Electoral Reform.* London: Anthony Wigram.

Fitzmaurice, John. 1996. *The Politics of Belgium: A Unique Federalism.* Boulder, Colo.: Westview.

Franck, Matthew J. 1996. *Against the Imperial Judiciary: The Supreme Court vs. the Sovereignty of the People.* Lawrence: University Press of Kansas.

Freedom House Survey Team. 1996. *Freedom in the World: The Annual Survey of Political Rights and Civil Liberties, 1995–1996.* New York: Freedom House.

Friedrich, Carl J. 1950. *Constitutional Government and Democracy,* rev. ed. Boston: Ginn.

Gadbois, George H., Jr. 1987. "The Institutionalization of the Supreme Court of India." In John R. Schmidhauser, ed., *Comparative Judicial Systems: Challenging Frontiers in Conceptual and Empirical Analysis,* 111–42. London: Butterworths.

Gallagher, Michael. 1991. "Proportionality, Disproportionality and Electoral systems." *Electoral Studies* 10, no. 1 (March): 33–51.

———. 1995. "Conclusion." In Michael Gallagher and Pier Vincenzo Uleri, eds., *The Referendum Experience in Europe,* 226–52. London: Macmillan.

Gallagher, Michael, Michael Laver, and Peter Mair. 1995. *Representative Government in Modern Europe,* 2d ed. New York: McGraw-Hill.

Gasiorowski, Mark J. 1996. "An Overview of the Political Regime Change Dataset." *Comparative Political Studies* 29, no. 4 (August): 469–83.

Gastil, Raymond D. 1989. *Freedom in the World: Political Rights and Civil Liberties, 1988–1989.* New York: Freedom House.
———. 1991. "The Comparative Survey of Freedom: Experiences and Suggestions." In Alex Inkeles, ed., *On Measuring Democracy: Its Consequences and Concomitants,* 21–46. New Brunswick, N.J.: Transaction.

Gerlich, Peter. 1992. "A Farewell to Corporatism." *West European Politics* 15, no. 1 (January): 132–46.

Gobeyn, Mark James. 1993. "Explaining the Decline of Macro-Corporatist Political Bargaining Structures in Advanced Capitalist Societies." *Governance* 6, no. 1 (January): 3–22.

Goldey, David, and Philip Williams. 1983. "France." In Vernon Bogdanor and David Butler, eds., *Democracy and Elections: Electoral Systems and Their Political Consequences,* 62–83. Cambridge: Cambridge University Press.

Goodin, Robert E. 1996. "Institutionalizing the Public Interest: The Defense of Deadlock and Beyond." *American Political Science Review* 90, no. 2 (June): 331–43.

Goodman, John B. 1991. "The Politics of Central Bank Independence." *Comparative Politics* 23, no. 3 (April): 329–49.

Gorges, Michael J. 1996. *Euro-Corporatism? Interest Intermediation in the European Community.* Lanham, Md.: University Press of America.

Grilli, Vittorio, Donato Masciandaro, and Guido Tabellini. 1991. "Political and Monetary Institutions and Public Financial Policies in the Industrial Countries." *Economic Policy: A European Forum* 6, no. 2 (October): 342–92.

Grimsson, Olafur R. 1982. "Iceland: A Multilevel Coalition System." In Eric C. Browne and John Dreijmanis, eds., *Government Coalitions in Western Democracies,* 142–86. New York: Longman.

Grofman, Bernard, and Peter van Roozendaal. 1997. "Modeling Cabinet Durability and Termination." *British Journal of Political Science* 27, no. 3 (July): 419–51.

Grosser, Alfred. 1964. "The Evolution of European Parliaments." In Stephen R. Graubard, ed., *A New Europe?* 219–44. Boston: Houghton Mifflin.

Gutmann, Emanuel. 1988. "Israel: Democracy Without a Constitution." In Vernon Bogdanor, ed., *Constitutions in Democratic Politics,* 290–308. Aldershot: Gower.

Gwartney, James, Robert Lawson, and Walter Block. 1996. *Economic Freedom of the World: 1975–1995*. Vancouver: Fraser Institute.

Haggard, Stephan, and Robert R. Kaufman. 1995. *The Political Economy of Democratic Transitions*. Princeton: Princeton University Press.

Hahm, Sung Deuk, Mark S. Kamlet, and David C. Mowery. 1996. "The Political Economy of Deficit Spending in Nine Industrialized Parliamentary Democracies: The Role of Fiscal Institutions." *Comparative Political Studies* 29, no. 1 (February): 52–77.

Hailsham, Lord. 1978. *The Dilemma of Democracy: Diagnosis and Prescription*. London: Collins.

Hall, Peter A. 1994. "Central Bank Independence and Coordinated Wage Bargaining: Their Interaction in Germany and Europe." *German Politics and Society*, Issue 31 (Spring): 1–23.

Hamilton, Alexander, John Jay, and James Madison. 1788. *The Federalist*. New York: McLean.

Hartlyn, Jonathan. 1989. "Colombia: The Politics of Violence and Accommodation." In Larry Diamond, Juan J. Linz, and Seymour Martin Lipset, eds., *Democracy in Developing Countries: Latin America*, 291–334. Boulder, Colo.: Lynne Rienner.

Hattenhauer, Hans, and Werner Kaltefleiter, eds. 1986. *Mehrheitsprinzip, Konsens und Verfassung*. Heidelberg: C. F. Müller Juristischer Verlag.

Hazan, Reuven Y. 1997. "Executive-Legislative Relations in an Era of Accelerated Reform: Reshaping Government in Israel." *Legislative Studies Quarterly* 22, no. 3 (August): 329–50.

Heller, William B. 1997. "Bicameralism and Budget Deficits: The Effect of Parliamentary Structure on Government Spending." *Legislative Studies Quarterly* 22, no. 4 (November): 485–516.

Hix, Simon. 1994. "The Study of the European Community." *West European Politics* 17, no. 1 (January): 1–30.

Holm, John D. 1988. "Botswana: A Paternalistic Democracy." In Larry Diamond, Juan J. Linz, and Seymour Martin Lipset, eds., *Democracy in Developing Countries: Africa*, 179–215. Boulder, Colo.: Lynne Rienner.

———. 1989. "Elections and Democracy in Botswana." In John D. Holm and Patrick Molutsi, eds., *Democracy in Botswana: The*

Proceedings of a Symposium Held in Gabarone, 1–5 August 1988, 189–202. Gabarone: Macmillan Botswana.

Holm, John D., Patrick P. Molutsi, and Gloria Somolekae. 1996. "The Development of Civil Society in a Democratic State: The Botswana Model." *African Studies Review* 39, no. 2 (September): 43–69.

Holmes, Kim R., Bryan T. Johnson, and Melanie Kirkpatrick. 1997. *1997 Index of Economic Freedom.* Washington, D.C.: Heritage Foundation.

Horwill, George. 1925. *Proportional Representation: Its Dangers and Defects.* London: Allen and Unwin.

Huber, John D. 1996. *Rationalizing Parliament: Legislative Institutions and Party Politics in France.* Cambridge: Cambridge University Press.

Huber, John D., and G. Bingham Powell, Jr. 1994. "Congruence Between Citizens and Policymakers in Two Visions of Liberal Democracy." *World Politics* 46, no. 3 (April): 291–326.

Huntington, Samuel P. 1991. *The Third Wave: Democratization in the Late Twentieth Century.* Norman: University of Oklahoma Press.

Inglehart, Ronald. 1977. *The Silent Revolution: Changing Values and Political Styles Among Western Publics.* Princeton: Princeton University Press.

———. 1997. *Modernization and Postmodernization: Cultural, Economic, and Political Change in Forty-Three Societies.* Princeton: Princeton University Press.

Inkeles, Alex, ed. 1991. *On Measuring Democracy: Its Consequences and Concomitants.* New Brunswick, N.J.: Transaction.

International IDEA. 1997. *Voter Turnout from 1945 to 1997: A Global Report on Political Participation.* Stockholm: International Institute for Democracy and Electoral Assistance.

International Labour Organization. 1996. *Yearbook of Labour Statistics 1996.* Geneva: International Labour Office.

Inter-Parliamentary Union. 1995. *Women in Parliaments, 1945–1995: A World Statistical Survey.* Geneva: Inter-Parliamentary Union.

Jackson, Keith, and Alan McRobie. 1998. *New Zealand Adopts Proportional Representation: Accident? Design? Evolution?* Aldershot: Ashgate.

Jaggers, Keith, and Ted Robert Gurr. 1995. *Polity III: Regime Change and Political Authority, 1800–1994* (computer file). Ann Arbor, Mich.: Inter-University Consortium for Political and Social Research.

Johnson, Nevil. 1998. "The Judicial Dimension in British Politics." *West European Politics* 21, no. 1 (January): 148–66.

Jones, Charles O. 1994. *The Presidency in a Separated System.* Washington, D.C.: Brookings Institution.

Jones, Mark P. 1995. *Electoral Laws and the Survival of Presidential Democracies.* Notre Dame, Ind.: University of Notre Dame Press.

Jung, Sabine. 1996. "Lijpharts Demokratietypen und die direkte Demokratie." *Zeitschrift für Politikwissenschaft* 6, no. 3: 623–45.

Kaiser, André. 1997. "Types of Democracy: From Classical to New Institutionalism." *Journal of Theoretical Politics* 9, no. 4 (October): 419–44.

Katz, Richard S. 1980. *A Theory of Parties and Electoral Systems.* Baltimore: Johns Hopkins University Press.

Katzenstein, Peter J. 1985. *Small States in World Markets: Industrial Policy in Europe.* Ithaca: Cornell University Press.

Kavanagh, Dennis. 1974. "An American Science of British Politics." *Political Studies* 22, no. 3 (September): 251–70.

Keeler, John T. S., and Martin A. Schain. 1997. "Institutions, Political Poker, and Regime Evolution in France." In Kurt von Mettenheim, ed., *Presidential Institutions and Democratic Politics: Comparing Regional and National Contexts,* 84–105. Baltimore: Johns Hopkins University Press.

King, Anthony. 1976. "Modes of Executive-Legislative Relations: Great Britain, France, and West Germany." *Legislative Studies Quarterly* 1, no. 1 (February): 11–36.

———. 1994. " 'Chief Executives' in Western Europe." In Ian Budge and David McKay, eds., *Developing Democracy: Comparative Research in Honour of J. F. P. Blondel,* 150–63. London: Sage.

Kirchner, Emil J. 1994. "The European Community: A Transnational Democracy?" In Ian Budge and David McKay, eds., *Developing Democracy: Comparative Research in Honour of J. F. P. Blondel,* 253–66. London: Sage.

Klingemann, Hans-Dieter. 1999. "Mapping Political Support in the 1990s: A Global Analysis." In Pippa Norris, ed., *Critical Cit-*

izens: Global Support for Democratic Government. Oxford: Oxford University Press.

Klingemann, Hans-Dieter, Richard I. Hofferbert, and Ian Budge. 1994. *Parties, Policies, and Democracy.* Boulder, Colo.: Westview.

Kothari, Rajni. 1970. *Politics in India.* Boston: Little, Brown.

Krauss, Ellis S. 1984. "Conflict in the Diet: Toward Conflict Management in Parliamentary Politics." In Ellis S. Krauss, Thomas P. Rohlen, and Patricia G. Steinhoff, eds., *Conflict in Japan,* 243–93. Honolulu: University of Hawaii Press.

Laakso, Markku, and Rein Taagepera. 1979. " 'Effective' Number of Parties: A Measure with Application to West Europe." *Comparative Political Studies* 12, no. 1 (April): 3–27.

Landfried, Christine. 1995. "Germany." In C. Neal Tate and Torbjörn Vallinder, eds., *The Global Expansion of Judicial Power,* 307–24. New York: New York University Press.

Lane, Jan-Erik, and Svante Ersson. 1994a. *Comparative Politics: An Introduction and New Approach.* Cambridge: Polity.

———. 1994b. *Politics and Society in Western Europe,* 3d ed. London: Sage.

———. 1997. "The Institutions of Konkordanz and Corporatism: How Closely Are They Connected?" *Swiss Political Science Review* 3, no. 1 (Spring): 5–29.

Lane, Jan-Erik, David McKay, and Kenneth Newton. 1997. *Political Data Handbook: OECD Countries,* 2d ed. Oxford: Oxford University Press.

LaPalombara, Joseph. 1987. *Democracy, Italian Style.* New Haven and London: Yale University Press.

Laver, Michael, and W. Ben Hunt. 1992. *Policy and Party Competition.* New York: Routledge.

Laver, Michael, and Norman Schofield. 1990. *Multiparty Government: The Politics of Coalition in Europe.* Oxford: Oxford University Press.

Laver, Michael, and Kenneth A. Shepsle. 1996. *Making and Breaking Governments: Cabinets and Legislatures in Parliamentary Democracies.* Cambridge: Cambridge University Press.

Lawson, Stephanie. 1993. "Conceptual Issues in the Comparative Study of Regime Change and Democratization." *Comparative Politics* 25, no. 2 (January): 183–205.

Lehmbruch, Gerhard. 1993. "Consociational Democracy and Corporatism in Switzerland." *Publius* 23, no. 2 (Spring): 43–60.

Lehner, Franz. 1984. "Consociational Democracy in Switzerland: A Political-Economic Explanation and Some Empirical Evidence." *European Journal of Political Research* 12, no. 1 (March): 25–42.

Leiserson, Michael. 1970. "Coalition Government in Japan." In Sven Groennings, E. W. Kelley, and Michael Leiserson, eds., *The Study of Coalition Behavior: Theoretical Perspectives and Cases from Four Continents,* 80–102. New York: Holt, Rinehart, and Winston.

Leonardi, Robert, and Douglas A. Wertman. 1989. *Italian Christian Democracy: The Politics of Dominance.* New York: St. Martin's.

Levine, Daniel H. 1989. "Venezuela: The Nature, Sources, and Prospects of Democracy." In Larry Diamond, Juan J. Linz, and Seymour Martin Lipset, eds., *Democracy in Developing Countries: Latin America,* 247–89. Boulder, Colo.: Lynne Rienner.

Levine, Stephen. 1979. *The New Zealand Political System: Politics in a Small Society.* Sydney: George Allen and Unwin.

Lewin, Leif. 1994. "The Rise and Decline of Corporatism: The Case of Sweden." *European Journal of Political Research* 26, no. 1 (July): 59–79.

Lewis, W. Arthur. 1965. *Politics in West Africa.* London: George Allen and Unwin.

Lijphart, Arend. 1984. *Democracies: Patterns of Majoritarian and Consensus Government in Twenty-One Countries.* New Haven and London: Yale University Press.

———. 1994. *Electoral Systems and Party Systems: A Study of Twenty-Seven Democracies, 1945–1990.* Oxford: Oxford University Press.

———. 1997a. "Dimensions of Democracies." *European Journal of Political Research* 31, nos. 1–2 (February): 195–204.

———. 1997b. "Unequal Participation: Democracy's Unresolved Dilemma." *American Political Science Review* 91, no. 1 (March): 1–14.

Lijphart, Arend, and Markus M. L. Crepaz. 1991. "Corporatism and Consensus Democracy in Eighteen Countries: Conceptual and Empirical Linkages." *British Journal of Political Science* 21, no. 2 (April): 235–46.

Linder, Wolf. 1994. *Swiss Democracy: Possible Solutions to Conflict in Multicultural Societies.* New York: St. Martin's.

Linz, Juan J., and Arturo Valenzuela, eds. 1994. *The Failure of Presidential Democracy.* Baltimore: Johns Hopkins University Press.

Lipset, Seymour Martin. 1960. *Political Man: The Social Bases of Politics.* Garden City, N.Y.: Doubleday.

Lipset, Seymour Martin, and Stein Rokkan. 1967. "Cleavage Structures, Party Systems, and Voter Alignments: An Introduction." In Seymour M. Lipset and Stein Rokkan, eds., *Party Systems and Voter Alignments: Cross-National Perspectives,* 1–64. New York: Free Press.

Lohmann, Susanne. 1998. "Federalism and Central Bank Independence: The Politics of German Monetary Policy, 1957–1992." *World Politics* 50, no. 3 (April): 401–46.

Longley, Lawrence D., and David M. Olson, eds. 1991. *Two into One: The Politics and Processes of National Legislative Cameral Change.* Boulder, Colo.: Westview.

Loosemore, John, and Victor J. Hanby. 1971. "The Theoretical Limits of Maximum Distortion: Some Analytical Expressions for Electoral Systems." *British Journal of Political Science* 1, no. 4 (October): 467–77.

Loughlin, John, and Sonia Mazey, eds. 1995. *The End of the French Unitary State? Ten Years of Regionalization in France (1982–1992).* London: Frank Cass.

Lowell, A. Lawrence. 1896. *Governments and Parties in Continental Europe.* Boston: Houghton Mifflin.

MacDonald, Scott B. 1986. *Trinidad and Tobago: Democracy and Development in the Caribbean.* New York: Praeger.

Mackie, Thomas T., and Richard Rose. 1991. *The International Almanac of Electoral History,* 3d ed. London: Macmillan.

Mackie, Thomas T., and Richard Rose. 1997. *A Decade of Election Results: Updating the International Almanac.* Glasgow: Centre for the Study of Public Policy, University of Glasgow.

McRae, Kenneth D. 1983. *Conflict and Compromise in Multilingual Societies: Switzerland.* Waterloo, Ont.: Wilfrid Laurier University Press.

———. 1986. *Conflict and Compromise in Multilingual Societies: Belgium.* Waterloo, Ont.: Wilfrid Laurier University Press.

———. 1997. "Contrasting Styles of Democratic Decision-Making: Adversarial versus Consensual Politics." *International Political Science Review* 18, no. 3 (July): 279–95.

Maddex, Robert L. 1995. *Constitutions of the World*. Washington, D.C.: Congressional Quarterly.

Mahler, Gregory S. 1997. "The 'Westminster Model' Away from Westminster: Is It Always the Most Appropriate Model?" In Abdo I. Baaklini and Helen Desfosses, eds., *Designs for Democratic Stability: Studies in Viable Constitutionalism*, 35–51. Armonk, N.Y.: M. E. Sharpe.

Mainwaring, Scott, and Matthew Soberg Shugart. 1997. "Introduction." In Scott Mainwaring and Matthew Soberg Shugart, eds., *Presidentialism and Democracy in Latin America*, 1–11. Cambridge: Cambridge University Press.

Mair, Peter. 1994. "The Correlates of Consensus Democracy and the Puzzle of Dutch Politics." *West European Politics* 17, no. 4 (October): 97–123.

Manglapus, Raul S. 1987. *Will of the People: Original Democracy in Non-Western Societies*. New York: Greenwood.

Mansbridge, Jane. 1980. *Beyond Adversary Democracy*. New York: Basic Books.

———. 1996. "Reconstructing Democracy." In Nancy J. Hirschmann and Christine Di Stefano, eds., *Revisioning the Political: Feminist Reconstructions of Traditional Concepts in Western Political Theory*, 117–38. Boulder, Colo.: Westview.

Mathur, Hansraj. 1991. *Parliament in Mauritius*. Stanley, Rose-Hill, Mauritius: Editions de l'Océan Indien.

———. 1997. "Party Cooperation and the Electoral System in Mauritius." In Brij V. Lal and Peter Larmour, eds., *Electoral Systems in Divided Societies: The Fiji Constitution Review*, 135–46. Canberra: National Centre for Development Studies, Australian National University.

Mauer, Marc. 1994. *Americans Behind Bars: The International Use of Incarceration, 1992–1993*. Washington, D.C.: Sentencing Project.

———. 1997. *Americans Behind Bars: U.S. and International Use of Incarceration, 1995*. Washington, D.C.: Sentencing Project.

Maxfield, Sylvia. 1997. *Gatekeepers of Growth: The International Political Economy of Central Banking in Developing Countries*. Princeton: Princeton University Press.

May, Clifford D. 1987. "Political Speechmaking: Biden and the Annals of Raised Eyebrows." *New York Times* (September 21): B8.

Messick, Richard E., ed. 1996. *World Survey of Economic Freedom, 1995–1996: A Freedom House Study.* New Brunswick, N.J.: Transaction.

Mill, John Stuart. 1861. *Considerations on Representative Government.* London: Parker, Son, and Bourn.

Moreno, Luís. 1994. "Ethnoterritorial Concurrence and Imperfect Federalism in Spain." In Bertus de Villiers, ed., *Evaluating Federal Systems,* 162–93. Dordrecht: Martinus Nijhoff.

Müller, Wolfgang C., and Kaare Strøm, eds. 1997. *Koalitionsregierungen in Westeuropa: Bildung, Arbeitsweise und Beendigung.* Vienna: Signum Verlag.

Munroe, Trevor. 1996. "Caribbean Democracy: Decay or Renewal?" In Jorge I. Domínguez and Abraham F. Lowenthal, eds., *Constructing Democratic Governance: Mexico, Central America, and the Caribbean in the 1990s,* 104–17. Baltimore: Johns Hopkins University Press.

Muravchik, Joshua. 1991. *Exporting Democracy: Fulfilling America's Destiny.* Washington, D.C.: AEI.

Nohlen, Dieter. 1978. *Wahlsysteme der Welt—Daten und Analysen: Ein Handbuch.* Munich: Piper.

——. 1984. "Changes and Choices in Electoral Systems." In Arend Lijphart and Bernard Grofman, eds., *Choosing an Electoral System: Issues and Alternatives,* 217–24. New York: Praeger.

Nohlen, Dieter, ed. 1993. *Enciclopedia electoral latinoamericana y del Caribe.* San José, Costa Rica: Instituto Interamericano de Derechos Humanos.

O'Donnell, Guillermo. 1994. "Delegative Democracy." *Journal of Democracy* 5, no. 1 (January): 55–69.

OECD. 1990. *OECD Economic Outlook,* 47. Paris: Organisation for Economic Co-operation and Development.

——. 1991. *OECD Economic Outlook,* 50. Paris: Organisation for Economic Co-operation and Development.

——. 1995. *Labour Force Statistics.* Paris: Organisation for Economic Co-operation and Development.

——. 1996a. *OECD Economic Outlook,* 60. Paris: Organisation for Economic Co-operation and Development.

———. 1996b. *Labour Force Statistics*. Paris: Organisation for Economic Co-operation and Development.

———. 1998. *OECD Economic Outlook*, 63. Paris: Organisation for Economic Co-operation and Development.

Ordeshook, Peter C., and Olga V. Shvetsova. 1994. "Ethnic Heterogeneity, District Magnitude, and the Number of Parties." *American Journal of Political Science* 38, no. 1 (February): 100–123.

Palmer, Monte. 1997. *Political Development: Dilemmas and Challenges*. Itasca, Ill.: Peacock.

Payne, Anthony. 1993. "Westminster Adapted: The Political Order of the Commonwealth Caribbean." In Jorge I. Domínguez, Robert A. Pastor, and R. DeLisle Worrell, eds., *Democracy in the Caribbean: Political, Economic, and Social Perspectives*, 57–73. Baltimore: Johns Hopkins University Press.

Peeler, John A. 1985. *Latin American Democracies: Colombia, Costa Rica, Venezuela*. Chapel Hill: University of North Carolina Press.

Pekkarinen, Jukka, Matti Pohjola, and Bob Rowthorn, eds. 1992. *Social Corporatism: A Superior Economic System?* Oxford: Clarendon.

Pempel, T. J. 1992. "Japanese Democracy and Political Culture: A Comparative Perspective." *PS: Political Science and Politics* 25, no. 1 (March): 5–12.

Peters, B. Guy. 1997. "The Separation of Powers in Parliamentary Systems." In Kurt von Mettenheim, ed., *Presidential Institutions and Democratic Politics: Comparing Regional and National Contexts*, 67–83. Baltimore: Johns Hopkins University Press.

Powell, G. Bingham, Jr. 1980. "Voting Turnout in Thirty Democracies: Partisan, Legal, and Socio-Economic Influences." In Richard Rose, ed., *Electoral Participation: A Comparative Analysis*, 5–34. Beverly Hills: Sage.

———. 1982. *Contemporary Democracies: Participation, Stability, and Violence*. Cambridge, Mass.: Harvard University Press.

———. 1989. "Constitutional Design and Citizen Electoral Control." *Journal of Theoretical Politics* 1, no. 2 (April): 107–30.

Power, Timothy J., and Mark J. Gasiorowski. 1997. "Institutional Design and Democratic Consolidation in the Third World." *Comparative Political Studies* 30, no. 2 (April): 123–55.

Premdas, Ralph R. 1993. "Race, Politics, and Succession in Trinidad and Guyana." In Anthony Payne and Paul Sutton, eds., *Modern Caribbean Politics*, 98–124. Baltimore: Johns Hopkins University Press.

Rae, Douglas W. 1967. *The Political Consequences of Electoral Laws*. New Haven: Yale University Press.

Rae, Douglas W., and Michael Taylor. 1970. *The Analysis of Political Cleavages*. New Haven: Yale University Press.

Ray, James Lee. 1997. "The Democratic Path to Peace." *Journal of Democracy* 8, no. 2 (April): 49–64.

Reed, Steven R., and John M. Bolland. 1999. "The Fragmentation Effect of SNTV in Japan." In Bernard Grofman, Sung-Chull Lee, Edwin Winckler, and Brian Woodall, eds., *Elections in Japan, Korea, and Taiwan Under the Single Non-Transferable Vote: The Comparative Study of an Embedded Institution*. Ann Arbor: University of Michigan Press.

Reich, Robert B. 1997. *Locked in the Cabinet*. New York: Alfred A. Knopf.

Reynolds, Andrew, and Ben Reilly. 1997. *The International IDEA Handbook of Electoral System Design*. Stockholm: International Institute for Democracy and Electoral Assistance.

Riker, William H. 1962. *The Theory of Political Coalitions*. New Haven: Yale University Press.

———. 1975. "Federalism." In Fred I. Greenstein and Nelson W. Polsby, eds., *Handbook of Political Science, 5: Governmental Institutions and Processes*, 93–172. Reading, Mass.: Addison-Wesley.

———. 1982. *Liberalism Against Populism: A Confrontation Between the Theory of Democracy and the Theory of Social Choice*. San Francisco: Freeman.

Rogowski, Ronald. 1987. "Trade and the Variety of Democratic Institutions." *International Organization* 41, no. 2 (Spring): 203–23.

Rose, Richard. 1974. "A Model Democracy?" In Richard Rose, ed., *Lessons from America: An Exploration*, 131–61. New York: Wiley.

———. 1992. *What Are the Economic Consequences of PR?* London: Electoral Reform Society.

Rose, Richard, and Dennis Kavanagh. 1976. "The Monarchy in Contemporary Political Culture." *Comparative Politics* 8, no. 4 (July): 548–76.

Roubini, Nouriel, and Jeffrey D. Sachs. 1989. "Political and Economic Determinants of Budget Deficits in the Industrial Democ-racies." *European Economic Review* 33, no. 5 (May): 903–38.

Rule, Wilma, and Joseph F. Zimmerman, eds. 1994. *Electoral Systems in Comparative Perspective: Their Impact on Women and Minorities.* Westport, Conn.: Greenwood.

Sartori, Giovanni. 1976. *Parties and Party Systems: A Framework for Analysis.* Cambridge: Cambridge University Press.

———. 1994a. *Comparative Constitutional Engineering: An Inquiry into Structures, Incentives, and Outcomes.* New York: New York University Press.

———. 1994b. "Neither Presidentialism nor Parliamentarism." In Juan J. Linz and Arturo Valenzuela, eds., *The Failure of Presidential Democracy,* 106–18. Baltimore: Johns Hopkins University Press.

Schmidt, Manfred G. 1996. "Germany: The Grand Coalition State." In Josep M. Colomer, ed., *Political Institutions in Europe,* 62–98. London: Routledge.

———. 1997. "Determinants of Social Expenditure in Liberal Democracies: The Post World War II Experience." *Acta Politica* 32, no. 3 (Summer): 153–73.

Schmitter, Philippe C. 1982. "Reflections on Where the Theory of Neo-Corporatism Has Gone and Where the Praxis of Neo-Corporatism May Be Going." In Gerhard Lehmbruch and Philippe C. Schmitter, eds., *Patterns of Corporatist Policy-Making,* 259–79. London: Sage.

———. 1989. "Corporatism Is Dead! Long Live Corporatism!" *Government and Opposition* 24, no. 1 (Winter): 54–73.

Scott, K. J. 1962. *The New Zealand Constitution.* Oxford: Clarendon.

Seliktar, Ofira. 1982. "Israel: Fragile Coalitions in a New Nation." In Eric C. Browne and John Dreijmanis, eds., *Government Coalitions in Western Democracies,* 283–314. New York: Longman.

Senelle, Robert. 1996. "The Reform of the Belgian State." In Joachim Jens Hesse and Vincent Wright, eds., *Federalizing Europe? The Costs, Benefits, and Preconditions of Federal Political Systems,* 266–324. Oxford: Oxford University Press.

Shapiro, Martin, and Alec Stone. 1994. "The New Constitutional Politics of Europe." *Comparative Political Studies* 26, no. 4 (January): 397–420.

Shugart, Matthew Soberg, and John M. Carey. 1992. *Presidents and*

Assemblies: Constitutional Design and Electoral Dynamics. Cambridge: Cambridge University Press.

Shugart, Matthew Soberg, and Scott Mainwaring. 1997. "Presidentialism and Democracy in Latin America: Rethinking the Terms of the Debate." In Scott Mainwaring and Matthew Soberg Shugart, eds., *Presidentialism and Democracy in Latin America*, 12–54. Cambridge: Cambridge University Press.

Siaroff, Alan. 1998. "Corporatism in Twenty-Four Industrial Democracies: Meaning and Measurement" (unpublished manuscript).

Siegfried, André. 1956. "Stable Instability in France." *Foreign Affairs* 34, no. 3 (April): 394–404.

Singh, V. B. 1994. *Elections in India, Volume 2: Data Handbook on Lok Sabha Elections, 1986–1991.* New Delhi: Sage India.

Steiner, Jürg. 1971. "The Principles of Majority and Proportionality." *British Journal of Political Science* 1, no. 1 (January): 63–70.

———. 1974. *Amicable Agreement Versus Majority Rule: Conflict Resolution in Switzerland.* Chapel Hill: University of North Carolina Press.

Stone, Alec. 1992. *The Birth of Judicial Politics in France: The Constitutional Council in Comparative Perspective.* New York: Oxford University Press.

Strøm, Kaare. 1990. *Minority Government and Majority Rule.* Cambridge: Cambridge University Press.

———. 1995. "Coalition Building." In Seymour Martin Lipset et al., eds., *The Encyclopedia of Democracy*, 1, 255–58. Washington, D.C.: Congressional Quarterly.

———. 1997. "Democracy, Accountability, and Coalition Bargaining." *European Journal of Political Research* 31, nos. 1–2 (February): 47–62.

Strøm, Kaare, Ian Budge, and Michael J. Laver. 1994. "Constraints on Cabinet Formation in Parliamentary Democracies." *American Journal of Political Science* 38, no. 2 (May): 303–35.

Strøm, Kaare, and Jørn Y. Leipart. 1993. "Policy, Institutions, and Coalition Avoidance: Norwegian Governments, 1945–1990." *American Political Science Review* 87, no. 4 (December): 870–87.

Taagepera, Rein. 1994. "Beating the Law of Minority Attrition." In Wilma Rule and Joseph F. Zimmerman, eds., *Electoral Systems in Comparative Perspective: Their Impact on Women and Minorities,* 236–45. Westport, Conn.: Greenwood.

Taagepera, Rein, and Bernard Grofman. 1985. "Rethinking Duverger's Law: Predicting the Effective Number of Parties in Plurality and PR Systems—Parties Minus Issues Equals One." *European Journal of Political Research* 13, no. 4 (December): 341–52.

Taagepera, Rein, and Matthew Soberg Shugart. 1989. *Seats and Votes: The Effects and Determinants of Electoral Systems.* New Haven and London: Yale University Press.

Tarlton, Charles D. 1965. "Symmetry and Asymmetry as Elements of Federalism: A Theoretical Speculation." *Journal of Politics* 27, no. 4 (November): 861–74.

Tate, C. Neal, and Torbjörn Vallinder, eds. 1995. *The Global Expansion of Judicial Power.* New York: New York University Press.

Taylor, Charles Lewis. 1986. *Handbook of Political and Social Indicators III: 1948–1982* (computer file), 2d ICPSR ed. Ann Arbor, Michigan: Inter-University Consortium for Political and Social Research.

Taylor, Charles Lewis, and David A. Jodice. 1983. *World Handbook of Political and Social Indicators,* 3d ed. New Haven and London: Yale University Press.

Taylor, Michael, and Valentine M. Herman. 1971. "Party Systems and Government Stability." *American Political Science Review* 65, no. 1 (March): 28–37.

Therborn, Göran. 1977. "The Rule of Capital and the Rise of Democracy." *New Left Review* 103 (May–June): 3–41.

Thorndike, Tony. 1993. "Revolution, Democracy, and Regional Integration in the Eastern Caribbean." In Anthony Payne and Paul Sutton, eds., *Modern Caribbean Politics,* 147–75. Baltimore: Johns Hopkins University Press.

Transparency International. 1997. *Corruption Perception Index.* Berlin: http://gwdu19.gwdg.de/~uwvw/rank-97.htm

Tschaeni, Hanspeter. 1982. "Constitutional Change in Swiss Cantons: An Assessment of a Recent Phenomenon." *Publius* 12, no. 1 (Winter): 113–30.

Tsebelis, George. 1995. "Decision Making in Political Systems: Veto Players in Presidentialism, Parliamentarism, Multicameralism and Multipartyism." *British Journal of Political Science* 25, no. 3 (July): 289–325.

Tsebelis, George, and Jeannette Money. 1997. *Bicameralism*. Cambridge: Cambridge University Press.

Tufte, Edward R. 1978. *Political Control of the Economy*. Princeton, N.J.: Princeton University Press.

Tummala, Krishna K. 1996. "The Indian Union and Emergency Powers." *International Political Science Review* 17, no. 4 (October): 373–84.

United Nations Development Programme. 1994. *Human Development Report 1994*. New York: Oxford University Press.

———. 1995. *Human Development Report 1995*. New York: Oxford University Press.

———. 1996. *Human Development Report 1996*. New York: Oxford University Press.

———. 1997. *Human Development Report 1997*. New York: Oxford University Press.

Vanhanen, Tatu. 1990. *The Process of Democratization: A Comparative Study of 147 States, 1980–88*. New York: Crane Russak.

———. 1997. *Prospects of Democracy: A Study of 172 Countries*. London: Routledge.

Varshney, Ashutosh. 1995. *Democracy, Development, and the Countryside: Urban-Rural Struggles in India*. Cambridge: Cambridge University Press.

Verba, Sidney. 1967. "Some Dilemmas in Comparative Research." *World Politics* 20, no. 1 (October 1967): 111–27.

Verney, Douglas V. 1959. *The Analysis of Political Systems*. London: Routledge and Kegan Paul.

Verougstraete, Ivan. 1992. "Judicial Politics in Belgium." *West European Politics* 15, no. 3 (July): 93–108.

von Beyme, Klaus. 1985. *Political Parties in Western Democracies*. New York: St. Martin's.

von Mettenheim, Kurt. 1997. "Introduction: Presidential Institutions and Democratic Politics." In Kurt von Mettenheim, ed., *Presidential Institutions and Democratic Politics: Comparing Regional and National Contexts*, 1–15. Baltimore: Johns Hopkins University Press.

Vowles, Jack, Peter Aimer, Susan Banducci, and Jeffrey Karp, eds. 1998. *Voters' Victory? New Zealand's First Election Under Proportional Representation*. Auckland: Auckland University Press.

Wada, Junichiro. 1996. *The Japanese Election System: Three Analytical Perspectives*. London: Routledge.

Warwick, Paul V. 1994. *Government Survival in Parliamentary Democracies*. Cambridge: Cambridge University Press.

Wheare, K. C. 1946. *Federal Government*. London: Oxford University Press.

———. 1964. *Federal Government*, 4th ed. New York: Oxford University Press.

Wiarda, Howard J. 1997. *Corporatism and Comparative Politics: The Other Great "Ism."* Armonk, N.Y.: M. E. Sharpe.

Wilensky, Harold L. 1990. "Common Problems, Divergent Policies: An Eighteen-Nation Study of Family Policy." *Public Affairs Report* 31, no. 3 (May): 1–3.

Wilson, Graham. 1990. *Interest Groups*. Oxford: Basil Blackwell.

———. 1994. "The Westminster Model in Comparative Perspective." In Ian Budge and David McKay, eds., *Developing Democracy: Comparative Research in Honour of J. F. P. Blondel*, 189–201. London: Sage.

———. 1997. "British Democracy and Its Discontents." In Metin Heper, Ali Kazancigil, and Bert A. Rockman, eds., *Institutions and Democratic Statecraft*, 59–76. Boulder, Colo.: Westview.

Wilson, Woodrow. 1884. "Committee or Cabinet Government?" *Overland Monthly*, Ser. 2, 3 (January): 17–33.

———. 1885. *Congressional Government: A Study in American Politics*. Boston: Houghton Mifflin.

Woldendorp, Jaap, Hans Keman, and Ian Budge. 1998. "Party Government in Twenty Democracies: An Update (1990–1995)." *European Journal of Political Research* 33, no. 1 (January): 125–64.

World Bank. 1992. *The World Bank Atlas: Twenty-fifth Anniversary Edition*. Washington, D.C.: International Bank for Reconstruction and Development.

———. 1993. *The World Bank Atlas 1994*. Washington, D.C.: International Bank for Reconstruction and Development.

———. 1994. *The World Bank Atlas 1995*. Washington, D.C.: International Bank for Reconstruction and Development.

———. 1995. *The World Bank Atlas 1996*. Washington, D.C.: International Bank for Reconstruction and Development.

———. 1997. *1997 World Bank Atlas*. Washington, D.C.: International Bank for Reconstruction and Development.

Index

Adedeji, Adebayo, 306
Almond, Gabriel A., 232n1, 307
Alternative vote, 71n6, 145–47, 148, 150–51, 157, 158, 198
Amati, Giuliano, 98n4
Anckar, Dag, 291–92
Anderson, Christopher J., 286–87
Apparentement, 156–57
Argentina, 54–55
Armingeon, Klaus, 38
Aron, Raymond, 121
Ashford, Douglas E., 192n1
Australia, 49–50, 52, 56, 59, 282, 288, 294–95; type of democracy in, 10, 248, 251, 255; party system of, 69–71, 75–77, 81, 84–85, 88; electoral systems of, 70, 71n6, 145–51 passim, 156–57, 161–69 passim, 285n5; executive in, 70, 108n8, 111–12, 133, 135, 138–40; parliament of, 119, 204–9 passim, 212, 214; interest groups in, 177, 182–83; federalism in, 187–94 passim, 198, 300; constitution of, 220, 222, 226–29 passim; central bank of, 236, 238, 241
Austria, 50, 56, 58, 59, 269, 277, 291; party system of, 77, 81, 82, 88; executive in, 106–7, 110–14 passim, 133, 138–39, 141; par-

liament of, 119, 121, 205, 207–9, 212–15 passim; electoral systems of, 145–46, 162, 168–69; interest groups in, 173, 177, 179, 181–83; federalism in, 187–94 passim, 198; constitution of, 220, 225–29 passim; central bank of, 236, 241; type of democracy in, 248, 251n4, 255, 307
Axelrod, Robert, 95, 97

Baar, Carl, 227
Bahamas, 50, 53, 56–57, 60, 189, 263, 298; party system of, 75, 77, 81–82, 88–89, 291; executive in, 111–12; 133, 138–40; parliament of, 119, 206, 210–14 passim; electoral system of, 145, 154–55, 162–69 passim; interest groups in, 177, 179, 182–83; constitution of, 220–21, 224–29 passim; central bank of, 236, 241; type of democracy in, 248, 250
Balladur, Edouard, 122
Barbados, 50, 53n3, 56–57, 60, 263, 276, 298; as example of majoritarian democracy, 7, 10, 27–30, 248, 250, 254n6; executive dominance in, 28, 35, 127, 133–35; executive in, 28, 110–12, 138–40; party sys-

Barbados (*continued*)
  tem of, 28–29, 32, 65, 75, 77, 81,
  88, 291; electoral system of, 29,
  145, 151, 154, 162–69 passim; interest groups in, 29–30, 177, 179,
  182–83; parliament of, 30, 119,
  200, 206, 210–14 passim; unitary
  government in, 30, 189; constitution of, 30, 219–21, 224–29 passim; central bank of, 30, 236, 241
Barco, Virgilio, 102
Bare-majority cabinets, 10–11, 21,
  28, 136. *See also* Minimal winning cabinets
Beer, Samuel, 258
Belgium, 50, 52, 56, 58, 277, 287,
  298; as example of consensus
  democracy, 7, 33–41, 248–49,
  252, 254–56, 307; executive in, 7,
  34–36, 70, 101–3, 107n6, 109–14
  passim, 132, 135, 138–40; party
  system of, 36–37, 69–71, 75–77,
  80, 82, 88; PR in, 37, 70, 145–48
  passim, 162–63, 169, 285n5; interest groups in, 37–38, 177, 182–
  83; federalism in, 38–39, 187–95
  passim, 197, 198; parliament of,
  39–40, 118–19, 127, 200, 206–9,
  210–14 passim; constitution of,
  40–41, 220, 225–29 passim, central bank of, 41, 237, 239, 241–42
Bicameralism. *See* Parliaments
Bienen, Henry, 129n5
Blackmail potential, 65–66, 78
Blair, Tony, 16, 17, 18
Block, Walter, 270
Blondel, Jean, 66–67, 69–70
Borrelli, Stephen A., 260
Botswana, 50, 53, 56–60 passim,
  189, 264–65, 276–83 passim, 295,
  298; party system of, 74–77, 81,
  84, 88, 291; executive in, 111–12,
  117, 126, 133–34, 138, 141; parliament of, 117, 119, 203, 212–14
  passim; electoral system of, 145,
  154–55, 162, 169; interest groups
  in, 177, 179, 182–83; constitution

of, 220–21, 224n2, 226, 229; cen-
  tral bank of, 237, 241; type of
  democracy in, 248, 254n6
Brass, Paul R., 72
Bräutigam, Deborah, 178
Brittan, Leon, 42
Budge, Ian, 100
Budget deficits, 267, 269–70
Busch, Andreas, 24–25
Bush, George, 275
Butler, David, 11, 231

Cabinet durability. *See* Cabinets
Cabinets, 10–11, 21, 28, 34–35, 42,
  90–111; and dimensions of
  democracy, 3, 62, 90, 243–46;
  classification of, 62, 74n7, 90–91,
  98, 103–8; durability of, 64, 73,
  129–34, 136–39, 261n2, 288–89;
  and party systems, 64, 112–13;
  and prime ministers, 113–15; and
  interest groups, 181–82. *See also*
  Executive-legislative relations
Caldera, Rafael, 128
Callaghan, James, 11
Canada, 50, 56, 269, 289, 298; type
  of democracy in, 10, 248–49, 255;
  party system of, 67, 77, 81, 82, 88;
  executive in, 111–12, 133, 135,
  138–40; parliament of, 119, 204,
  206–9, 212, 214; electoral system
  of, 145, 151, 162, 167, 169; interest groups in, 177, 180, 182–83;
  federalism in, 187–90 passim,
  193–98 passim, 300; constitution
  of, 220, 222, 226–29 passim; central bank of, 236, 241
Cappelletti, Mauro, 227
Castles, Francis G., 260
Central banks, 20–21, 24–25, 30, 41,
  46–47, 232–40; and federalism, 5,
  240–42; and dimensions of
  democracy, 5, 243–46, 306; and
  inflation, 233–36, 273, 301
Chirac, Jacques, 122
Churchill, Winston, 11, 92, 100
Clinton, Bill, 52, 107, 143–44, 232

Coalition cabinets, 74n7, 90–91, 104–9, 136–39. *See also* Cabinets
Coalition potential, 65–66, 78, 87
Coalition theories, 91–103
Cohen, William, 107
Colombia, 50–52, 56, 58, 189–90, 277, 282, 286, 289; party system of, 72–73, 75–77, 80–88 passim; cabinets in, 102, 103, 107n6, 110–12; presidentialism in, 106, 118–19, 127–28, 132–36 passim, 138, 281, 303n1; electoral systems of, 145–46, 155–63 passim, 168–69; interest groups in, 177, 179, 182–83; bicameralism in, 205, 206, 210, 212–15 passim; constitution of, 220–22, 226–29 passim; central bank of, 237, 241; type of democracy in, 248, 250, 254–55
Committee on the Constitutional System, 121, 123, 124
Compulsory voting, 285
Connally, John B., 107
Consensus democracy, 2–8, 31–47; dimensions of, 3–5, 243–57; effects of, 131, 258–302
Constitutions, 19, 24, 30, 40–41, 45–46, 216–23; and federalism, 4, 187–88, 230; and dimensions of democracy, 4, 243–46; and referendums, 217–22 passim, 230–31; and judicial review, 223–30
Coppedge, Michael, 179
Corporatism. *See* Interest groups
Corruption, 279, 288–89
Costa Rica, 50, 56, 111–12, 189, 269, 282; party system of, 77, 81, 82, 88; presidentialism in, 106, 118–19, 127–28, 132–36 passim, 138–39, 281, 303n1; electoral systems of, 145–48 passim, 154–55, 160–63 passim, 168–69, 285n5; interest groups in, 177, 179, 182–83; unicameralism in, 202, 212, 214; constitution of, 220, 226, 229; central bank of, 236, 241; type of democracy in, 248, 250, 254–55

Crepaz, Markus M. L., 177n1, 260
Criminal justice, 275, 296–98, 299–300
Crisp, Brian, 179
Crossman, R. H. S., 223
Cukierman, Alex, 233, 235–39
Cultural-ethnic issue dimension, 14, 27, 37, 80–81, 83–84
Cultural influence, British, 9–10, 21, 27–28, 250–52. *See also* Political culture
Cyprus, 54–55
Czech Republic, 54, 306

Dahl, Robert A., 6, 48–49, 191, 252, 276–78, 280, 291, 299
Death penalty, 275, 296, 298
Decentralization. *See* Division of power
de Gaulle, Charles, 222, 230, 250–51
Democracy: defined, 1–2, 32, 48–49; quality of, 7–8, 275–93, 301; conceptual map of, 7, 246–57; performance of, 7–8, 258–74, 293–301; models of, 9–47; incidence of, 49–57
Democratic peace, 298n12
Denmark, 50, 56, 277, 286, 289, 291–92, 299; party system of, 67, 76–77, 80–88 passim; executive in, 101, 110–14 passim, 132, 137–39; parliament of, 119, 202, 206, 212–15 passim; PR in, 145, 152, 162, 169; interest groups in, 177, 182–83; decentralization in, 189–94 passim, constitution of, 220, 226–29 passim; central bank of, 236, 241; type of democracy in, 248, 250, 255
Diamond, Larry, 51
Dicey, A. V., 19
Dillon, C. Douglas, 107
Dini, Lamberto, 108n7
Disproportionality, index of, 74n7, 157–58
District magnitude, 150–52, 153

Division of power, 3–4, 17–18, 23–
24, 30, 38–39, 45–47, 185–99; and
dimensions of democracy, 3, 185–
86, 243–46; and bicameralism, 4–
5, 187–88, 213–15; and central
banks, 5, 240–42; and population
size, 24, 30, 61, 195, 215
Dixon, Robert G., Jr., 5
Dodd, Lawrence C., 131–32
Dogan, Mattei, 130
Druckman, James, N., 73
Duchacek, Ivo D., 4, 188
Duverger, Maurice, 121–22, 155,
164–65, 210

Economic development, 56, 60–61,
177–78, 180, 238–39, 262–73
passim, 277–300 passim
Economic freedom, 267, 270
Economic growth, 234, 264–66, 270
Ecuador, 54–55
Effective number of parties, 57n6,
64, 67–69, 74–77. See also Elec-
toral systems; Party systems
Elazar, Daniel J., 4, 187–88
Electoral formulas, 144–49
Electoral systems, 14–16, 22–23,
25–27, 29, 37, 43–44, 143–64;
and dimensions of democracy, 3,
243–46, 303–5; and party sys-
tems, 64, 164–70; and constitu-
tions, 220–21; and turnout, 286n7
Electoral thresholds, 152–53, 305
Emerson, Rupert, 308
Environmental policies, 275, 295–
97
Equality, 278, 282–84
Ersson, Svante, 192, 194–95
Esping-Andersen, Gøsta, 294–95
Estonia, 54, 306
European Union, 14, 16, 20, 85, 262;
as example of consensus system,
7, 33–34, 42–47
Executive dominance. See
Executive-legislative relations
Executive-legislative balance. See
Executive-legislative relations

Executive-legislative relations, 11–
12, 21–22, 28, 35–36, 42, 102,
116–35, 175; and dimensions of
democracy, 3, 243–46; and cabinets, 134–39. See also Cabinets;
Parliaments
Executives. See Cabinets
Executives-parties dimension, 2, 5,
30, 62–63, 89, 135–36, 171, 243–
57; and government performance,
258–71, 274, 276–99, 301–3, 306

Factions. See Party systems
Family policy, 278, 281–82
Federalism. See Division of power
Federalist Papers, 259
Federal-unitary dimension, 2–5, 30,
185, 200, 216, 232–33, 243–57;
and government performance,
272–73, 293, 299–302, 306
Feldstein, Martin, 47
Fenno, Richard F., 107
Figueres, José, 128
Finer, S. E., 6, 259–60
Finland, 50, 56, 58, 269, 277, 283,
289; cabinets in, 7, 103, 108n7,
110–12, 132, 138; party system of,
67, 76, 80–88 passim; semipresi-
dentialism in, 114n9, 119, 122,
141; electoral systems of, 145–48
passim, 162, 169; interest groups
in, 174, 177, 182–83; decentralization in, 189–94 passim; unicameralism in, 202, 212–15 passim; constitution of, 220, 226–30
passim; central bank of, 237, 241;
type of democracy in, 248, 250,
255
Ford, Gerald R., 128
Foreign policy issue dimension, 14,
80–81, 85–86
France, 42, 46, 50–53 passim, 56,
58, 269, 282; presidentialism in,
12n1, 106, 114n9, 118–19, 121–
23, 125, 127–29, 133–39 passim,
281, 303n1; party system of, 66,
71, 76–77, 80–88 passim; elec-

toral systems of, 71*n6*, 145–51 passim, 155–64 passim, 168–69, 291*n10;* cabinets in, 97, 101, 107*n6*, 111–12, 130, 136, 304; interest groups in, 176–77, 182–83; unitary government in, 189–94 passim; bicameralism in, 201, 205, 210–15 passim; constitution of, 218–22 passim, 225, 226–29 passim; central bank of, 237, 241; type of democracy in, 248, 250–51, 254–56
Freedom House, 50–52, 54–55, 270, 276
Friedrich, Carl J., 4
Foreign aid, 276, 296, 298–99

Gallagher, Michael, 17, 157–58
Gasiorowski, Mark J., 51
Gastil, Raymond D., 72
Gerlich, Peter, 173
Germany, 42, 50, 52, 55–56, 58, 277, 287*n8;* executive in, 7, 70, 97, 101, 107*n6*, 109–14 passim, 132, 138, 141; PR in, 26, 44, 70, 145–48 passim, 153, 156, 162, 169, 305; central bank of, 41, 232*n1*, 236, 239, 241; constitution of, 46, 220, 222, 225–26, 229–30; party system of, 67, 69–71, 75–77, 80–89 passim; parliament of, 117–20 passim, 125–26, 204–9 passim, 212, 214, 304; interest groups in, 177, 179, 182–83; federalism in, 187–94 passim, 198–99; type of democracy in, 247–49, 251*n4*, 254–55
González, Felipe, 98*n4*
Goodin, Robert E., 5
Goodman, John B., 72, 240
Gorges, Michael J., 44–45
Government-voter proximity, 279, 287–88
Great Britain. *See* United Kingdom
Greece, 50, 53, 55–56, 265, 268, 269, 273, 287; party system of, 77, 81, 85, 88; executive in, 111–14 passim, 132, 138–39; parliament of,

119, 202–3, 212, 214; PR in, 145, 162–63, 168–70, 285*n5;* interest groups in, 176–77, 182–83; unitary government in, 189–94 passim, constitution of, 220, 223–24, 226, 229; central bank of, 236–37, 239, 241; type of democracy in, 248, 250, 303
Greenspan, Alan, 232
Grilli, Vittorio, 233, 238
Grimsson, Olafur R., 85
Grofman, Bernard, 89
Grosser, Alfred, 175
Guillory, Christine A., 286–87
Guinier, Lani, 143
Gurr, Ted Robert, 51, 276
Gwartney, James, 270

Haggard, Stephan, 178
Hahm, Sung Deuk, 260
Hailsham, Lord, 12, 28
Hall, Peter A., 240
Hartlyn, Jonathan, 72
Hattenhauer, Hans, 5–6
Heads of state, 40*n1*, 126–27, 139–42
Heller, William B., 211*n4*
Herman, Valentine M., 100, 130*n6*
Holm, John D., 179
Holmes, Kim R., 270
Horwill, George, 150
Huber, John D., 287–88, 306
Human development index, 56, 60, 61, 264. *See also* Economic development
Hungary, 54, 306
Huntington, Samuel P., 6, 55, 57

Iceland, 50, 56, 60, 189, 193, 263; party system of, 76, 81, 84, 85, 88; executive in, 109–14 passim, 132, 138, 141; parliament of, 119, 121, 201–2, 212–14; electoral systems of, 145–46, 154, 156, 162, 169; interest groups in, 177, 182–83; constitution of, 220, 226, 229; central bank of, 237, 241; type of democracy in, 248, 250, 255

Incarceration, 275, 296–98, 299–300

India, 50–51, 53, 56–61 passim, 269, 282, 289, 297, 298; party system of, 71, 72–73, 75–77, 80–88 passim; executive in, 108n8, 110–12, 131n7, 132, 135, 138, 141, 291n10; parliament of, 119, 205–06, 207–9, 212, 214; electoral system of, 145, 151–52, 162, 168–69; interest groups in, 177, 180, 182–83; federalism in, 187–90 passim, 195–97, 198; constitution of, 219–21, 226–27, 229–30; central bank of, 236, 241; type of democracy in, 248, 251, 252, 304, 307

Inflation, 25, 233–36, 240, 262, 265–68, 272–74, 301

Inglehart, Ronald, 86

Interest groups, 16–17, 23, 29–30, 37–38, 44–45, 171–80; and dimensions of democracy, 3, 171, 243–46, 306; and cabinets, 181–82; and party systems, 181–84

Ireland, 17, 50, 56, 282, 283, 288; party system of, 67, 77, 81–88 passim; executive in, 101, 110–14 passim, 117, 132, 135, 138, 141; parliament of, 117–21 passim, 206, 210–11, 212, 214; electoral systems of, 145–48 passim, 153, 157, 161–62, 169; interest groups in, 177, 182–83; unitary government in, 189, 193–94; constitution of, 220, 226, 229; central bank of, 236, 241; type of democracy in, 248, 255, 303

Israel, 50–51, 52, 55–56, 58, 59, 269, 271n5, 298; executive in, 7, 106n5, 110–12, 123–24, 126–27, 132, 138–39; party system of, 76–77, 80–88 passim; parliament of, 118–19, 125, 202, 212–15 passim; electoral systems of, 145–56 passim, 160–62, 164, 169; interest groups in, 174, 177, 182–83;

semifederalism in, 189, 191; constitution of, 217–18, 220, 226, 229; central bank of, 236, 241; type of democracy in, 248–49, 251, 255, 307

Issue dimensions, 14, 22, 28–29, 36–37, 78–89

Italy, 42, 50, 52, 55–56, 58, 268, 269, 273, 286–87; executive in, 7, 98n4, 108n7, 110–14 passim, 132, 138; party system of, 66, 67, 71, 72–73, 75–77, 80–88 passim; parliament of, 118–19, 205–6, 210–15 passim; PR in, 145–49 passim, 162, 169, 285; interest groups in, 177, 181–84; unitary government in, 189–94 passim; constitution of, 220–21, 225–29 passim; central bank of, 237, 241; type of democracy in, 248, 255

Jaggers, Keith, 51, 276

Jamaica, 50, 53n3, 56, 60, 189, 271, 282, 298; party system of, 74–77, 81, 85, 88, 291; executive in, 111–12, 133, 138–40; parliament of, 119, 206, 210–14 passim; electoral system of, 145, 154–55, 158n9, 163–69 passim; interest groups in, 177, 179, 182–83; constitution of, 220–21, 225–29 passim; central bank of, 237–38, 241; type of democracy in, 248, 250, 254–55

Japan, 50, 52, 56, 57, 282, 295, 298; party system of, 72–73, 74–77, 80–88 passim; executive in, 108, 110–12, 132, 138–40; parliament of, 117, 119, 205–06, 210–14 passim; electoral systems of, 145, 148–49, 156–63 passim, 166–70 passim, 303; interest groups in, 177, 182–83; decentralization in, 189–90, 193–94; constitution of, 220, 222–23, 226, 229; central bank of, 237, 241; type of democracy in, 248, 251n4, 252, 255

Jenkins, Lord, 16
Johnson, Bryan T., 270
Johnson, Lyndon B., 129
Jospin, Lionel, 122
Judicial review, 19–20, 24, 30, 41,
   46, 223–28; and federalism, 4,
   187–88, 230; and dimensions of
   democracy, 5, 243–46; and constitutions, 228–30

Kaltefleiter, Werner, 5–6
Kamlet, Mark S., 260
Katzenstein, Peter J., 38, 172, 174–
   75, 260
Kaufman, Robert R., 178
Kavanagh, Dennis, 140
Keeler, John T. S., 129
Kekkonen, Urho, 122
Kelsen, Hans, 225
Kennedy, John F., 107
Kilbrandon, Lord, 17
King, Anthony, 114, 127
Kinnock, Neil, 42
Kirkpatrick, Melanie, 270
Klingemann, Hans-Dieter, 286
Korea, 54–55
Kothari, Rajni, 197

Laakso, Markku, 68
Lane, Jan-Erik, 192, 194–95
LaPalombara, Joseph, 181–82
Latvia, 54, 306
Laver, Michael, 17, 96, 97–98
Lawson, Robert, 270
Lawson, Stephanie, 6
Legislatures. See Parliaments
Lehmbruch, Gerhard, 38
Lehner, Franz, 231
Leiserson, Michael, 94
Leopold III, King, 140
Levine, Daniel H., 190
Levine, Stephen, 22
Lewis, Sir Arthur, 31, 33, 253, 308
Limited vote, 145, 149, 210
Lincoln, Abraham, 1, 49
Linder, Wolf, 39
Lipset, Seymour Martin, 82, 83

List proportional representation,
   145, 147–48, 149, 152, 210
Lowell, A. Lawrence, 64, 65, 259
Luxembourg, 50, 56, 59, 189, 192,
   263, 284n4, 291; executive in, 7,
   107n6, 109–14 passim, 125, 133,
   138–40; electoral systems of, 44,
   145, 154, 162, 169, 285n5; party
   system of, 67, 76, 81, 82, 88; parliament of, 119, 202, 212, 214;
   interest groups in, 177, 182–83;
   constitution of, 220, 226, 229–30;
   central bank of, 237, 241; type of
   democracy in, 248, 255, 256–57

Maastricht Treaty, 41, 234, 262
MacArthur, Douglas, 251n4
McKinney, Cynthia, 198
McNamara, Robert S., 107
Macro-economic policy, 7–8, 258–
   70, 274, 301
Mainwaring, Scott, 124n3, 134
Mair, Peter, 17, 256
Majoritarian democracy, 2–30;
   dimensions of, 3–5, 243–57;
   effects of, 130–31, 258–302
Malapportionment, 155–56
Malta, 50, 53n3, 56–57, 189, 263,
   276, 298; party system of, 75–77,
   81–88 passim, 292; executive in,
   111–12, 133, 138, 140; parliament
   of, 119, 202, 212, 214; PR in, 145–
   48 passim, 154, 157, 161–62,
   168–69; interest groups in, 177,
   179, 182–83; constitution of, 220,
   226–27, 229; central bank of, 236,
   241; type of democracy in, 248,
   254n6, 303–4
Mandela, Nelson, 126
Manglapus, Raul S., 308
Mansbridge, Jane, 6, 293
Manufactured majorities, 15, 23, 29,
   166–68
Maori, 22, 25, 26, 27, 49, 152
Marbury v. Madison, 223
Marshall, John, 223
Masciandaro, Donato, 233, 238

Mathur, Hansraj, 178–79
Mauritius, 50, 53, 56, 59, 189, 269;
party system of, 71, 77, 81, 88;
executive in, 110–13, 132, 135,
138, 140, 291n10; parliament of,
119, 202, 212, 214; electoral system of, 145, 151–52, 154–55,
162–63, 169; interest groups in,
177–80, 182–83; constitution of,
220–21, 224n2, 226–29 passim;
central bank of, 236, 238, 241;
type of democracy in, 248, 251,
304
Maxfield, Sylvia, 234
May, Clifford D., 1n1
Mill, John Stuart, 279, 289–92
Minimal winning cabinets, 74n7,
90–96, 136–39. See also Cabinets
Minority cabinets, 90–91, 96–104,
136–37. See also Cabinets
Mitterrand, François, 101, 121,
190
Mixed member proportional sys-
tem, 26, 145, 147–49, 152, 158,
210
Molutsi, Patrick P., 179
Monarchs. See Heads of state
Monetary policy. See Central banks;
Inflation
Money, Jeannette, 43, 202, 211
Moreno, Luís, 191
Mowery, David C., 260
Multiparty systems. See Party sys-
tems
Munroe, Trevor, 28

Netherlands, 50, 52, 56, 58, 59, 284,
289, 295; executive in, 7, 101,
110–14 passim, 125, 126–27, 132,
138–40; party system of, 66n4, 67,
76, 80–88 passim; parliament of,
119, 201n1, 206–7, 210–14 passim; PR in, 145–48 passim, 152–
56 passim, 161–62, 165, 169,
285n5; interest groups in, 177,
182–83; semifederalism in, 189,
191, 193–94; constitution of, 220,

224, 226–30 passim; central bank
of, 236, 241; type of democracy in,
248, 255–56
New Zealand, 49–50, 56, 59, 119,
289, 292, 294–95, 297; as example
of majoritarian democracy, 7, 10,
21–27, 247–48, 255; executive in,
21–22, 27, 110–12, 138–40; executive dominance in, 21–22, 35,
127, 133, 135; party system of, 22,
27, 32, 65, 67, 75, 77, 81, 88; electoral systems of, 22–23, 25–27,
145–53 passim, 162–63, 167, 169,
290; interest groups in, 23, 177,
182–83; unitary government in,
23–24, 189, 192; unicameralism
in, 24, 200, 202, 204n2, 212, 214;
constitution of, 24, 217–18, 220,
226, 229; central bank of, 24–25,
237–38, 241
Neyapti, Bilin, 233, 235–39
Nixon, Richard M., 107, 129, 234
Northern Ireland, 14, 15, 17–18, 33,
44, 58, 86, 271
Norway, 50, 56, 262, 269, 286, 291–
92, 299; party system of, 67, 76–
77, 80–89 passim; executive in,
101, 111–14 passim, 125, 132,
137–40, 281; parliament of, 119,
124n3, 125, 126, 201–3, 212–15
passim; PR in, 145, 152–56 passim, 162, 169; interest groups in,
177, 180–83 passim; decentralization in, 189–94 passim; constitution of, 220, 226–27, 229; central
bank of, 237, 241; type of democracy in, 248, 250, 254–56

O'Donnell, Guillermo, 12n1
One-party cabinets. See Cabinets
Oversized cabinets, 90, 99–103,
136–39. See also Cabinets

Palmer, Monte, 295
Papua New Guinea, 50–51, 53, 56,
59–61, 280, 284, 291, 298; party
system of, 74–76, 80, 85, 88;

executive in, 101, 110–12, 132, 135, 138–40, 281; parliament of, 118–19, 202, 212–15 passim; electoral system of, 145, 151, 158n9, 162, 168–69; interest groups in, 177, 179, 181–83; semifederalism in, 189, 191; constitution of, 220–21, 226–29 passim; central bank of, 236, 238, 241; type of democracy in, 248, 251

Parliamentary government, 11–12, 35–36, 52n1, 198–99; defined, 104–6, 117–24; other traits of, 124–27, 303–5

Parliaments, 18–19, 24, 30, 39–40, 45, 175, 200–213; and dimensions of democracy, 3, 215, 243–46; and federalism, 4–5, 187–88, 213–15; sizes of, 153–55, 163. *See also* Executive-legislative relations

Party systems, 12–14, 22, 28–29, 32, 36–37, 43, 62–77; and dimensions of democracy, 3, 62–63, 243–46; and issue dimensions, 14, 87–89; and cabinets, 64, 112–13; and electoral systems, 64, 164–70; and allied or factional parties, 69–74, 75n9, 159n9, 167n12; and interest groups, 181–84

Payne, Anthony, 30

Peeler, John A., 72, 179

Pempel, T. J., 108

Pérez, Carlos Andrés, 108n7

Pluralism. *See* Interest groups

Plurality rule. *See* Electoral systems

Plural societies, 56–59, 83–84, 168, 262, 271; and type of democracy, 32–33, 46–47, 61, 251–53, 302

Political culture, 306–09

Political parties. *See* party systems

Population size, 52, 55, 60–61, 154–55, 215, 252; and government performance, 262–73 passim, 291–92, 299

Portugal, 50, 56–57, 248, 265, 269, 299; party system of, 71, 76–77,

80–88 passim; executive in, 110–14 passim, 132, 138, 141; parliament of, 119, 121, 202, 212, 214; electoral systems of, 145–46, 162, 169; interest groups in, 176–77, 181–83; unitary government in, 189–94 passim; constitution of, 220, 225–29 passim; central bank of, 237, 239, 241

Postmaterialism, 80–81, 86–87

Powell, G. Bingham, Jr., 6, 122n2, 232n1, 260–61, 285, 287–88, 306

Power-sharing. *See* Cabinets

Presidential cabinets, 104–8, 113, 118. *See also* Cabinets

Presidential government, 12n1, 51–52, 110–11, 113, 198; defined, 104–6, 117–24; other traits of, 124–29, 141–42, 155, 159–61, 281, 292, 303

Presidents. *See* Heads of state; Presidential government

Prime ministers, 113–15. *See also* Parliamentary government

Proportional representation. *See* Electoral systems

Rae, Douglas W., 15, 68n5, 165–67

Ranney, Austin, 231

Referendums, 24, 26, 40, 217–22 passim, 230–31

Regime support dimension, 80–81, 85

Reich, Robert B., 232

Religious issue dimension, 14, 27, 36–37, 80–83

Riker, William H., 6, 92, 99, 186–87, 191

Rogowski, Ronald, 260

Rokkan, Stein, 83

Rose, Richard, 9, 25, 140, 260–62

Roubini, Nouriel, 260

Royed, Terry J., 260

Sachs, Jeffrey D., 260

Sartori, Giovanni, 65–66, 78, 113–15, 124

Satisfaction with democracy, 279, 286–87
Schain, Martin A., 129
Schmidt, Manfred G., 70, 295
Schmitter, Philippe C., 171–72, 175
Schofield, Norman, 96, 97–98
Scotland, 14, 16, 18
Seliktar, Ofira, 86
Senelle, Robert, 41
Sentencing Project, 297
Shapiro, Martin, 46
Shepsle, Kenneth A., 96
Shugart, Matthew S., 124n3, 134, 150
Siaroff, Alan, 174, 176–77, 269n3
Siegfried, André, 130
Single nontransferable vote, 145, 149, 150, 161–63, 210, 303
Single transferable vote, 145, 148, 151n4, 157, 158, 161–62, 198, 209, 303–4
Size principle, 92–93, 99–100
Slovenia, 54, 306
Socioeconomnic issue dimension, 14, 22, 28–29, 37, 79–82, 83
Solomon Islands, 54
Somolekae, Gloria, 179
South Africa, 54–55, 126
Spain, 42, 50–51, 53, 56, 58, 265, 268, 269, 291; party system of, 77, 80, 82, 88; executive in, 98n4, 101, 109–14 passim, 133, 138–40, 142; parliament of, 119, 204, 210, 212, 214; PR in, 145–48 passim, 153, 156, 162–63, 168–70; interest groups in, 176–77, 182–83; semi-federalism in, 189–94 passim; constitution of, 220, 225–29 passim; central bank of, 237, 241; type of democracy in, 248, 250, 303
Steiner, Jürg, 6, 35
Stone, Alec, 46
Strikes, 23, 267, 269
Strøm, Kaare, 104
Sweden, 50, 56, 280, 282, 289, 294–95; party system of, 67, 76, 80–88 passim; executive in, 101, 109–14

passim, 133, 137–39, 141; parliament of, 119, 201–6 passim, 212–15 passim; PR in, 145, 152–56 passim, 162, 169; interest groups in, 173, 177, 181–83; decentralization in, 189–94 passim; constitution of, 220–22, 226–29 passim; central bank of, 237, 241; type of democracy in, 248, 250, 254–56
Switzerland, 50, 52, 56, 58, 269, 285, 291, 297; as example of consensus democracy, 7, 33–41, 248–49, 255, 307; executive in, 7, 34–35, 97, 109–15 passim, 132–36 passim, 138, 141, 231; separation of powers in, 35, 119–20, 127, 303; party system of, 36–37, 67, 75–77, 80–88 passim; PR in, 37, 145, 156, 162–63, 168–69; interest groups in, 37–38, 177, 180, 182–83; federalism in, 38, 45, 187–95 passim, 196, 198–99; bicameralism in, 39, 44, 200–10 passim, 212, 214; constitution of, 40–41, 220, 222, 226–30 passim; central bank of, 41, 236, 239–41

Taagepera, Rein, 68, 88–89, 150, 280
Tabellini, Guido, 233, 238
Tarlton, Charles D., 195
Taylor, Michael, 68n5, 130n6
Thatcher, Margaret, 12, 17
Therborn, Göran, 49
Thorndike, Tony, 29
Transparency International, 289
Trinidad and Tobago, 50–51, 53, 56, 59, 269, 297, 298; party system of, 74–77, 81–82, 88, 291; executive in, 111–12, 133, 138, 140; parliament of, 119, 204, 206, 210–14 passim; electoral system of, 145, 154–55, 158n9, 162–69 passim; interest groups in, 177, 179–80, 182–83; unitary government in, 189–91; constitution of, 220–221, 224, 226, 229; central bank of,

236, 238, 241; type of democracy in, 248, 250, 254–55
Tsebelis, George, 5n2, 43, 202, 211
Tufte, Edward R., 79, 252, 291, 299
Turnout, 159, 261n2, 278, 284–86
Two-party systems. See Party systems

Unemployment, 234, 236, 240, 266, 268–69
Unicameralism. See Parliaments
Unitary government. See Division of power
United Kingdom, 42, 50, 52, 56, 58–59, 259, 262, 271, 288–98 passim; as example of majoritarian democracy, 7, 9–21, 247–48, 255; executive in, 10–11, 92, 100–01, 108n8, 110–14 passim, 131n7, 138–39; executive dominance in, 11–12, 35, 118–19, 125, 127, 133–34, 136; party system of, 13–14, 32, 65, 67, 75–77, 81–88 passim; electoral system of, 14–16, 44, 145–69 passim; interest groups in, 16–17, 177, 180, 182–83; unitary government in, 17–18, 189–94 passim; bicameralism in, 18–19, 200–06 passim, 212, 214; constitution of, 19–20, 217, 220, 226–29 passim; central bank of, 20–21, 237, 241
United States, 50, 52, 56, 283, 294–300 passim; type of democracy in, 9, 247–50, 252, 254–55; presidentialism in, 12n1, 106, 118–20, 123–24, 127–29, 132–39 passim, 281, 305; central bank of, 41, 232, 236, 239–41; bicameralism in, 45n3, 204–10 passim, 212–14 passim; party system of, 72–73, 75–77, 81–89 passim; cabinets in, 107–8, 110–13 passim; electoral systems of, 143–45, 151–62 passim, 164, 167, 169, 198, 285; interest groups in, 177, 182–83; federalism in, 187–95 passim, 198; constitution of, 220, 222, 224, 226, 229

Unwritten constitutions, 19, 24, 217–28. See also Constitutions
Urban-rural issue dimension, 80–81, 83, 84–85
Uruguay, 54–55, 120

van de Walle, Nicolas, 129n5
Vanhanen, Tatu, 277–80, 283–84
Velásquez, Ramón, 108n7
Venezuela, 50–52, 53, 56, 277, 282; party system of, 76, 81, 82, 88; presidentialism in, 106, 118–19, 127–28, 132–36 passim, 138–39, 281, 303n1; cabinets in, 107n6, 108n7, 111–12; electoral systems of, 145–49 passim, 155, 160–63 passim, 168–69, 285n5; interest groups in, 177, 179–83 passim; federalism in, 187, 189–90, 198; bicameralism in, 205, 207–9, 212, 214; constitution of, 220, 226, 229; central bank of, 237, 241–42; type of democracy in, 248, 250, 254–56
Verba, Sidney, 307
Violence, control of, 51, 260, 267, 270–71, 274, 301
von Beyme, Klaus, 72
von Mettenheim, Kurt, 27
Voting participation. See Turnout

Wada, Junichiro, 72
Wales, 14, 16, 18, 58
Warwick, Paul V., 129–30, 131n7
Webb, Steven B., 233, 235–39
Webster, Daniel, 1n1
Welfare policy, 275, 294–96, 299–300
Westminster model, 9–30, 89, 133. See also Majoritarian democracy
Wheare, K. C., 4, 190
Wiarda, Howard J., 174
Wilensky, Harold L., 281–82
Wilson, Graham, 16
Wilson, Woodrow, 9–10, 129
Women's representation, 52, 278, 280–82

Patterns of Democracy

Government Forms and Performance in Thirty-Six Countries

AREND LIJPHART

In this updated and expanded edition of his highly acclaimed book *Democracies*, Arend Lijphart offers a broader and deeper analysis of worldwide democratic institutions than ever before. Examining thirty-six democracies during the half-century from 1945 to 1996, Lijphart arrives at important—and unexpected—conclusions about what type of democracy works best. Although conventional wisdom suggests that majoritarian democracies like those in the United States and Great Britain are superior to consensual systems like those in Switzerland and Israel, Lijphart shows this is not so. In fact, consensual systems stimulate economic growth, control inflation and unemployment, and limit budget deficits just as well as majoritarian democracies do. And consensus democracies clearly outperform majoritarian systems on measures of political equality, women's representation, citizen participation in elections, and proximity between government policies and voter preferences.

Systematically comparing cabinets, legislatures, parties, election systems, supreme courts, and—for the first time in this volume—interest groups and central banks, Lijphart demonstrates that the more consensual a democracy, the "kinder and gentler" it is when addressing such issues as welfare, the environment, criminal justice, and foreign aid. These findings are of far-reaching import not only for countries designing their first democratic constitutions but also for established democracies seeking practical approaches to reform.

"I can't think of another scholar as well qualified as Lijphart to write a book of this kind. He has an amazing grasp of the relevant literature, and he's compiled an unmatched collection of data."—**Robert A. Dahl,** Yale University

Arend Lijphart is research professor of political science at the University of California, San Diego, and the author or editor of more than twenty books.

Yale University Press   New Haven & London   *http://www.yale.edu/yup/*